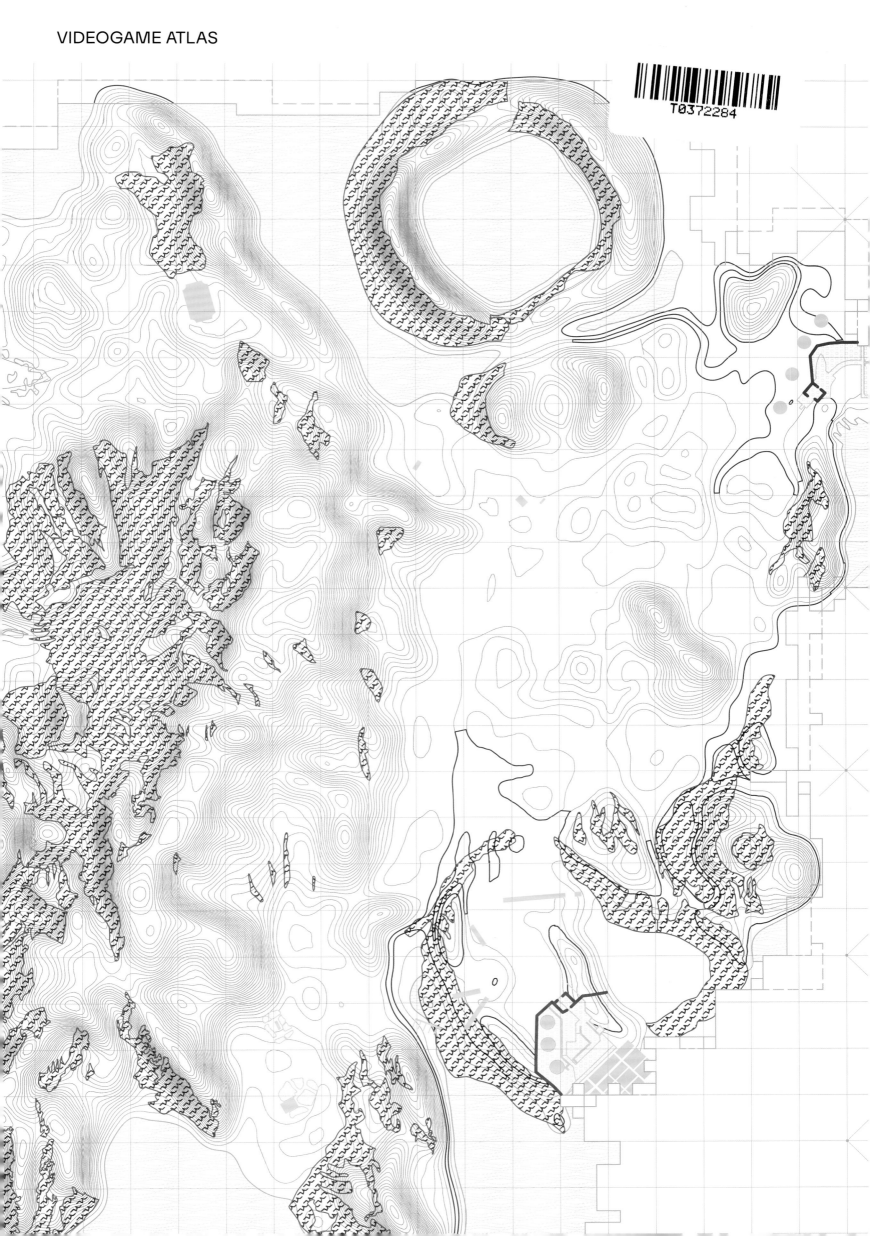

T0372284

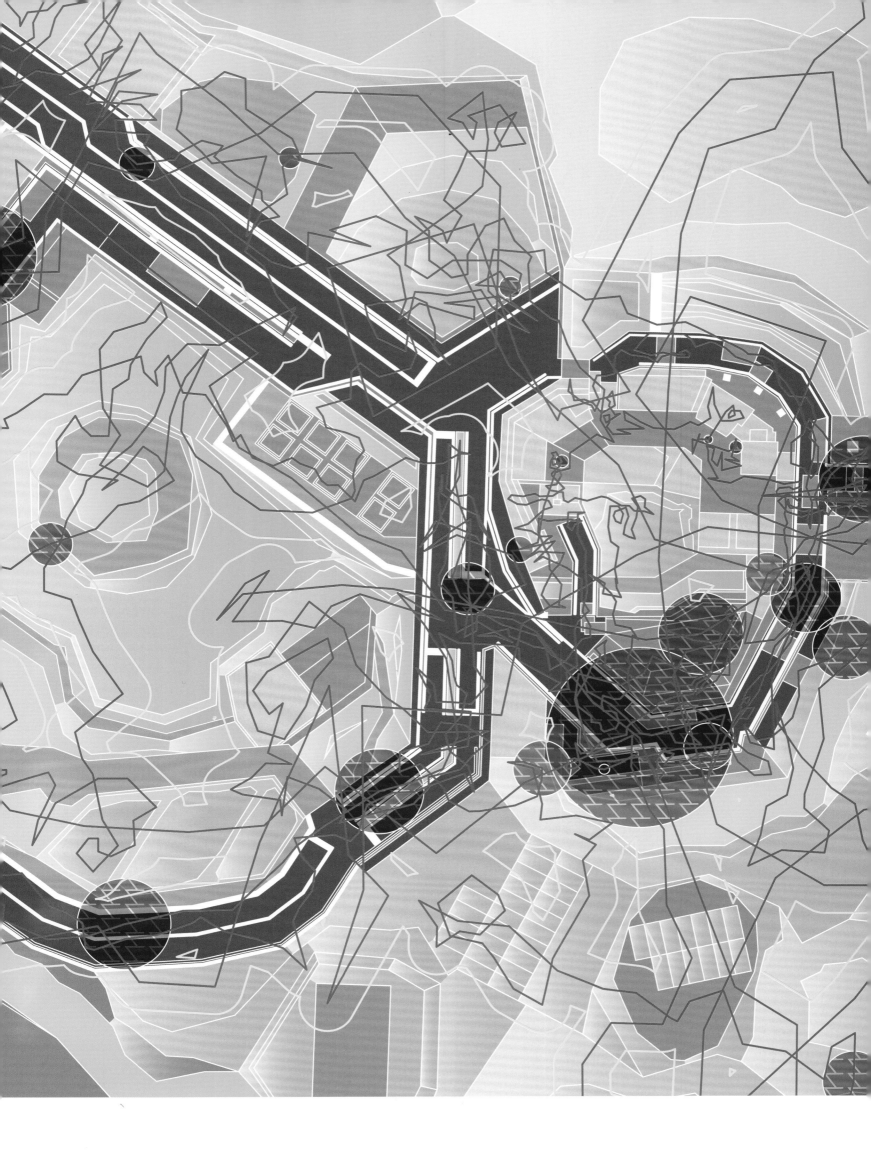

Death Stranding (previous page)
A map of America as shown in the game, see pages 80–101.

Katamari Damacy (above)
Plan showing the route taken by a katamari in the game, see pages 166–187.

VIDEOGAME ATLAS

Mapping Interactive Worlds

Luke Caspar Pearson
Sandra Youkhana

Foreword by Marie Foulston
With 484 illustrations

Dark Souls
A map of Lordran, see pages 56–79.

◯ Contents

◯ Foreword
◯ Marie Foulston

One of my earliest, and fondest, videogame memories is playing *The Legend of Zelda: A Link to the Past* with my father. In this memory my hands clutch not at a controller, but at a printed map. My father steers Link around Hyrule while I sit by his side as navigator, with the game's paper map laid out on the table in front of me. We play as a team. My role is to remember shortcuts and routes not yet taken, to familiarise myself with the geography and landscapes and to recognise anything that is out of the ordinary to help uncover any hidden secrets. Freed from the demands of hand-eye coordination or combat, I am granted the ability to experience and perceive the world of the game in an entirely different way.

In *Videogame Atlas*, Luke Caspar Pearson and Sandra Youkhana offer that same shift in perspective. As digital cartographers, they draw on their expertise across both architecture and gaming to layer insights, data and research playfully and precisely onto a wealth of iconic videogame worlds.

We are at a point in history where it is estimated that just under half of the global population[1] play videogames. The recent pandemic has left many more people open to and appreciative of embodied digital experiences and we are now living in a world where tech corporations are eager to bring the next predicted phase of the internet, the Metaverse, into existence. We have arrived at a point in history where the significance of virtual worlds has never been greater.

Interrogating and understanding these sites of shared digital heritage is not just fascinating but essential. Even if these digital spaces are seemingly ephemeral, they are still real. We have played in them, moved through them, explored them; they are places where we have died and been reborn, places we have both destroyed and co-created. These are places where we have *lived*.

Fostering greater literacy and understanding of these worlds gives weight to the experiences and memories born within them. Demystifying and humanizing the way games are created highlights the skills and craft of the many designers, players, modders, fans and audiences who have played a part in their design and evolution.

Whether we find ourselves building civic infrastructure in Fluxburgh, battling through Midgar, or rolling through the cosmos, each virtual world is 'a space neither separate from real space nor simply a continuation of it'.[2] Each videogame world imperfectly reflects the 'physical' world that surrounds us. In giving ourselves permission to take these spaces of play seriously, and to study them in depth, we can understand and re-imagine the 'real' world in new and diverse ways.

In the chapters that follow, Youkhana and Pearson weave together expert knowledge, language and theory to navigate us through intricate geographies and landscapes. With colourful curiosity and intrigue, they offer us a fresh perspective on familiar places we have frequented before, as well as drawing us in to places that are foreign and new. We travel through each game not with a controller in hand but, instead, a paper atlas – a portal through which to experience videogame worlds in a different light.

1   Newzoo, *Global Games Market Report*, 2021
    newzoo.com/insights/trend-reports/newzoo-global-
    games-market-report-2021-free-version
2   Julie E. Cohen, 'Cyberspace As/And Space',
    *Georgetown Public Law and Legal Theory
    Research Paper*, No. 898260, 2007.
    scholarship.law.georgetown.edu/cgi/viewcontent.
    cgi?article=1822&context=facpub

Every day, millions of people travel to strange and wonderful worlds, diving into intense, escapist universes full of puzzles and adventure – where they can undertake grand battles, assuming new abilities and identities to experience stories unfolding around them. They can participate in simulated societies while also belonging to collective spaces that create new social structures. These are the worlds of videogames, synthetic environments that challenge our conception of space and how we interact with it. The aesthetic experience of videogames is immersive yet fragmentary, inconsistent and often seemingly illogical. We might die thousands of times in a game world but also feel at home there. This is precisely what attracts players to these virtual places and gives videogame worlds their power to move people. Jesper Juul calls these worlds 'half-real',[1] where fictional stories meet stringent rules, and as Katherine Isbister argues, these worlds 'may be imaginary, but the social dynamics are not'.[2]

As co-authors of this book, we appreciate game worlds in a similar way, because this aligns with our own personal experiences. Prior to studying and working in architecture, we grew up playing videogames at a time when technological innovations in the industry transformed the depiction of game worlds from flat graphics to compelling three-dimensional worlds. While 2D games were actually closely connected to techniques of architectural drawing (like the carved cross-sections of *Lemmings* or Shigeru Miyamoto's *Mario* level designs), these three-dimensional environments closed the distance between virtual space and real-world architecture. This was a time when Mario's movement was liberated in *Super Mario 64,* and the world opened to us in unforeseen new ways. We could feel like we knew New York or Hong Kong by playing *Deus Ex*, sneaking up from the city streets to explore people's private apartments and read their secrets. Or we could explore the spaces of a Mexican film noir through the vivid visuals of *Grim Fandango*'s Land of the Dead. Each of these games had its own method of evoking space, resulting in diverse ways of creating a virtual environment for us to explore and dream within.

With these interests underpinning our architectural careers, we began to see more opportunities for convergence between both fields and have since sought out new ways for communicating space using game engines in our own work. Software used in game design and architecture has become more interchangeable, with architects increasingly utilizing real-time virtual environments in their design process.

This can lead to a productive relationship between the two industries. With so much data organizing our contemporary lives, games offer a unique model for breaking down complex systems through storytelling. At the same time, architecture and its history enables game designers to understand how cities and spaces came to be, in order to create more potent and credible worlds, from vernacular architectural styles or nifty wayfinding techniques to more accurately crafted façade details. This exchange of information is blurring the boundaries of what belongs to the physical or the virtual world, with principles from both sides transferring either way.

Certain aspects of architecture have been challenged by the rising prevalence of videogames, making them ideal settings for the act of speculation. For many years architects were imaginers of new worlds and societies, producing 'paper architecture' projects that conjured up alternative worlds for humanity. Italian architect Giovanni Battista Piranesi would create strange, paradoxical prisons with impossible geometry. The Metabolist group of architects from Japan proposed cities as giant organisms, and designed house-size robots. Countercultural designers such as American collective Ant Farm drew cities to be inhabited by both humans and dolphins. Congolese artist Bodys Isek Kingelez made models of fantastical cities looking at the future of African urbanism, and Madelon Vriesendorp created many influential paintings of New York with buildings as characters, including a famous picture of the Empire State and Chrysler buildings in bed together.[3]

Most videogames foreground fantastical environments because they are entertainment media designed to draw players into imagined and novel systems. However, in doing so, and in hosting so many people in their worlds, games re-establish the importance of utopian architecture that was used to hold a mirror up to society. In this book, we seek to uncover how those fantasies are facilitated, and what games might be telling us about their architecture and society as we explore their worlds.

AN ATLAS
By presenting this visual analysis of these twelve game worlds through the medium of an atlas, we want to celebrate their unique environments by developing a cartographic understanding of the spaces they allow us to play in.

Game worlds are entirely synthetic – everything is made from scratch, with the developers deciding on the world's edges and limitations, and determining what aspects from reality (physics, climate, human mobility, society) will be simulated. This makes them extraordinary sites for evaluation, as each game holds its own idiosyncratic logic to be exposed. To properly examine this, our mapping process and cartographic approaches follow Mark Monmonier's argument that 'a map must offer a selective, incomplete view of reality'.[4] This means that we make a series of very specific mappings and analyses of different aspects of each game world, which highlight the unique ways in which it deals with space. Just as each game offers a divergent view of the world, each chapter uses different types of drawing and information to explore them. This idea is intrinsic to the methods by which the information is presented in this book, but also to game worlds themselves, as alternative or 'incomplete' versions of reality.

Alongside the 'physical' qualities of the game worlds, the presence of players also defines their urbanism, creating social spaces for people to inhabit. These spaces can exist both within the game and in the communities that surround the game. In each case, this means there is collective intelligence that inhabits each game world, as well as the interactions between players within that world, which further expands the game's extent.

As such, this book is an attempt to unravel these game worlds in the same way an architect or an urban designer would analyse a real site or space, by seeking to grasp their conditions and complexities. The aim of this is to understand these worlds as they are presented to us by the game – as its citizens, forming our own judgments and interpretations from what is offered, and to discover our capacity to affect the environment within its given constraints.

In this regard, this book is not a guidebook, and does not offer strategies for succeeding at the game or a comprehensive walkthrough of an entire game world. It is also not a 'behind the scenes' developer's log, as there are many titles of this nature for all the games that are featured within. You will likely not play the game better because of this atlas, but instead we intend to offer a deep insight into specific aspects of the worlds these games establish, and how this connects out to architecture, urbanism, anthropology and history. Through the many drawings and diagrams contained within this book, we also hope to use visual communication as a key tool to understand these relationships, to reveal systems and structures in a way that can also sit independently of our text.

Our analytical techniques have been broad and adaptive, producing around 200 drawings based on hundreds of hours playing the games contained within this book, capturing thousands of screenshots, recordings and other data about their worlds. In this time, we have also learned to play these games in ways unintended by their developers to extract key information, by testing the limits of the world.[5] From retracing paths already taken and creating new ones, to 'noclipping'[6] our way outside of various game worlds, we have taken unorthodox journeys to generate this information.

We have counted steps and surveyed different sites, climbed up and jumped from buildings hundreds of times, and driven back and forth over hills. We employed data-mining techniques and camera tools to reveal angles and information that would not normally be presented to the player but are key to maintaining their experience of the world. While what we present may not be perfect compared to the picture that the developers could give us, we see this as a record of the limitations and possibilities that each game world affords. If a game is harder to get a particular type of information from, then that in itself is interesting. We seek to test these limits and play with the possibilities of understanding these worlds using the resources the game does provide, while also inventing new ways to read them.

Beyond our own primary research, a book such as this could not be produced without the vast bodies of information created around each game by its player communities. Much of this information is fragmented, hiding in Discord channels, Reddit boards, game wikis, forums and YouTube clips. While we do feature quotes and sources from game developers to understand certain systems first-hand, much of the prevailing knowledge of these games is unofficial and developed through research made by players. This book cannot hope to cover every single part of the expansive 'folksonomies'[7] that surround games, but instead seeks to make sense of and build on this body of knowledge.

There is, of course, no *one* game that could cover all these themes. Videogames are diverse in their mechanisms, aesthetics and narratives, and so each chapter within this book exposes a distinct set of logics unique to each game world, that may contradict or challenge another game.

In *Assassin's Creed Unity*, we explore the game world as a form of historical re-enactment, accessing architectural landmarks in ways that are impossible in reality. As we find, *Unity*'s Paris is a carefully designed landscape of movement, where historical fidelity meets possibilities for parkour.

We move on to examine the ways in which *Cities: Skylines* operates a power structure and ruleset that reveals an Americanized urban model. Here we also explore how the game's community has challenged this model, by extending the game in many ways that contradict its existing systems. In *Dark Souls* we encounter another game with an active community, drawn to an uncaring and deadly world through very specific architectural strategies that create a picturesque landscape of death. Here we find an environment that combines multiple architectural reference points and painstakingly assembled circulation routes to evoke a harsh and ruined existence.

In our study of *Death Stranding*, we interrogate the desolate geographies and blank spaces of logistics in a post-apocalyptic world. By revealing new ways of reading the American landscape, we outline the impact of non-human architecture on our society and environment. This emphasis on landscape leads us on to a world constructed entirely from scratch: the procedural cities, societies and histories of *Dwarf Fortress*. By looking at both the symbolic visual language of the game and the architecture produced by its notoriously complex systems, we analyse how players design for this most inhospitable of worlds.

As a layered radial city built around a towering corporate headquarters, we assess how Midgar, the city from *Final Fantasy VII* and its *Remake*, physically represents the hierarchy of its society. By also analysing two versions of a city designed twenty-three years apart, we showcase the challenges in updating its urbanism while preserving its unique character. As an environment undergoing more constant updates, the world of *Fortnite* is dictated by an ever-evolving storyline that influences its physical development as well as its overriding narrative. Governed by catastrophic events and various climatic forces, the world is presented as an example of self-destruction and iterative repair.

Going on to *Katamari Damacy*, we find a tale of consumerism within a messy, seemingly illogical world, assembled from thousands of everyday objects. We break down the chaos of the rolling ball to understand the world as a spatial choreography, where objects, buildings and landscape can all be subsumed by the player.

Moving from the ball to the block, we peel apart the expansive world of *Minecraft* by studying three different servers that showcase the spatial and social desires of players. From fantasy realms to an apocalyptic wasteland, we examine the morphology of each of these servers and how it is defined by both their constraints and their player culture. Following this we take our explorations to the planetary scale by examining how the procedural system of *No Man's Sky* generates landscapes so vast that players strive to establish social spaces and connections to give themselves some form of foothold in the universe.

We then shift to contemporary Japan with *Persona 5*, demonstrating a world that fuses the supernatural with the everyday, comparing the game's city to its real-world counterpart. Here we will witness how the architecture of ego and the depths of the mind are in a symbiotic relationship with the tight and twisting spaces of Tokyo.

Finally, we flee the city in favour of a life on the rural homestead in *Stardew Valley*, nurturing the landscape square by square with relief from both human and mythical forces. Through gentle lessons in labour, we are taught the value of time and given the choice to bypass it in favour of accelerated production.

Each chapter, while operating as an independent piece of analysis, adds to our complete understanding of the urbanism of interactive game worlds, unravelling all the many messages we receive from the moment we pick up the controller and start a new journey. We hope you enjoy taking that journey with us.

1   Jesper Juul, *Half-Real* (Cambridge, MA & London: MIT Press, 2005).

2   Katherine Isbister, *How Games Move Us: Emotion by Design* (Cambridge, MA & London: MIT Press, 2017), 53.

3   Madelon Vriesendorp, *Flagrant délit* (1975).

4   Mark Monmonier, *How to Lie with Maps* (Chicago and London: The University of Chicago Press, 1991), 25.

5   Such methods have been called 'counterplay', ways of playing games to reveal new knowledge about them, as discussed in *The Fiberculture Journal*, Issue 16: *Counterplay* (2010).

6   Noclip is broadly defined as the suspension of game physics allowing 'ghosting' through walls. A definition from Doom creator John Carmack was referenced by Twitter user @me_irl following an email conversation with @ID_AA_Carmack (John Carmack) posted 11:50 PM - 16 Nov 2012. 'john carmack on 'no clipping''. pastebin.com/8sj4RAxq

7   Oxford Languages defines a folksonomy as 'a user-generated system of classifying and organizing online content into different categories by the use of metadata such as electronic tags.'

○ VIDEOGAME ATLAS

Sections

ASSASSIN'S CREED UNITY

Details

Year	2014
Developer	Ubisoft Montreal
Publisher	Ubisoft

Platforms

PlayStation 4

Microsoft Windows   Xbox One

Google Stadia

In *Assassin's Creed Unity*, Paris becomes a landscape of movement, a compressed city where windows are doors, rooftops are path-ways and gathered crowds create new urban territories.

☐ Maps:

07 Districts
21 Viewpoints

1.1   Parisian Parkour

The planning of videogame cities often involves a set of considerations that would never normally enter an architect's vocabulary. For some games, urban space becomes not only a visual anchor for the action taking place, but a key protagonist working to facilitate the game itself. The *Assassin's Creed* series, with its emphasis on stealth and combat in historical urban locations, is a significant example of this. While many of the urban features the games portray are true (or reasonably approximate), the emphasis on unique modes of navigation truly shapes the city.

While the 2014 game *Assassin's Creed Unity* is not necessarily considered the best game in the series and was beset with glitches and issues on its release, it has one of the most developed and fluid free-running systems of all the *Assassin's Creed* titles. The game is placed within late-18th-century Paris, at the time of the French Revolution and the rise of figures such as Napoleon. As a Helix initiate reliving the virtual memories of Arno Dorian, the player must perform a series of assassinations that centre around famous monuments in Paris including Notre-Dame, the Palais du Luxembourg or Palais-Royal, and now-destroyed buildings such as the Tuileries Palace. By structuring the city around these notable buildings, the game presents a version of Paris that becomes progressively distorted as one navigates away from the central islands of Île de la Cité and Île Saint-Louis [Fig. 1].

The game also provides brief flashes of Paris in different times, accessed through Helix Rifts, server anomalies that allow Arno to travel to other eras including the Belle Époque of the late 19th century and occupied Paris during the Second World War. Here we see the city framed much more tightly, with the Second World War sections taking place exclusively around the iconic Eiffel Tower. But it is clear through the story of the game that we are mainly focused on Paris at a time of extreme and historically significant unrest. This is emphasized through the design of the game world and its systems, with *Unity* creating a warren of narrow streets, sloping rooftops and squares filled with baying crowds around the historical monuments we might recognize today. As such it is both the story and the technical innovations behind the game that tie its world to this key period of French history.

1

Map of Paris showing the different districts of the city with borders defined by monumental Viewpoints.

+ 250%

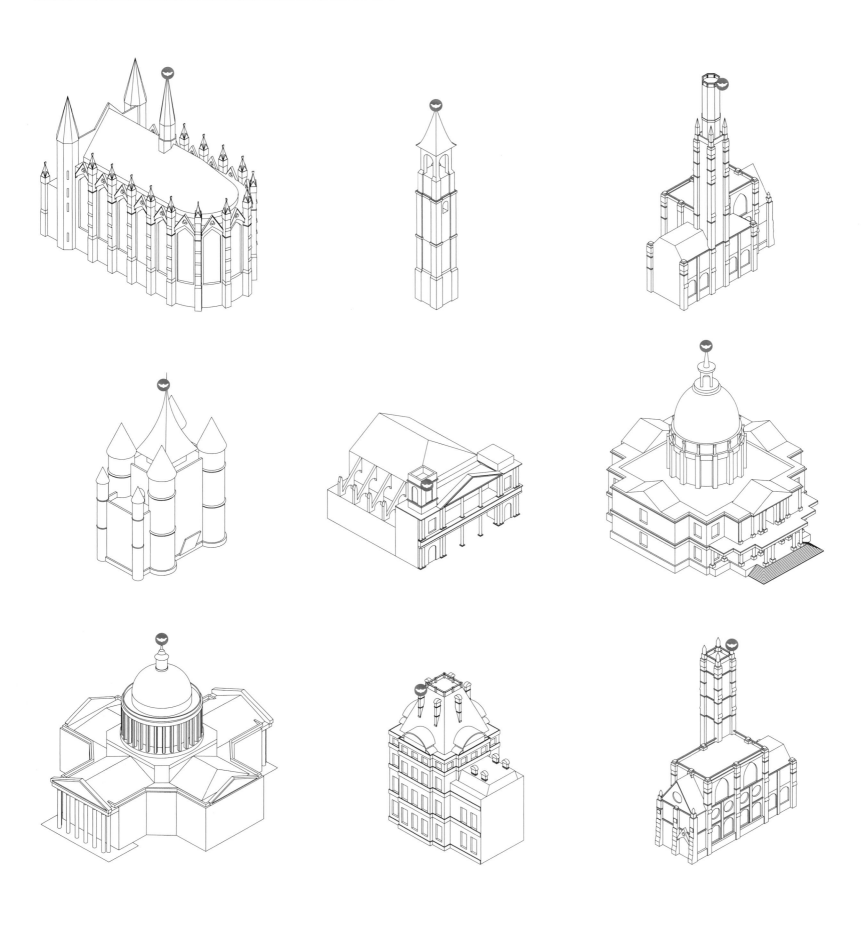

2

Diagram showing a selection of monumental buildings that provide Viewpoints for players to ascend.

1.2   Monumental Viewpoints

As with most *Assassin's Creed* games, the open world is punctuated by a series of high vantage points where players can 'unlock' parts of the main map. *Unity* has twenty-three such Viewpoints – twenty-one in Paris and two in Versailles – that can be used to reveal the map to the player while establishing fast travel points. These generally take the form of monuments one can still find in Paris, aside from a few that have been lost in the years between the game's setting and the real city we see today. By reconstructing some of these Viewpoints, we can see that they clearly trend towards the type of buildings that would also have provided marker points in the real city, such as churches and cathedrals alongside notable public and institutional buildings [Fig. 2]. As we scale each of these buildings, we find common features – the player typically 'synchronizes' the Viewpoint with Arno's memories from a projecting timber ledge, or a crucifix at the top of a spire. At this point the game's camera zooms out and orbits around Arno, giving us an aerial overview of the city and unlocking that portion of the map, showing how engagements at a smaller, architectural scale have a larger urban impact. As we encounter these monuments in-game, their similarity to reality can be startling. As detailed in an article in *The Verge*, Notre-Dame was the product of designer Caroline Miousse working for fourteen months to recreate it,[1] and the in-game building is covered in tiny details. Yet if we approach the building while holding down our controller's RT and A buttons, Arno will start to rapidly climb its face. The navigation system of *Unity* turns every building in Paris into a new territory; a set of vertical surfaces for us to traverse and use to move ourselves quickly around space. While Arno moves 'magnetically' towards handholds in a general direction, the system still places some limits on where we can climb, requiring the player to identify elements in the façade to grab on to and lift themselves to a higher vantage point.

On the façade of Notre-Dame, for example, we can see elements that the player cannot grab hold of, even though some, such as pipe-like columns, would presumably be trivial for Arno to utilize. This draws the player up into the centre of the building towards a series of scaffolds, which allow the player to ascend to the top of the cathedral's famous towers [Fig. 3]. Although the game's developers have said that they did not have to design set paths given that the navigation system is highly flexible,[2] we can still see elements that Arno does not recognize as climbable, even if they would seem to be in reality.

One example of this would be the way the game treats windows, with the leaded frames of certain windows being surmountable while others, including some on Notre-Dame's face, remain inaccessible. The augmentation of the building is not limited to the addition of non-original climbing elements, but also includes the combining of multiple historical stages of the building. The cathedral's original spire, built in the 13th century, had degraded and was removed around a decade before the events of *Unity*, while the lead-covered timber version that players can climb in the game was only started some fifty years later, and was completed in 1859, collapsing in the fire of 2019.[3]

By comparison, the Bourse de Commerce has more clearly delineated boundaries in its circular façade, with players able to climb every pillar flanking entrance gates. Things become a little less well defined on the dome of the building, where Arno can lever himself upwards using the frames of windows, but at any other point on the surface he simply slides back down again [Fig. 4]. Just as with Notre-Dame, the player can look and find elements on the surface of the building that can be climbed in order to play a route upwards, but in both cases the contextual nature of the climbing system means Arno tends to ascend smoothly upwards, finding handholds in the general direction the player moves him.

The interiors of famous buildings have also been augmented to facilitate the player's mobility. The very first mission as an assassin involves Arno tracking a target through Notre-Dame, perhaps following their path from the ropes strung across the space. In later side missions we can go inside the Pantheon, where we find many scaffolds, ladders and rope walks, while the edging and cornices of the space are also made wide enough for Arno to walk along or hang from. Seen from the top of the dome, we understand that the architecture itself has been thoroughly modulated to allow for the player to explore it in new ways. At the same time, we find many of the buildings in the game to be in a perpetual state of construction or occupied by elements that just so happen to be climbable [Fig. 5].

1   Andrew Webster, 'Building a Better Paris in Assassin's Creed Unity', *The Verge*, theverge.com/2014/10/31/7132587/assassins-creed-unity-paris
2   YouTube, IGN, 'Making Assassin's Creed Unity: Part 4 – Gameplay Evolution', youtube.com/watch?v=kCM_8ee2bpU
3   Karen Zraick and Heather Murphy, 'Notre-Dame Cathedral: Facts and a Brief History', *The New York Times*, nytimes.com/2019/04/15/world/europe/notre-dame-cathedral-facts.html

Elevation of Notre-Dame cathedral showing areas for climbing and those that are inaccessible for Arno. Here we can see how the design of the navigational areas forces players up the centre of the building.

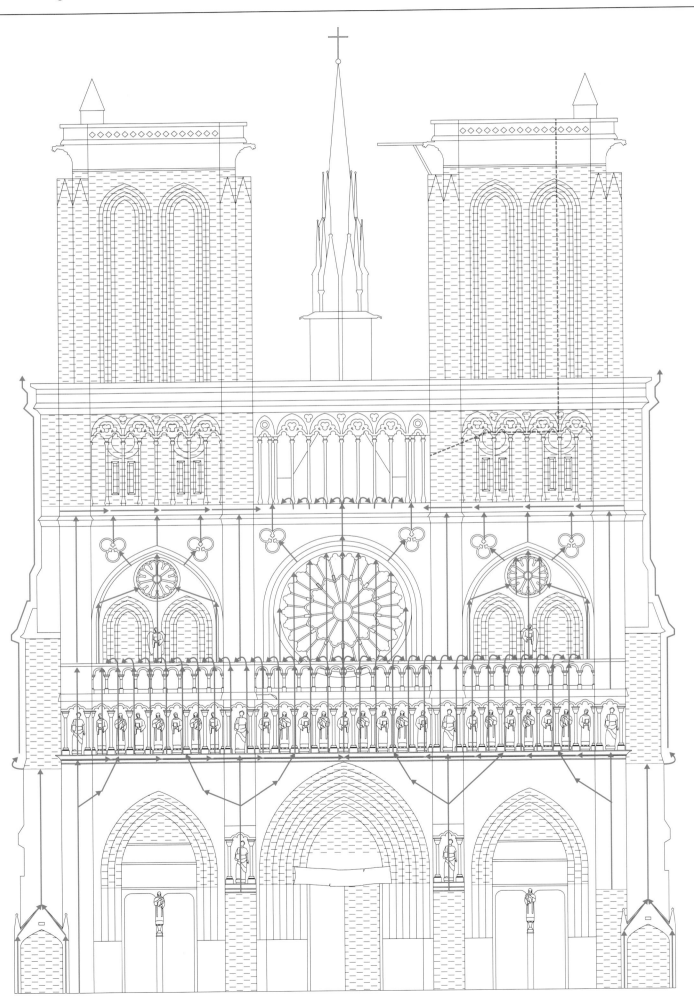

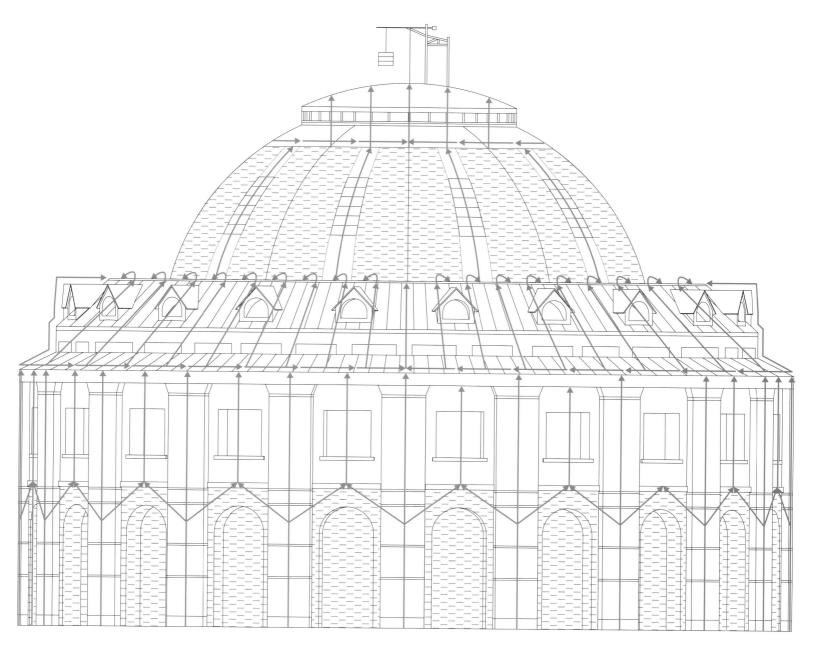

Elevation of the Bourse de Commerce, indicating climbable and non-climbable areas. The dome must be climbed by means of a window, otherwise players will slide down.

View of the Pantheon's interior showing the climbing infrastructure inserted into the space to aid navigation, including exaggerated ledges, rope wires and scaffold constructions.

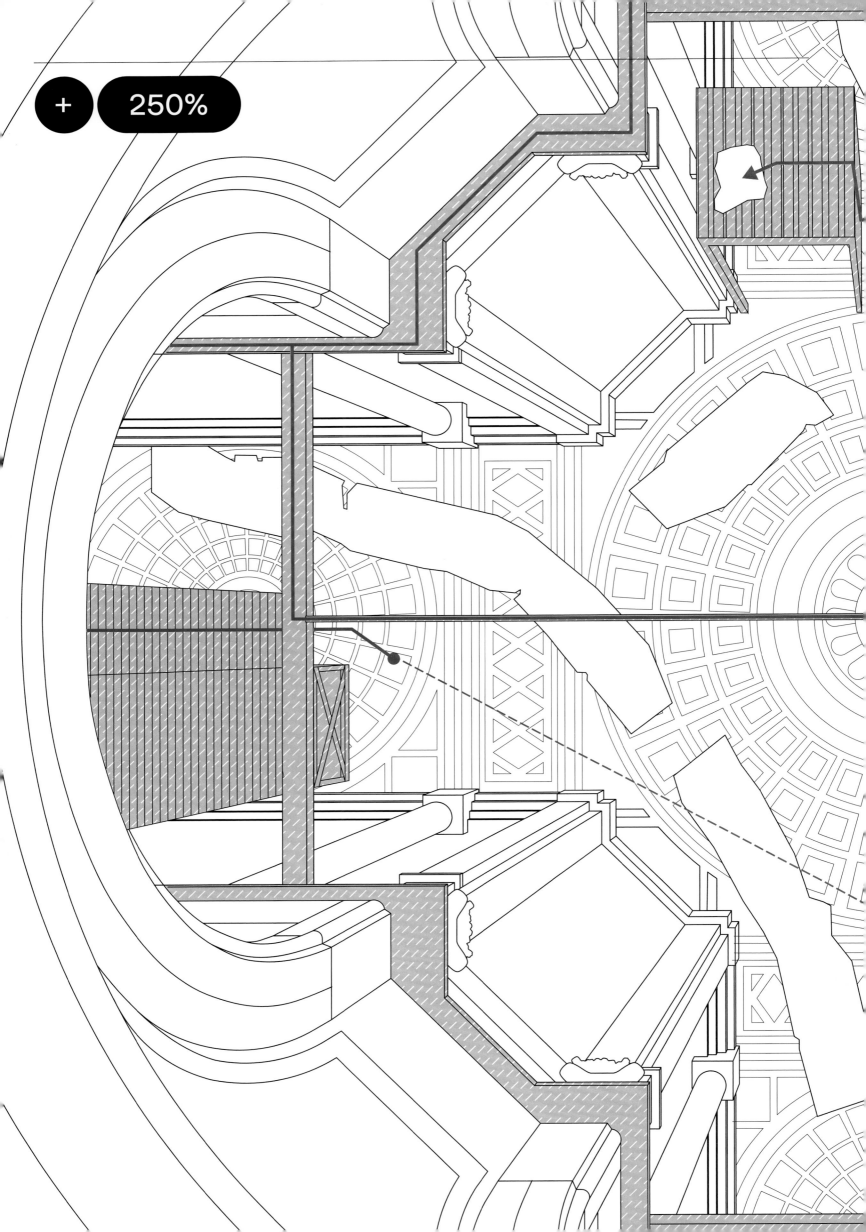

1.3 A Procedural Paris

While the historical monuments provide key reference points for the world of *Unity*, many other buildings and streets have since disappeared, reworked in the Haussmann renovation of Paris. Recreating the milieu of the 18th-century city thus took advantage of procedural techniques, using generative software to create blocks and buildings from a toolkit of parts [Fig. 6]. The developers themselves describe using their House Block Generator as a way of taking street plan shapes and generating sequences of buildings to populate them.[4] Designers could then cycle through possibilities to create unique streets that also allowed for smooth movement across rooftops. Here the tool allows for the creation of dense approximations of Parisian urbanism while also providing the necessary ability to shape the roofscape, which is one of the most significant thoroughfares in the game.

There are certain forms of Parisian architecture that lend themselves well to parkour. These include the city's famous double-sloping mansard roofs, a design innovation emerging around the 17th century that allowed for additional interior floors within a building, secreted within the roof. Many streets within *Assassin's Creed Unity*'s Paris are just wide enough for Arno to jump from the top slope of a mansard to the facing building's guttering line, and this distance of roughly 7.5 m (24 ft 7¼ in.) comes to define the spacing of many blocks, particularly in the central districts of the map. The world is compressed using what has been described as 'radial scaling.' Working out from the Notre-Dame, the relative gap between notable buildings in their real and in-game positions increases with distance from the centre [Fig. 7].

While the infill buildings are generated through the procedural tool, much of the mobility of the game is facilitated by various repeated elements that are incorporated into buildings of all types. Together these elements create a new symbolic language, where even as we walk slowly through Paris, we can see repeated signs of the parkour landscape above us, allowing the player to move and act quickly at a moment's notice. This is a language of scaffolds, pulleys, flagpoles, handholds and gargoyles that are regularly deployed across the city to keep Arno moving with ease [Fig. 8]. The most incongruous – thus overtly revealing this infrastructure – are the hay-filled wagons that Arno can dive into from the tops of tall buildings. These carts are placed around the city, typically at the foot of monuments, Viewpoints and mission zones. Sometimes, as with the Tuileries Palace, the wagon appears entirely unsuited to the contextual surroundings, sitting as it does just outside the front door of a palatial façade. The strange contextual placing of

parkour elements can also be seen in the Belle Époque levels, where the same hay-filled carts and pulley lifts are present despite the presumed technological innovations that have taken place in the intervening century.

Observed together, this procedural system and the language of bolt-on elements form blocks of buildings where both the façade and the roof become surfaces for navigation. While such blocks do sometimes contain interior spaces with windows that Arno can vault through, more often the inside of the building – the space normally dedicated to circulation and the movement of people – is closed off while the exterior of the building, usually dedicated to keeping out the elements, is entirely dedicated to movement [Fig. 9]. This is, however, the movement of (typically) one person. While some characters will also navigate rooftops with Arno, most enemies will not attempt to climb and follow. The architecture of *Unity*'s Paris is a manifestation of the way a parkour traceur sees the city.

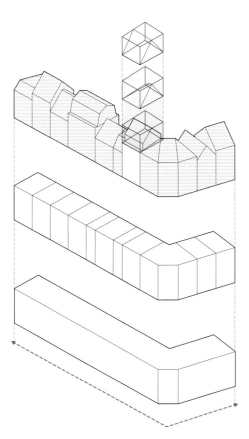

6

The House Block Generator used by the developers enables the creation of procedural streetscapes using architectural archetypes.

4   YouTube, IGN, 'Making Assassin's Creed Unity: Part 2 – Next Generation Technology', youtube.com/watch?v=QGA0WZLp_08

7

Map comparing the position of monuments in *Unity* to their real-life location. Here we can see the 'radial scaling' employed by the designers in action, as comparative distances grow larger towards the edge of the city.

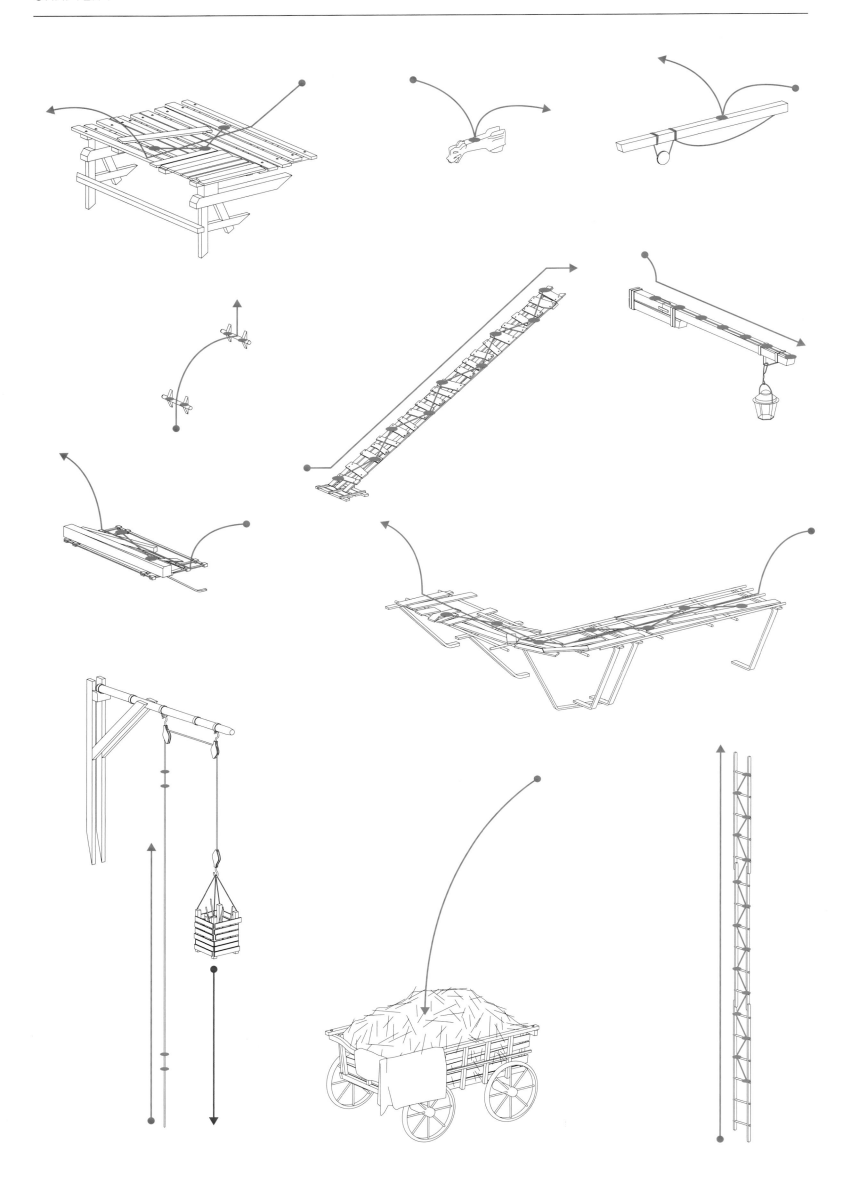

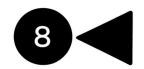

Examples of climbing elements that are reused across Paris. These components are attached to many types of buildings to promote navigation.

The combination of procedurally generated blocks and attached climbing components can be seen in a slice of Paris, allowing Arno to quickly ascend and descend the architecture as needed.

☐ Elements:

07 Social Clubs
07 Helix Rifts
15 Crime Scenes

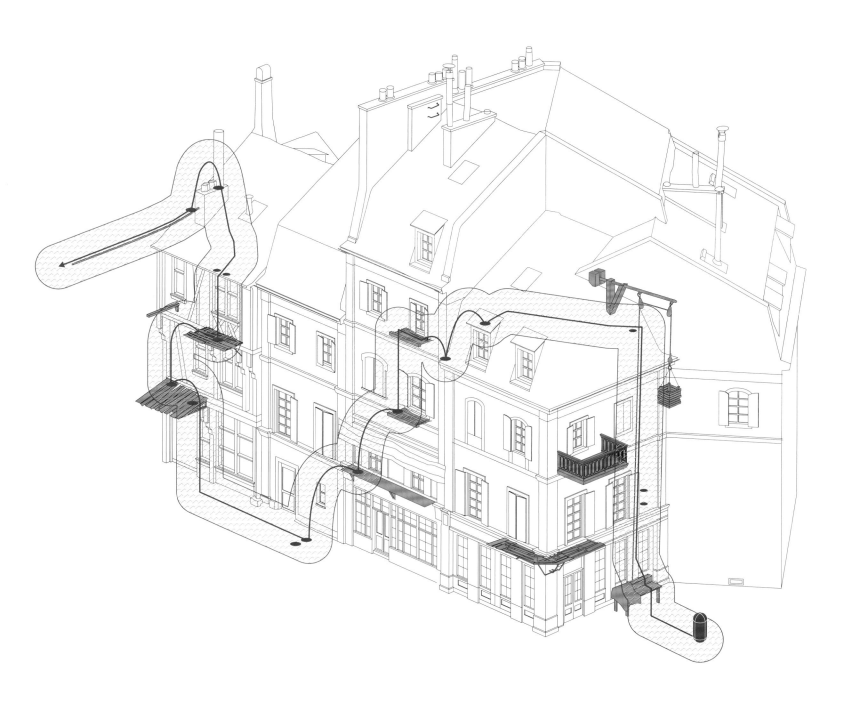

Architectural details made for specific chase missions, such as a landscape of chimney points placed in convenient locations that the player uses to chase a hot-air balloon across the rooftops.

At other points in the game, we can see that the language and placement of objects is clearly more handcrafted, to direct the player on a particular journey. This still fits within the language of the city, appearing as a kind of spatial 'coincidence' as the player moves through Paris at high speed. In the mission 'The Escape', Arno must chase an out-of-control hot-air balloon, jumping between houses and dodging guards as he tries to catch up with Elise's flightpath. Near the end of the chase, chimney pots pile up and cluster together, allowing Arno to hop from foot to foot in a sprint [Fig. 10]. Chimneys, typically placed within the party wall of two buildings, are instead scattered across the rooftops of the building at the precise distances of Arno's leaps. While in the game this facilitates Arno's forward movement, in reality this would create an internal space below that is inconveniently compromised by these heavy structural elements.

In another mission, entitled 'Starving Times', players must chase a boat along the River Seine, barrelling through a bridge before hopping across a series of mooring posts and jumping from boat to boat. In a similar fashion to the chimney pots, here the distribution of built elements belies their real function, with several moorings that appear to be inaccessible to boats due to their position, but prove highly useful for Arno to jump from one jetty to another [Fig. 11].

While both missions require us to move rapidly so as not to lose the target and desynchronize memories, if we return to the mission areas afterwards we can see that these same quirks of design remain in the city. Much like the game-world cliché of 'chest-high walls'[5] these architectural details might appear to be strange errors were it not for our understanding of how they are closely linked to Arno's mobility at a specific point in time, and this holds true for other aspects of the game world's design.

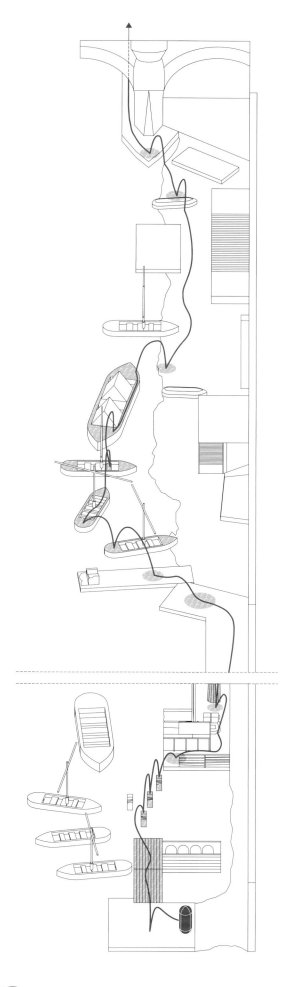

Boats and moorings are carefully placed together to form a choreographed route that players must use to follow another boat along the banks of the Seine.

5   Giant Bomb, 'Concept: Chest-High Walls', giantbomb. com/chest-high-walls/3015-4410/

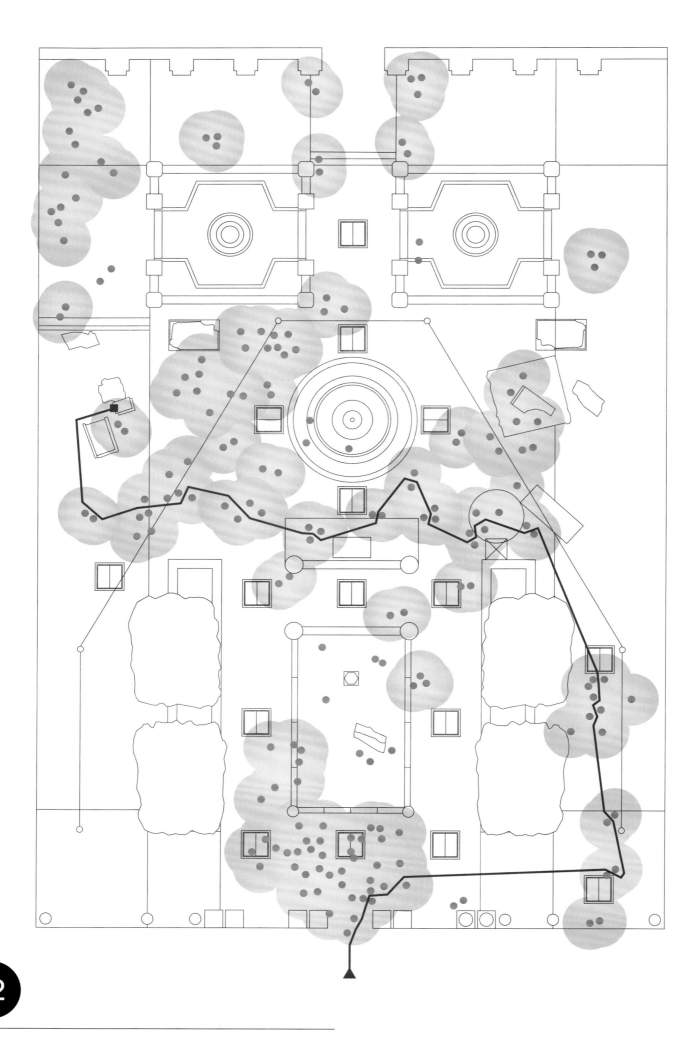

12

Plan of the Palais Royal showing the spaces occupied by
the crowd. Players can disappear from the view of guards
by carefully tracing a path through the densest areas.

1.4   Space of the Crowd

Another form of space that is ubiquitous in the *Assassin's Creed* series is the space of the crowd. Groups of people together automatically conceal Arno from guards, allowing him to enter buildings and areas undetected. While in the design of real cities, many architectural designers focus on the movement of crowds through their building using digital simulations (including analytical groups such as Space Syntax[6]), in *Unity* crowds can also be used as static zones, with the positioning of non-player characters (NPCs) creating an invisible landscape of stealthy space for Arno to utilize. The study of crowds and their sociology is closely tied to the time period depicted in *Unity*, with a number of influential theorists and texts on crowds having used the French Revolution as the starting point for their critical analysis.[7]
In the mission 'A Dinner Engagement', we can see this clearly demonstrated in plan where the courtyard of the Palais Royal is filled with revellers, allowing the player to trace a path through the space. We can therefore consider the crowds to be integral to the architectural design of the environment, as much a part of the space as the hedges, statues or trees [Fig. 12]. By using consumables such as the money purse, players can start to move this crowd space around Arno, attracting people to the area through thrown coins.

To integrate crowds as a spatial tool, the developers needed to create a system that could accommodate many people in an area at once. As detailed in a GDC talk, a system using abstracted figures called 'bulks' means that the game can scale NPCs up and down both visually and in the complexity of their AI routines in real time.[8] As Arno traverses this landscape of people, they change from mute, blocky objects in space, to walking and talking characters [Fig. 13]. These techniques are very similar to those typically used to render the world itself, such as level of detail (LOD) models, which reinforces the notion that crowds can be considered a key part of the architectural setting within the game.

In the mission that follows, 'The Execution', this space of the crowd is extended out to a colossal scale, with many thousands of NPCs gathering in the Tuileries Garden to witness the execution of the king. By mapping the areas covered by this sea of people, we can clearly see that the space the player is concerned with is not the ornate and symmetrical form of the garden with its hedges so much as it is the scattering of people across the grounds of the park, providing a complex territory for scouting and searching for the target [Fig. 14].

While it is easy to read *Unity*'s Paris through the architecture of iconic monuments and historical buildings, to create a city of movement for Arno the designers of the world have had to maintain several different parallel layers to the space. As we move through the city, we are not only scaling buildings but also thousands of smaller supporting details. By pushing through a crowd we might alternate between being inside and outside of its collective space. While Paris originally gained the nickname 'City of Lights', seemingly in part due to 17th-century innovations designed to make public space safer through infrastructure, in *Unity* we experience a city of crowds, a city of balconies or even a city of chimneys, all working as one.

6   Space Syntax is an academic/industry partnership based in London, employing various techniques in the analysis of urban space. spacesyntax.com

7   In *The Politics of Crowds: An Alternative History of Sociology* (Cambridge: Cambridge University Press, 2012), Christian Borch traces the formation of modern theories on crowd behaviour back to influential French figures in the field such as Gustave Le Bon, and *Germinal*, an 1885 novel by Émile Zola.

8   YouTube, GDC, 'Massive Crowd on Assassin's Creed Unity: AI Recycling', youtube.com/watch?v=Rz2cNWVLncl

☐ Crowds:

10,000 People
3 Scales
1 Target

Assassin's Creed Unity uses a system where people in crowds dynamically scale in visual and AI complexity depending on their distance from the player, enabling lifelike interactions with huge numbers of people.

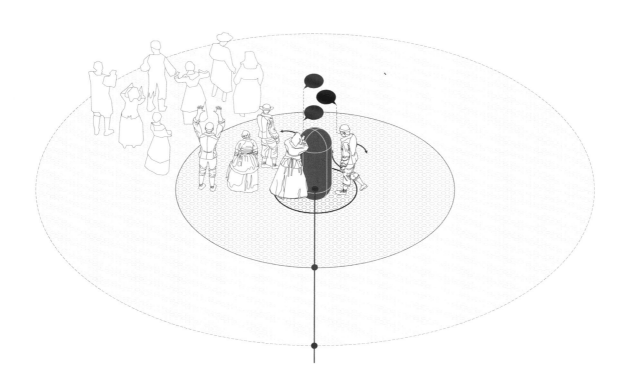

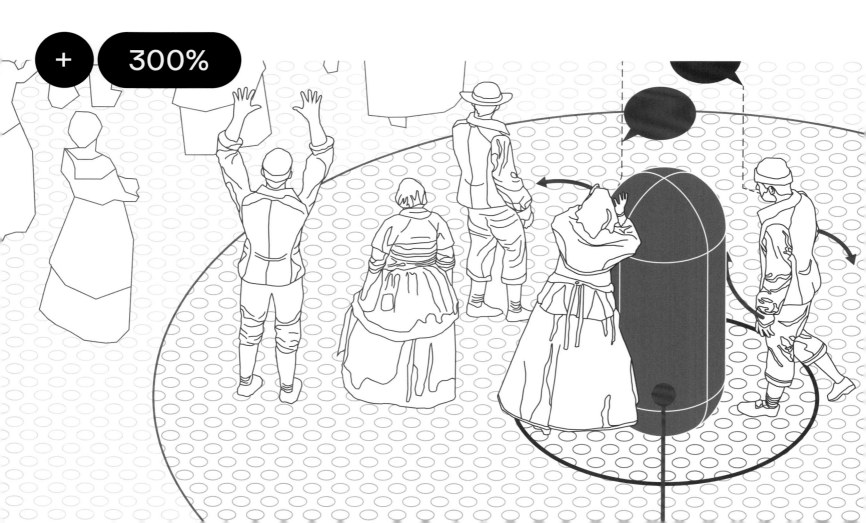

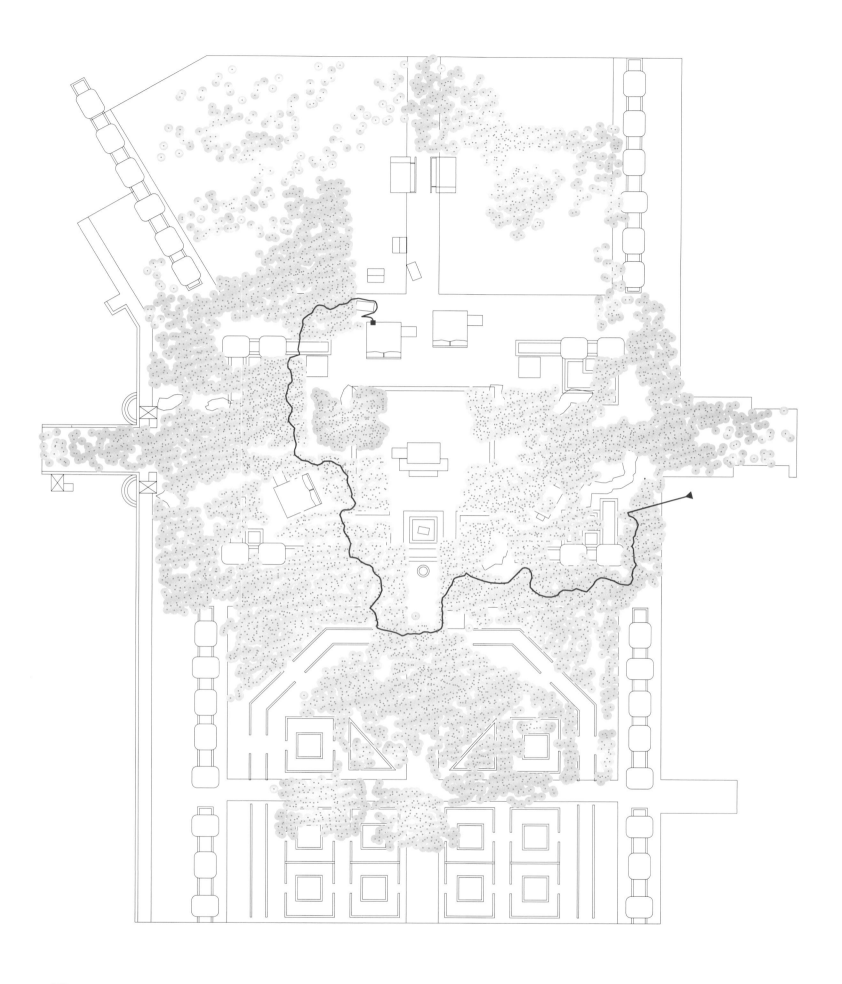

14

Plan of the Tuileries Garden showing a crowd of
approximately 10,000 NPCs, which Arno uses as
a space to mask his approach to a target.

○ VIDEOGAME ATLAS

Sections

CITIES: SKYLINES

Details

Year	2015
Developer	Colossal Order
Publisher	Paradox Interactive

Platforms

PlayStation 4   macOS

Microsoft Windows   Linux

Nintendo Switch   Xbox One

By expanding the original game, the player communities of *Cities: Skylines* are enabling new urban forms through tens of thousands of home-brewed modifications, from the practical and infrastructural to the fantastical.

☐ Maps:

12 Base
45+ DLC
48,000+ Community

2.1   Default Geographies

Cities: Skylines is a game that could draw many comparisons to the *SimCity* series, yet in the seven years since its release it has grown organically not only through the efforts of its developers, but through the energy of a huge and prolific modding community that has transformed and extended the capability of Colossal Order's urban simulation. Built on the widely accessible *Unity* engine and providing built-in editing tools, the game was set up to receive the creativity of its user base, who have responded by producing huge numbers of alterations (over 265,000 as of 2021). To understand the systems of *Cities: Skylines*, and the types of cities it promotes, we should examine what is provided in the base 'vanilla' game, and what has been expanded by the efforts of the community.

When we look at a city created in the game, such as the popular 'pre-made' city Fluxburgh, (by Steam Workshop user 'Flux'), we can see a complex urban system represented to the player through the traditional 'god view' oversight [Fig. 1]. With the intricate systems of roads, developed shorelines and suburban drift, it is easy to mistake a *Cities: Skylines* city for a real-life counterpart, albeit somewhat more compressed than we might expect.

It is unlikely that players will spend much of their time simply gazing at their city, for the trade-off for having the godlike overview is the requirement to delve into all of its systems in a way a real-life mayor would never be likely to. The *Cities: Skylines* user interface provides us with many diagnostic maps and data analysis tools – we can design and connect our water systems and electricity, build transit and waste systems, and mediate the culture and leisure of the city's inhabitants. Being able to rapidly sort through these layers [Fig. 2] and parse their information is important to the success of any given design. As real-life cities increasingly rely on big data, with the risk that huge amounts of computer-analysed information 'might generate spectacular results but offer no new human-readable insights into the subject at hand',[1] *Cities: Skylines* requires that we, as human players, negotiate this information and intuit how to proceed.

The game provides players with a series of vanilla base maps of 5x5 active tiles, giving the player a possible play area of 92.16 km^2, which is comparable to the size of Zürich, Switzerland. While some of these maps are non-geographical, others are based on portions of real-world locations including Hong Kong, Washington, DC and Istanbul. In these instances, key landforms and water bodies are extracted from the cities while being simplified and adapted to the playable scale of the game [Fig. 3]. Each map comes with its own challenges and opportunities through features such as undulating terrain, coastline, climate and raw materials, which might not fall within the immediately playable area of the map. As a result, the community considers some base maps to be easier than others, setting the scene for a well-balanced city. Other maps are immediately more demanding, with intersecting rivers and steep terrains requiring more complex responses – with the different choices catering to a range of players and abilities. These challenges can also be social. *Cities: Skylines* has been regularly referenced (and played) by real-life urban planners, but sometimes these discussions emphasize what the game might make difficult in terms of the type of society it promotes. An article in the *Guardian*, for example, focused on the challenges of building a socialist city within the game.[2] By looking further into *Cities: Skylines* and its systems, alongside the type of communities it generates both within the game and outside, in the player base, we can start to understand more about how its simulations work and how far they mirror (or do not) what types of cities might be possible today.

1   Ed Finn, *What Algorithms Want: Imagination in the Age of Computing* (Cambridge, MA & London: MIT Press, 2018), 90.

2   Finn Williams, 'The Guardian Cities: Skylines challenge – can I build a truly anti-capitalist city?' accessed 16/08/21, theguardian.com/cities/2015/aug/06/guardian-cities-skylines-challenge-build-anti-capitalist-post-growth-city

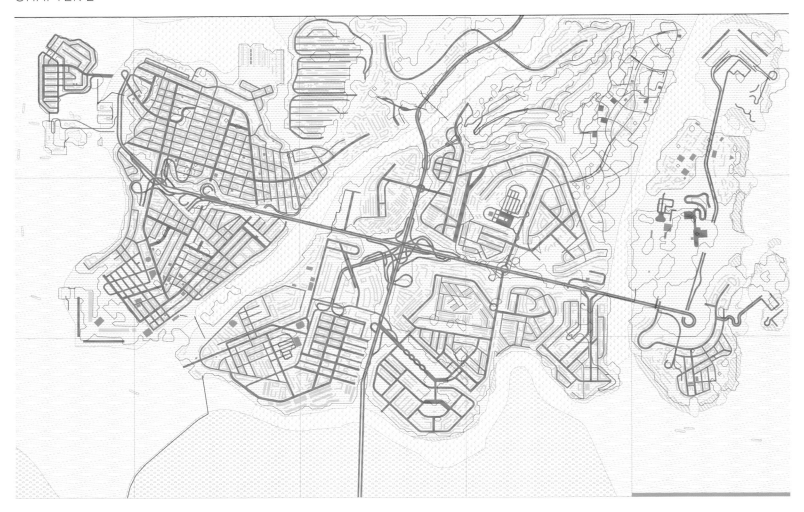

Map of Fluxburgh, one of the most popular
'pre-made' saves that players can download from
Steam Workshop.

+ 350%

Layers of infrastructure in Fluxburgh, separating water, waste, fire, electricity and unique buildings as systems that sustain the city's growth.

Selection of 'vanilla' base maps available for the player to select when they start the game that are based on real-world locations. These diagrams compare the real geographies of Stockholm, Hong Kong, St Louis, Venice, Istanbul, Washington, DC, Greece and San Francisco to how they are translated in the game.

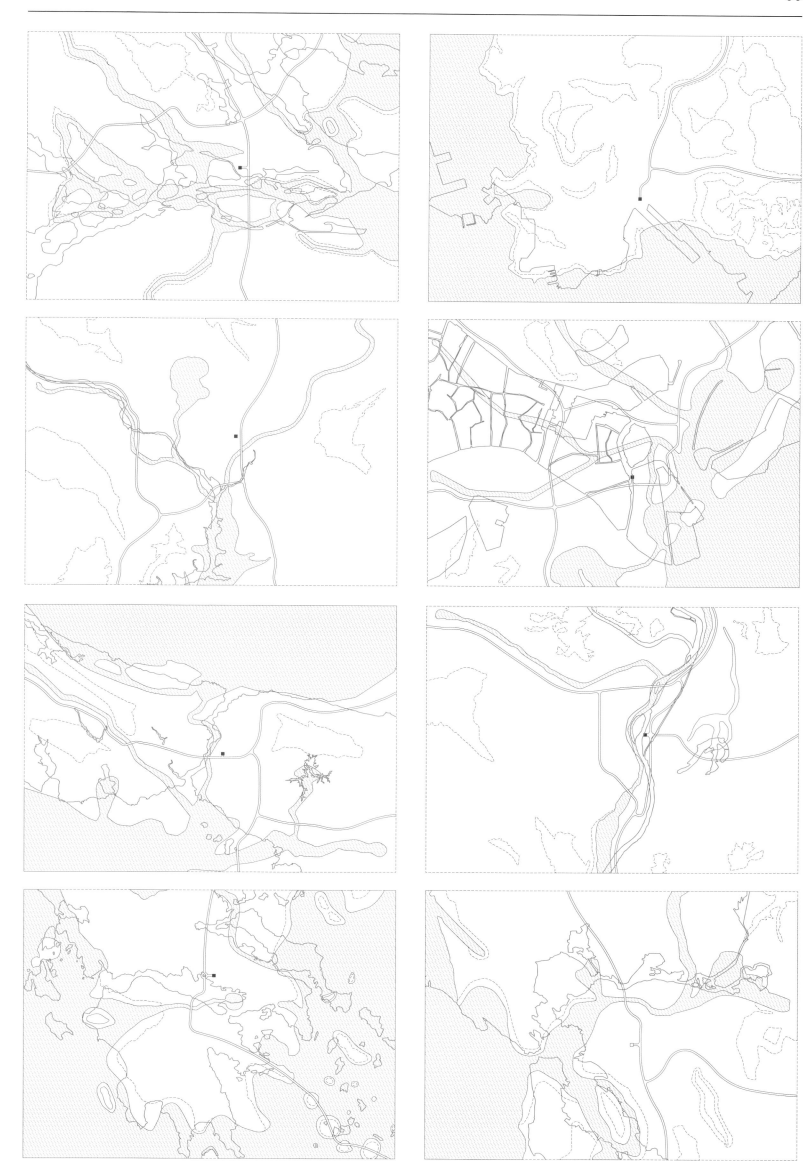

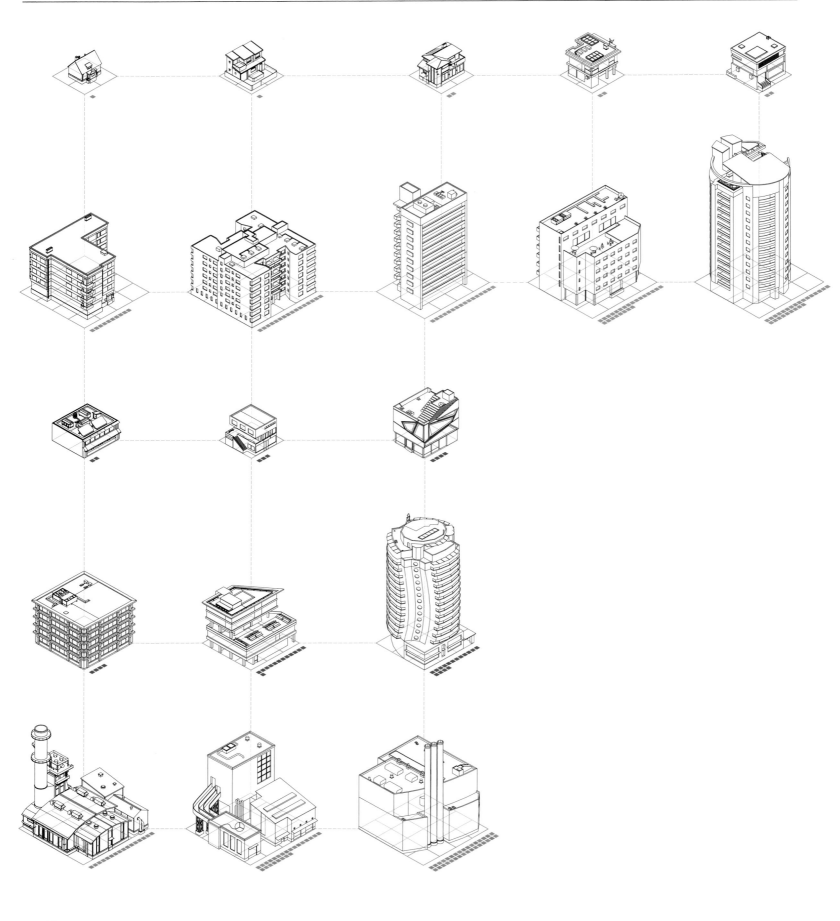

4

Analysing the growth of residential, commercial
and industrial buildings as they level up in the game,
and how this transforms their appearance,
occupancy and scale.

2.2   Augmenting the Zone

Cities: Skylines uses a model of urban zoning to designate various parts of the city to different functions. While zoning is a technique used in many countries to organize different forms of development, the game simulates what is known as 'non-hierarchical' zoning, where each different zoning type is attached to a different function.[3] In real urban design, and within the game's simulation, this means that zones are designated for discrete uses – so a low-rise residential zone will have no commercial buildings, and vice-versa. This is a mirror to games such as *Cities: Skylines* or *SimCity*, described by Daniel Lobo as 'a reflection of the most extreme tendencies of development in the USA'.[4] This produces clearly defined areas of building types not appropriate to many cities, while zoning large areas at once encourages the game to fill spaces with bigger 4x4 building units that may also produce a scale not in sync with its surroundings.

All buildings in *Cities: Skylines* also have levels, and as these levels increase, buildings start to become more economically valuable to the city. Residential buildings, for example, will be able to accommodate more families and their residents will be better educated and wealthier as the levels increase. By mapping the various building typologies and levels present in the game, we can see how these buildings are upgraded, and replaced by newer, smarter-looking structures as their level and occupancy grows [Fig. 4]. The game suggests that these plots of land are to be continually redeveloped to progress both its urban scale and the advancement of its society, with buildings being destroyed and rebuilt several times before a zoned area reaches its highest level. Such an approach may not fully reflect the realities of cities with large and sought-after historical housing stock, instead leaning towards a hyper-intensified version of property development trends.

The influential urban theorist Jane Jacobs argued that city districts required 'more than one primary function', attracting 'the presence of people who…are in the place for different reasons', and advised 'mingling' the age and style of buildings.[5] Some of the *Cities: Skylines* community appear to agree. In response to the strict zoning distinction, the game's communities have developed guides to how to subvert the system by changing individual grid squares [Fig. 5].[6] By first applying a chequerboard pattern of one- to two-square zones, the game will automatically fill these with smaller buildings, allowing for more authentic low-rise districts to be created. This can be taken further by limiting things to single spaces, enabling players to produce tighter terraced streets as are common in British cities such as London and Manchester. Here we can see players 'gaming' the zoning systems, downscaling them in a way that allows for control over individual buildings, but in turn subverting the whole principle of zoning itself.

Once players reach certain milestones within the game, they can apply various policies to different districts to affect their growth and operation. One of the most visually significant policies is the High-rise Ban, which prevents a building from reaching its highest level [Fig. 6]. Players have utilized this policy to create transitional zones between high-level buildings and low-level buildings, to prevent such extreme changes in height between two districts. The High-rise Ban is therefore used as a facilitator for mid-rise buildings, filling a typological gap in the games' architectural toolkit. By mediating the heights of buildings more gradually, the skyline can appear more blended in its scale. Cities are frequently shaped by the regulations bestowed on them, visible most notably in the skyscrapers of New York City. In 1916 the city passed zoning laws that regulated the height and mass of the building's envelope, visualized by draughtsman Hugh Ferriss.[7] The characteristic skyscrapers we see today are therefore products of both economics and regulation, and this logic is paralleled in the game.

3   Lichfields planning consultants Think Tank, 'Should zoning be introduced in England?', *Lichfields*, lichfields.uk/blog/2018/may/14/should-zoning-be-introduced-in-england/

4   Daniel G. Lobo, 'Playing With Urban Life: How SimCity Influences Planning Culture', *Space Time Play: Computer Games, Architecture and Urbanism: The Next Level* (Basel: Birkhäuser Verlag, 2007), 208.

5   Jane Jacobs, *The Death and Life of Great American Cities* (New York: Vintage Books, 1961), 150-151.

6   Steam Guide by user 'simonmd', 'Zoning areas. making good use of smaller buildings', posted 21 March 2015, steamcommunity.com/sharedfiles/filedetails/?id=411155282

7   Hugh Ferriss, *The Metropolis of Tomorrow* (Ives Washburn, 1929).

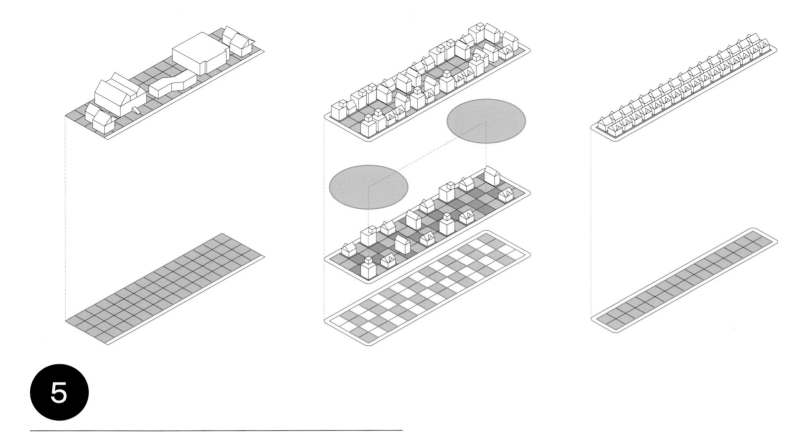

5

Diagram showing how players manipulate the zoning system by placing individual squares to promote different types of urban form, such as terraced housing, that are impossible in the game's base system.

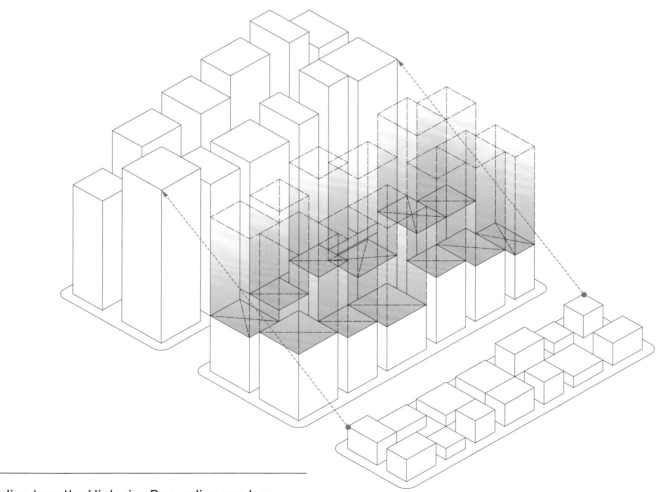

6

Understanding how the High-rise Ban policy can be applied to different districts by preventing buildings from reaching their maximum level. This offers players the ability to create a mediating buffer between low-rise and skyscraper building blocks.

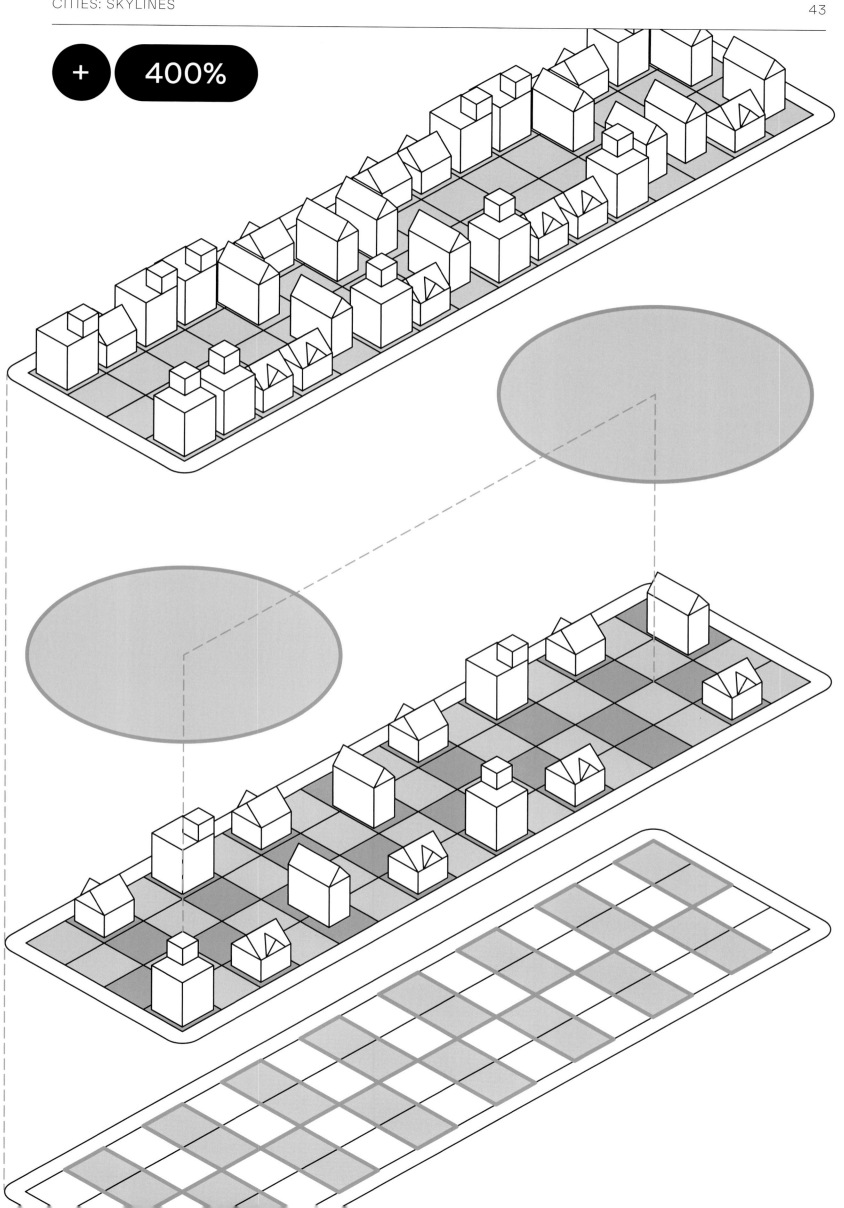

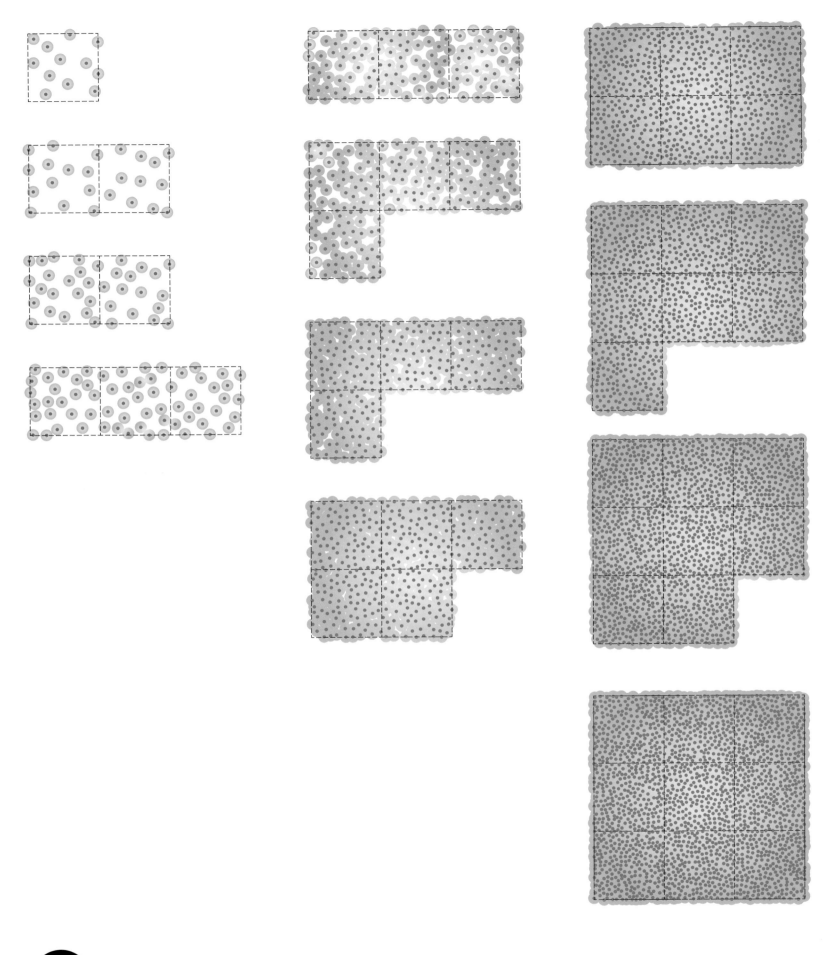

7

Population density is tied to the area of the city, reaching new milestones to expand from a Little Hamlet to a full-blown Megalopolis.

2.3   Constructing a Community

Cities: Skylines allows players to expand their city by unlocking new 'milestones', with a total of nine grid squares to occupy without mods. By reaching a minimum population limit, the territory can grow from a Little Hamlet, which has a required population of 120–480, to a Megalopolis, with 20,000–90,000 inhabitants. With each milestone the player gains access to new services, buildings, policies, finance and zones, increasing their ability to affect the city. As the area expands, so too does the level of occupation, creating a unique relationship between population density and expanse [Fig. 7]. Cims represent the non-player characters (NPCs) of the game, leading different lifestyles that are affected by the decisions of the player. Each cim has its own identity, complete with a name, level of education, life stage, place of residence, employment or education, and current activity. The game allows the player to track each individual cim as they go about their daily life. As individuals as well as a populace, cims can feed back their level of happiness to the player, who must respond to these fluctuating levels to ensure that their city's industry remains stable through a healthy, happy workforce. As mayor, players are given explicit insights into the predicaments of the society they are creating. The complexity of this system and the real-time nature of the feedback given suggests that more direct communication between real-world citizens and policymakers must surely be possible through game interfaces such as *Cities: Skylines*.

Many of the cims' life stages have interesting spatial relationships within the city [Fig. 8]. When the player starts the game, the 'pioneer' cims reside in a single household composed of two adults and two or three children. As a young adult, a child must have moved out of their family home and be married by the age of twenty-five, or they are removed from the game. For this to happen, the player needs to zone new types of housing, such as apartment blocks, to enable multiple residents to cohabit. As a result of zoning this type of housing, external cims migrate into the city to provide suitable partners for the existing cims. Because pioneer cims are not able to marry one another, this zoning progression is critical to facilitate the cims in the next stage of their lives.

As the cims reach their senior years, finally able to live alone, players can increase their lifespan by approximately 10% with Eldercare that provides ample health benefits within close range of the cims' home. Once a cim dies, the critical Deathcare infrastructure transports deceased citizens to cemeteries and crematoriums. The player must ensure that their transportation network is efficient enough to allow for the constant movement of hearses from different residential properties to transport deceased cims to their resting place. If the hearse is unable to pick up the deceased cim, the house becomes abandoned, which means it cannot be immediately re-occupied, and may require demolition. Players also need to manage extreme fluctuations in the cim population known as 'deathwaves', a cyclical phenomenon where large numbers of deaths occur within a city near-simultaneously, putting considerable strain on the Deathcare services.[8] By growing the city at a slower pace, the player can avoid such increases to populations of a similar age, who will ultimately live, grow and die together.

8   Skylines Wiki, 'Healthcare' accessed 16/08/21, skylines.paradoxwikis.com/Healthcare

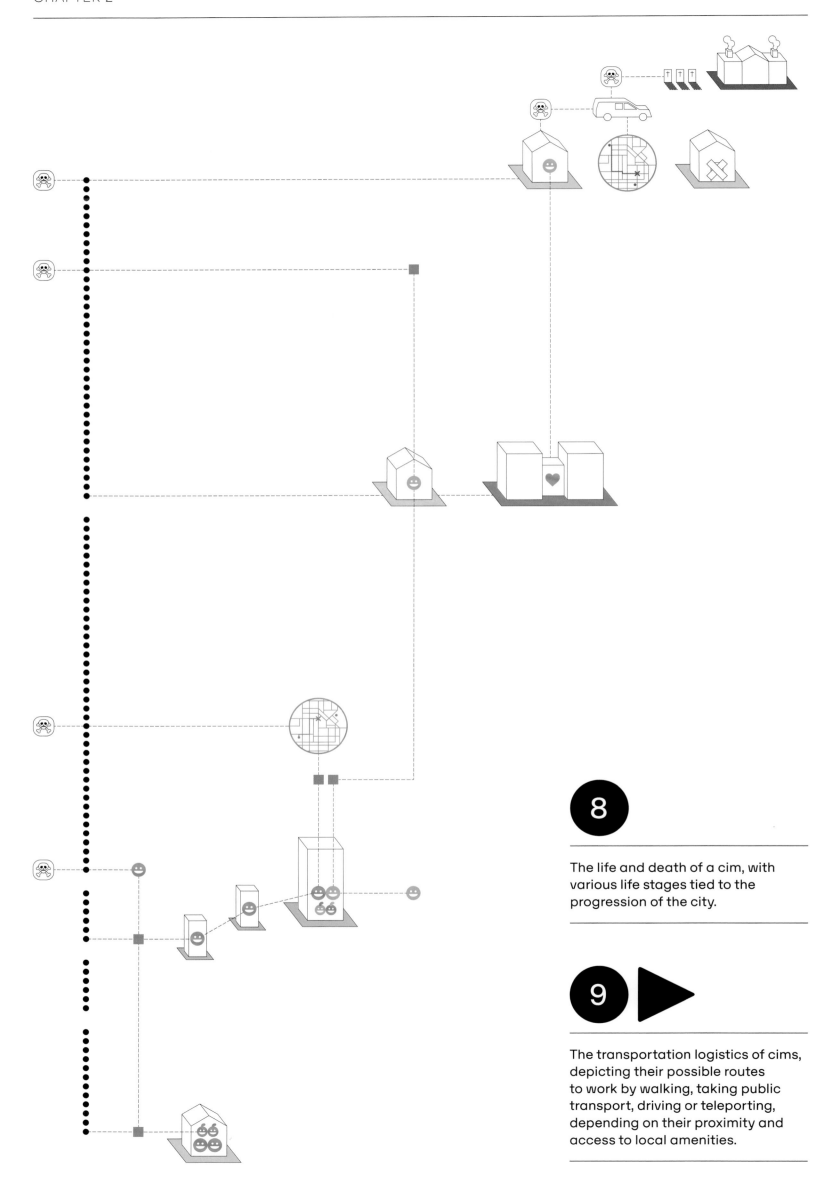

8

The life and death of a cim, with various life stages tied to the progression of the city.

9 ▶

The transportation logistics of cims, depicting their possible routes to work by walking, taking public transport, driving or teleporting, depending on their proximity and access to local amenities.

As the population is made physically visible to the player in the game, with cims inhabiting the streets and driving cars, the game has several mechanics to alleviate heavy loads on the CPU caused by this simulation. By placing a maximum limit on the number of cars allowed on the road within the game, vehicles stuck in gridlock caused by the player's infrastructural actions 'despawn' from the roads to avoid heavy traffic jams. The player is still made aware of the issues within their road systems through the UI, but the physical impact is removed from the game. The movement of cims is also governed by similar logics, through 'teleportation'[9] mechanics. Cims can walk to work within a 1-km (⅔-mile) radius of their home, but if their workplace is further away, they take public transportation. If no transportation links are provided at all, a cim teleports straight to work from their home. These various scenarios often create illogical urban consequences in the game, as players negotiate between mobility, distance and infrastructure [Fig. 9].

Implausible scenarios take place on the streets too when these mechanics collide. Depending on their distribution, if a bus stop gets too full, or a subway takes too long, cims can spawn cars from their pockets to get to work [Fig. 10]. This leads to a sudden influx of people and cars on the streets in certain areas, simulating extreme high-density traffic scenarios. In this way, the overcrowding of real cities is paralleled, but in the game, it is generated by an unlikely virtual circumstance with strange results.

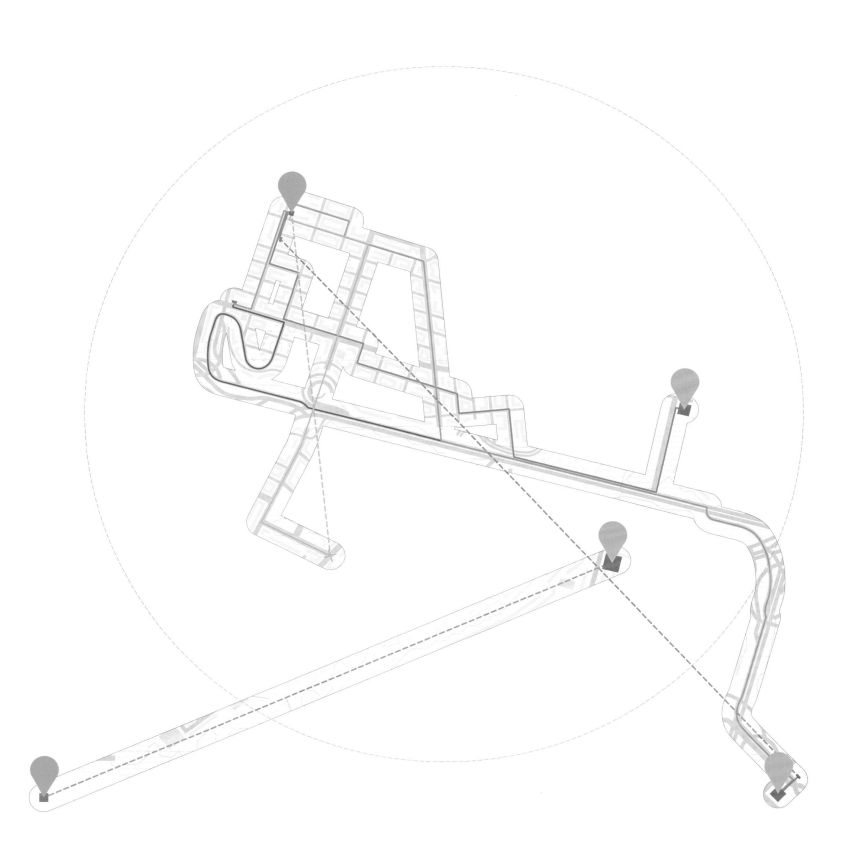

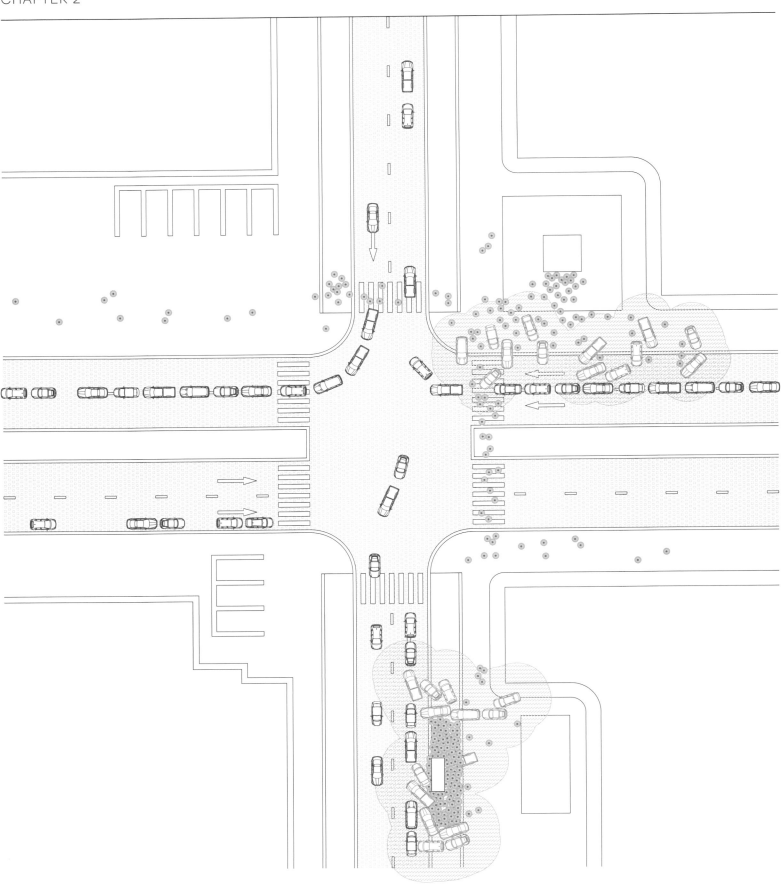

10

The phenomenon created on roads by the spawning of cars, occurring when public transportation hubs become overcrowded, preventing the cim from getting to work.

☐ Vehicles:

16,383 Moving
32,767 Parked

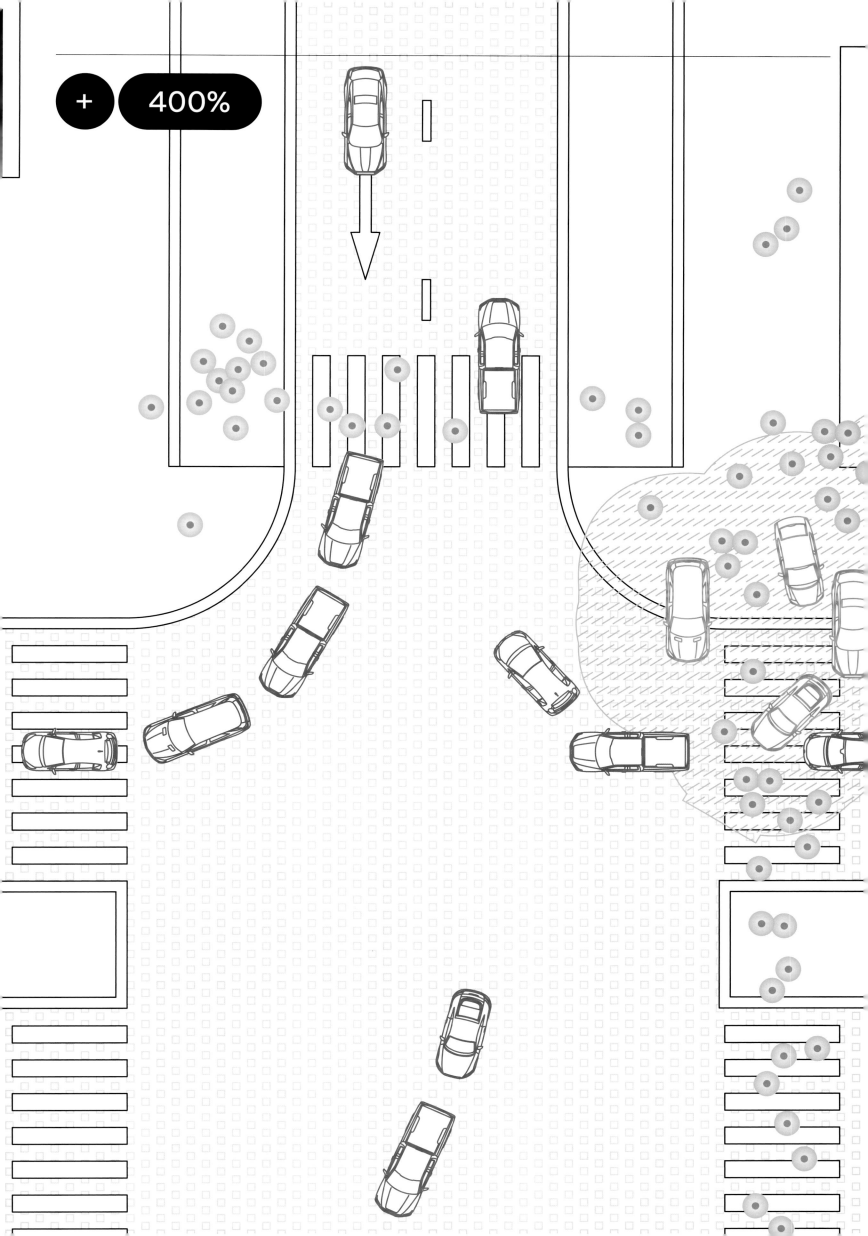

Top ten user-created base maps, each with their own unique geography and combination of landforms, infrastructure and natural resources.

2.4 Workshops of Style

The base version of *Cities: Skylines* offers two styles of city to the player: American and European. As discussed, there are certain logics to the game that prioritize American-style urbanism despite the more European appearance of architecture. The game can also be extended through several sets of downloadable content (DLC) that add different elements, including the 'Natural Disasters', 'Green Cities' or 'Campus' packages. Yet these two styles and DLC additions are dwarfed by the innumerable possibilities offered by the game's connection to Steam Workshop, a community-led portal where different users can create new extensions and modifications to the base game. Adding new buildings or functionality into the game simply requires a player to 'subscribe' to that modification, allowing for the game to be extended in many ways. Through the mods and assets on Workshop, we can start to understand the design desires and interests of the community by tracking what they make, what is popular, and what mechanics they want to change and improve in the base simulation of the city.

In addition to the game's vanilla maps, there are tens of thousands of user-created maps available for download, providing players with a range of different environments in which to situate their cities. The most popular of these, Riverdale by the user Mechalic, has nearly a quarter of a million subscribers and is loosely based on the area of Devonport in New Zealand, situated just outside Auckland. Many other popular environments are not based on real cities in the same way, but instead the authors create maps around resources. This might be the number of highways entering the area or the prevalence of water sources. The proliferation of maps encourages players who wish to pursue a certain type of city to download an environment that fits their desires. Within the most popular maps, we still tend to see landscape forms that match quite closely to those that have assisted the growth of many major cities in reality – proximity to the coastline, rivers and easy access to agricultural land all tend to feature heavily [Fig. 11].

District Styles are complete packages that contain many buildings, allowing players to apply those styles to different areas of the city. These modifications will have many individual models and combinations within them, which then replace the base buildings in the game. The most subscribed District Style of all time is the 'American Eclectic Theme' by the user BoldlyBuilding, with over 130,000 players using the package.[10] Other highly popular styles include 'Baroque Buildings', 'Berlin-inspired', 'Central European', 'Dutch Buildings', 'Japan Urban', 'South of France' and 'Soviet', with another most-subscribed style being 'Army Base Style' [Fig. 12]. By taking samples of these styles, we can see the ways in which the community seeks to enhance the game, introducing new forms of urbanism that are impossible in the *Cities: Skylines* default format.

While District Styles can be assigned to a whole area, we can see how their application affects the architecture of the city right down to the smallest built scale, a 1x1 grid-sized low-density residential unit. These buildings give us further insight into the architectural sensibilities of the community. As expected for a low-density building, these tend towards the suburban, with styles such as 'Midatlantic Victorian', 'Belgian Village Housing', 'UK Village' and 'Brazilian Home' sitting alongside more idiosyncratic types of housing such as 'Viking Peasant Hut' or even 'Squidward's Home' for players seeking to create a Spongebob Squarepants-themed metropolis. These stylistic tropes, often inspired by fantasy, begin to blur the lines between reality and imagination, giving the player authority over the aesthetic rationale of their city and its credibility [Fig. 13].

9   Antti Lehto, Damien Morello, Karoliina Korppoo, 'Game Design Deep Dive: Traffic systems in Cities: Skylines', *Game Developer*, gamedeveloper.com/design/game-design-deep-dive-traffic-systems-in-i-cities-skylines-i-

10 Data obtained from 'Cities: Skylines' Steam Workshop page, steamcommunity.com/workshop/browse/?appid=255710&browsesort=totaluniquesubscribers&section=readytouseitems&requiredtags%5B0%5D=District+Style&actualsort=totaluniquesubscribers&p=1

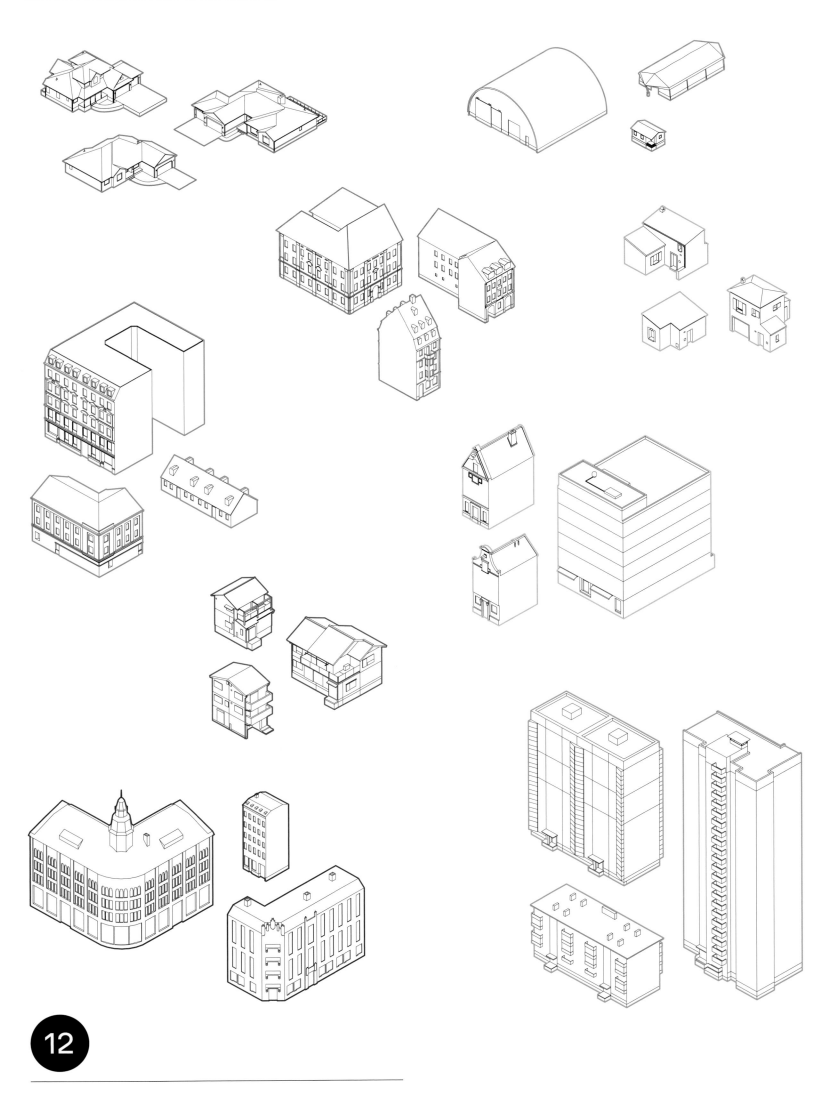

12

Top ten District Styles showing the deviations from
European styles offered by the game itself.

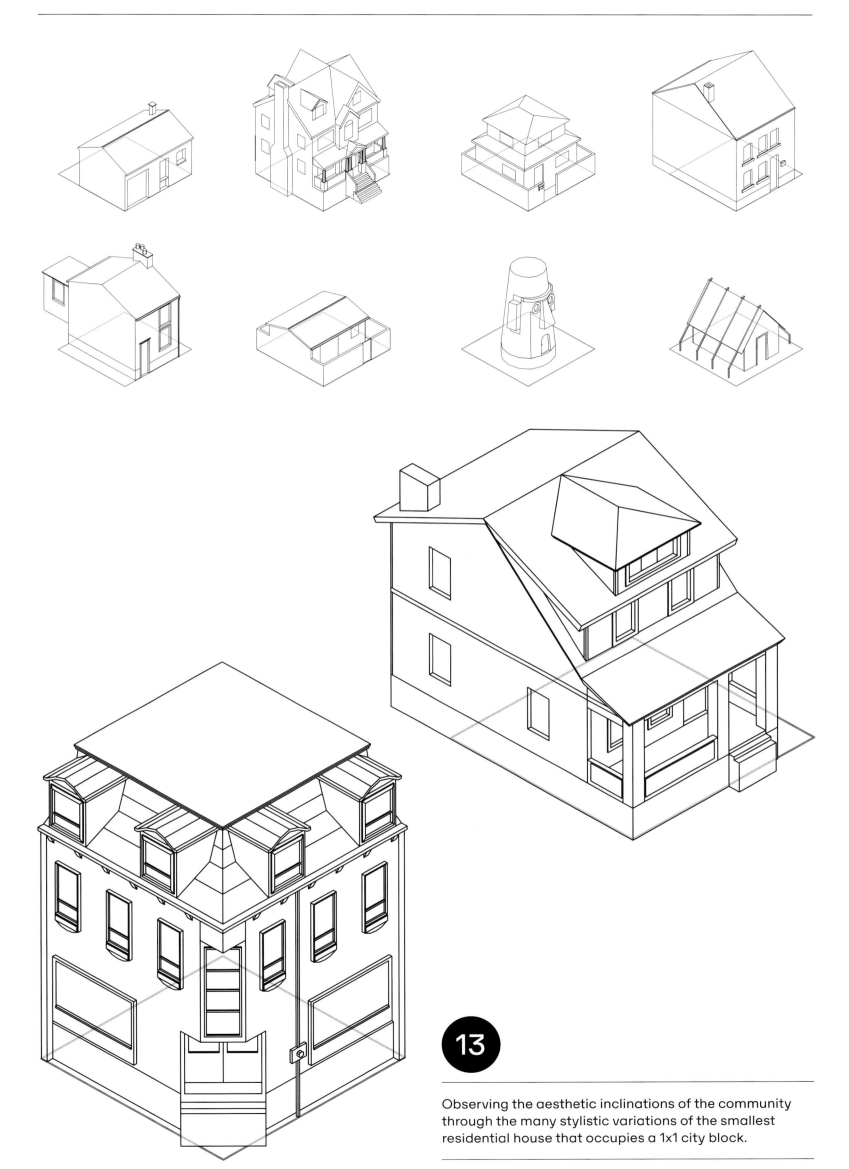

13

Observing the aesthetic inclinations of the community through the many stylistic variations of the smallest residential house that occupies a 1x1 city block.

The same is true for the ten most popular Unique Buildings available on the Workshop. These distinctive pieces of architecture bring a set of special benefits to the city, adding to an Entertainment value that boosts the Leisure rating of surrounding buildings and increasing the attractiveness of the city to tourists who help to drive the city's economy. The most subscribed Unique Building is a recreation of Seattle's Space Needle by the user x3/Alvin, with around 260,000 players using the mod. By collecting other top-rated buildings, we can see distinctions between Unique Buildings that are more in the realm of 'iconic' structures that we might expect, and others that are more everyday, yet contribute to the systems of the city in a complementary manner. Other popular buildings are IKEA by Ozo, REAL Supermarket, 'Loss' Casino and Hotel (based on Las Vegas's Wynn), Medium Football Stadium, Community Center and the hulking San Francisco Hyatt Hotel, designed by architect John Portman, famous for his huge indoor atrium structures. In this sense, players can begin to define what is uniquely iconic to them, and discover whether others place a similar value on these types of buildings.

These modifications do not only affect buildings, but can fundamentally change the systems of the game, from 'Traffic Management: President Edition' and 'Roundabout Builder' for creating and managing road systems to 'Extra Landscaping Tools' or 'Quay Anarchy' for altering the natural landscape and shorelines. There are also community creators of elements such as road intersections, allowing players to place pre-designed road sections in rather than designing these solutions themselves. A user named Timboh appears to be by far the most prolific author of road intersections, having created the top thirty-four most popular assets in the Intersection category of the Workshop. With Timboh's favoured designs we can see the increasing complexity of traffic management offered to players, all the way up to a giant pentagram-shaped junction with a complexity that dwarfs even some of Los Angeles' most complicated spaghetti intersections [Fig. 14].

As a platform, *Cities: Skylines* caters for a different type of player – one who thrives in the slower, more complex and gradual development of systems in a virtual environment. While many of these processes take decades to enable in real cities, perpetuated by bureaucratic and economic influences, players can come to understand some of these considerations and play them out at an accelerated rate. Through its endless sandbox exploration, it is possible for players to have kept and maintained the same city for years, and for that city to be shaped not only by the game's designers and players, but by a whole catalogue of elements being constantly produced by an army of virtual architects and urbanists.

Top ten road interchanges demonstrating the complexity of infrastructural networking within the game.

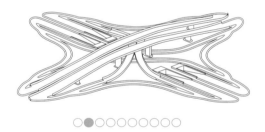

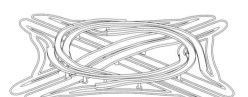

□ Workshop:

42,000+ Buildings
46,000+ Intersections
31,000 Parks

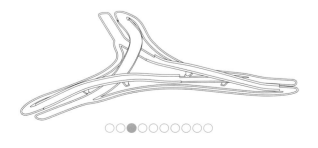

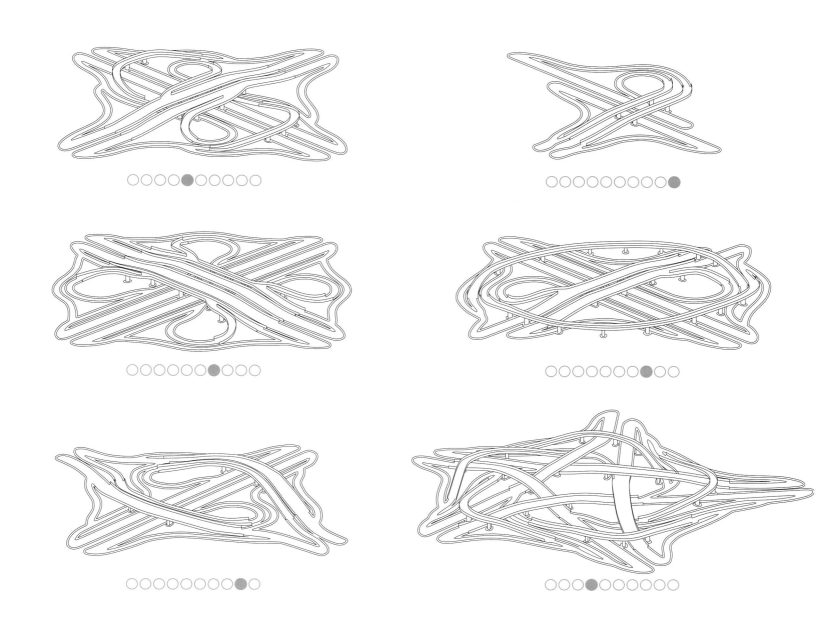

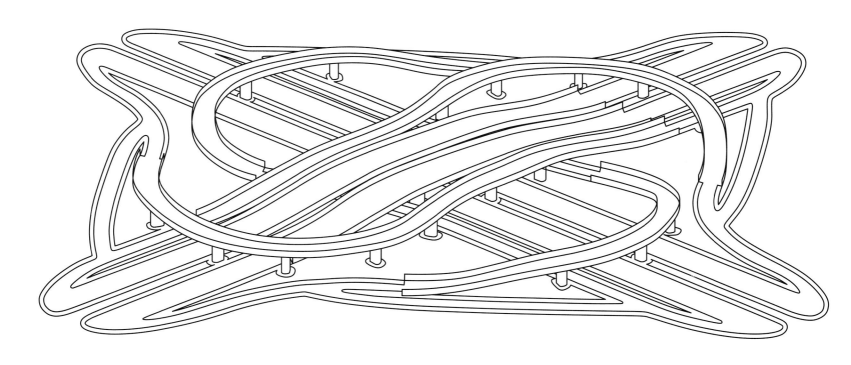

○ VIDEOGAME ATLAS

Sections

DARK SOULS

Details

Year	2011
Developer	FromSoftware
Publisher	Namco Bandai Games

Platforms

Microsoft Windows

PlayStation: 3/4   Xbox One

Xbox 360   Nintendo Switch

Lordran is an exemplar of 'picturesque' design in videogames – a landscape of death and decay woven from architectural ruins and fragments, experienced through complex and carefully controlled pathways.

☐ Maps:

30 Locations
26 Bosses

3.1   Ruins and Rebirth

There are few videogames whose spatial storytelling receives as much interest and praise as that of *Dark Souls*. FromSoftware's series is regularly cited as an exemplar of environmental communication, with architecture playing a key role in its sprawling and opaque lore. *Dark Souls* is set in the realm of Lordran, constructed by the 'Four Lords' who founded the world following the Age of Ancients – where everlasting dragons ruled over an unformed land – becoming the Age of Fire. At Lordran's centre sits Anor Londo, the city of the gods and an emblem of a world kept alive by the First Flame. As the 'Chosen Undead', players are asked to journey to Lordran and kindle the First Flame, preventing the world falling into the Age of Dark, where humanity rather than gods will prevail.

Although *Dark Souls* ostensibly provides an open world in which to pursue that goal, it is different from the horizontally spread landscapes we typically encounter in 'sandbox' games. Lordran is a tightly knit and interconnected world that is highly vertiginous. Comprising thirty different locations, the game's map is approximately 1.3 km (¾ miles) in linear size from north to south, and yet players will also experience around 900 m (2952 ft 9⅛ in.) of vertical level change should they visit every area [Fig. 1]. Such measurements are inadequate in defining Lordran, because the aesthetic experience of the world is shaped by both pathways and views. Lordran's ruined landscapes and gleaming central city, with 'god rays' of light shooting down, create an atmosphere approaching the sublime or picturesque.

To see Lordran as picturesque connects it to historical principles used in architecture and landscape design. Picturesque design was an 18th- and 19th-century movement in architecture that developed many of the aesthetic principles we observe in *Dark Souls*. The prized scenic views, unconventional pathways and architectural motifs such as ruins communicate a symbolism of deep time and mythology. Alongside the movement, artists such as Robert Hubert or Giovanni Battista Piranesi created images that embraced both the romantic and paradoxical potential of ruined space, with Piranesi's *Carceri D'Invenzione* bearing a startling resemblance to some of Lordran's dungeon areas.[1]

Despite these influences being European, we might speculate that FromSoftware's understanding of the power of ruination also comes from a deeper fascination with such subjects in Japanese culture. Chie Hiraizumi demonstrates that 'as far back as […] the 8th century, there are waka poems about cities already in ruins'.[2] Alongside poetry was *kusozu*, Buddhist imagery of decomposing cadavers that communicated 'the consequences of rebirth in the human world – death'.[3] Writing in *Japan-ness in Architecture*, Arata Isozaki argues that this sensibility is key to Japanese aesthetics in embracing 'the frozen landscape of death' by 'observing the process of decay and then deliberately pulling the end nearer'.[4] As Gareth Damian Martin argues, 'every architectural space […] seems to oscillate between the state of tomb and room'.[5] Lordran's emphasis on enigmatic views of the dead and dying seems to straddle both sensibilities and combine them into a new aesthetic form.

1   Royal Academy collection, *Carceri D'Invenzione Di G. Battista Piranesi Archit Vene*, royalacademy.org.uk/art-artists/book/carceri-dinvenzione-di-g-battista-piranesi-archit-vene

2   Chie Hiraizumi, 'Is There a Japanese Tradition of Painting Ruins? From the Edo Period to Today', in *Beyond the End: Ruins in Art History* (Tokyo: The Shoto Museum of Art, 2018), 141.

3   Gail Chin, 'The Gender of Buddhist Truth: The Female Corpse in a Group of Japanese Paintings', in *Japanese Journal of Religious Studies*, vol. 25, no. 3/4 (Autumn, 1998), 277–317.

4   Arata Isozaki, *Japan-ness in Architecture* (Cambridge, MA & London: MIT Press, 2011), 88–89.

5   Gareth Damian Martin, 'An obituary for the architecture of Dark Souls' eternally dying land', *Eurogamer*, eurogamer.net/articles/2017-06-18-an-obituary-for-the-architecture-of-dark-souls-eternally-dying-land

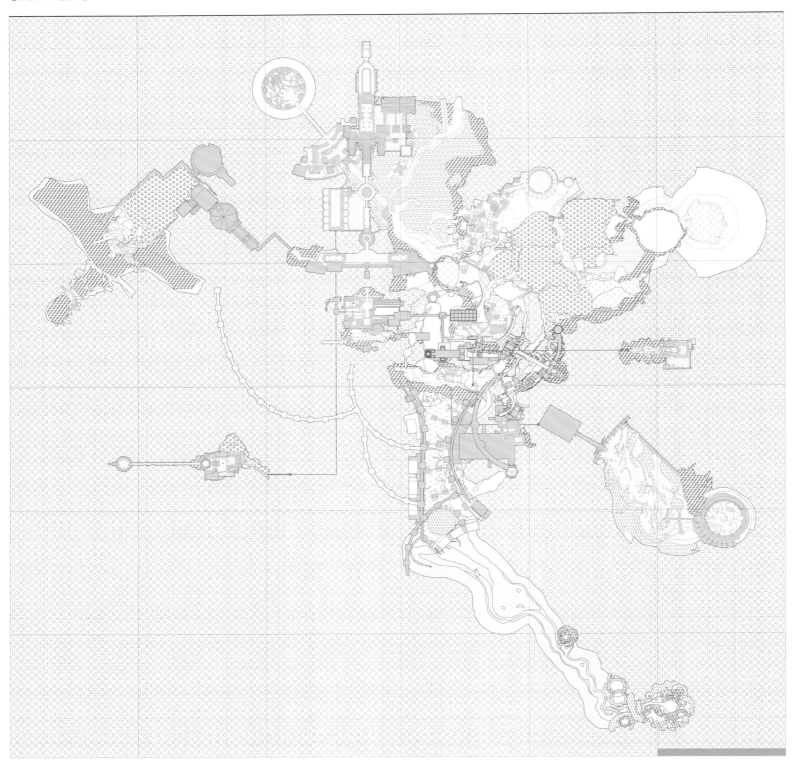

1

A map of Lordran through its interior spaces shows it to be a dense and interlinked world, with many areas weaving together vertically to create a spatially rich environment.

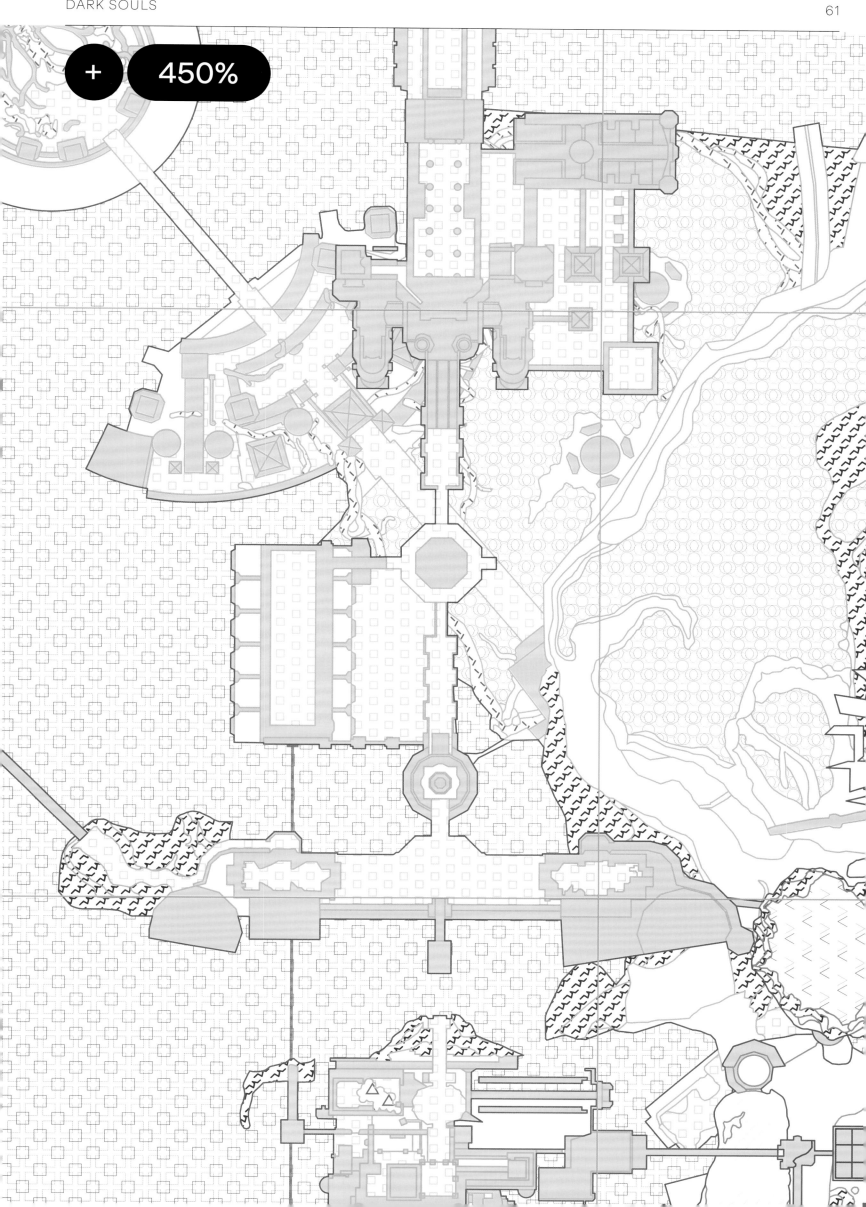

2

Isometric mapping of bonfire locations throughout the world, showing how they form a network of points that provide respite and security for the player in an overwhelmingly uncaring world.

3.2 Fire and Fog

Underpinning Lordran's motifs of flame and ruin, and the game's mechanics of death and undeath, are bonfires, the game's equivalent to save points. Resting at bonfires replenishes the player's health and spells, but also resets all non-boss enemies in the area. Death returns us to a bonfire in 'hollow' form, with less health but certain other advantages. By allowing us to die and repeat, *Dark Souls* turns death into something 'that can be observed, contemplated, and slowly experienced'.[6] Bonfires provide moments where the world shelters us, as architecture should. Olga Medvedkova's studies into Vitruvius' 1st-century writing on architecture reveal fire to her as 'the locus for architecture, the symbolic hearth of civilization'.[7] By mapping out the bonfires of Lordran we can see that they form a network – one that provides not only the practical facility to save one's game, but that also provides moments of reward and respite [Fig. 2]. There are forty-four such bonfires scattered across the world of *Dark Souls*, twenty-one of which are sites the player can 'warp' between once they have obtained the Lordvessel in Anor Londo, providing further protection by enabling them to bypass dangerous journeys.

While bonfires help to divide the continuous world of Lordran into a series of smaller areas, players will also encounter 'fog doors' that occlude pathways forward and demarcate significant areas such as boss battles. These are ubiquitous in the *Dark Souls* series, where players are invited to 'traverse the white light'. Boss doors are typically grander in scale, although some are smaller – opening out into huge areas beyond as a form of 'spatial gesture',[8] amplifying the grandiosity of the battle arena. Fog doors are also used to block an area when another player's spirit invades the world, with progress halted until the aggressor has been banished. Rather than hiding sight lines or denoting significant points, here the fog doors impose a temporary spatial limitation of the kind not typical to the rest of the game.

☐ Bonfires:

44 Bonfires
21 Warp Points
01 Lordvessel

6   Daniel Podgorski, 'Unchosen Undead: A Thorough
     Existentialist Philosophical Analysis of FromSoftware's
     Original Dark Souls', *The Gemsbok*, thegemsbok.com/
     art-reviews-and-articles/dark-souls-from-software-
     existentialism-philosophy/
7   Olga Medvedkova, 'In the Beginning, There was Fire:
     Vitruvius and the Origin of the City', in *Wounded Cities:
     The Representation of Urban Disasters in European Art
     (14th–20th Centuries)* (Leiden: Brill, 2015), 19.
8   Alban Janson & Florian Tigges, *Fundamental Concepts
     of Architecture: The Vocabulary of Spatial Situations*
     (Birkhäuser, 2014), 144–45.

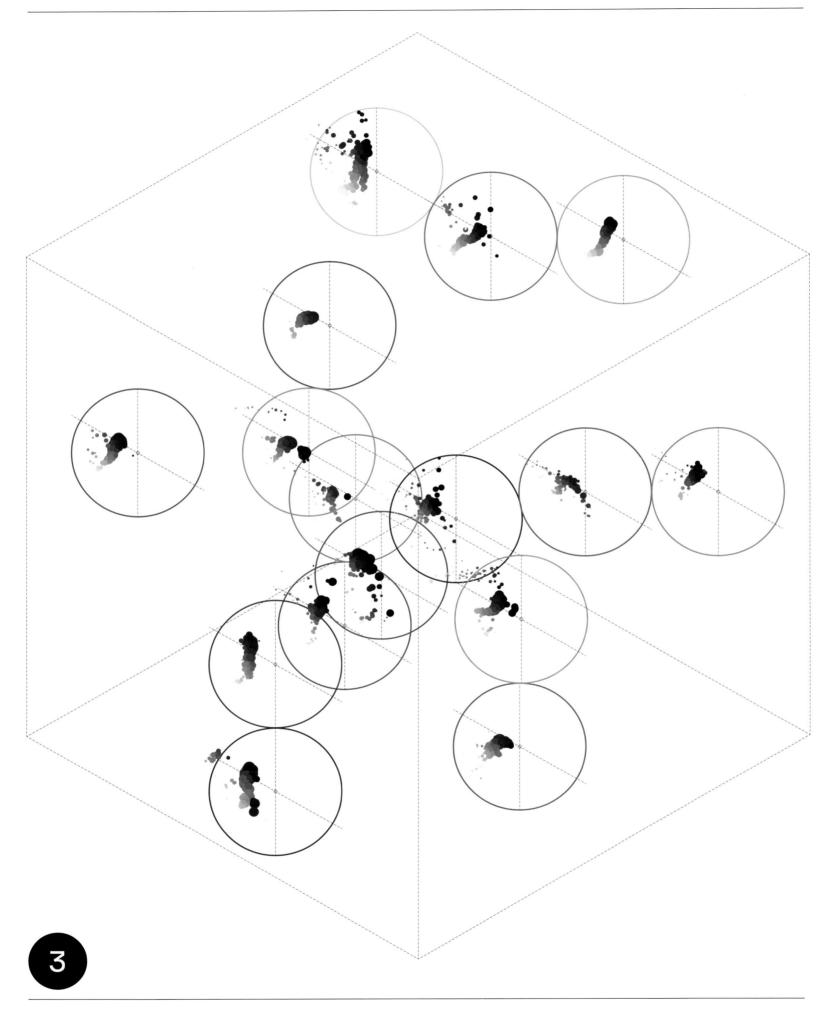

3

Colour analysis of Lordran using the game's 2D
textures geolocated into an isometric diagram.
Through this method we can see the predominant
tones used in the design of each area.

3.3   Order and Chaos

Dark Souls is a game prized for the beauty of its world, and yet if we look at the materials and tones used in Lordran we could find this landscape of decay to be somewhat drab and dull. By unpacking the game's 2D textures in an area-by-area study, we use colour analysis software[9] to understand the relative tonal balance of the materials used in each area of the game [Fig. 3]. By comparing this to the average colour of a screenshot image from each location in the game we build a picture of the colour tones that define each area. This difference demonstrates the importance of lighting in generating scenic atmospheres – Anor Londo, for example, gleams very differently in-game than its textures would suggest. But although many of Lordran's environments are dank and appalling, this does not preclude them from being picturesque. Indeed, scholars of picturesque design argue that the movement was 'largely concerned with the celebrated ability of art to fix the disgusting, allowing it to be converted to visual pleasure, that is, making disgusting things a source for art'.[10]

An artistic method associated with picturesque design was *capriccio*, paintings combining depictions of buildings from different time periods to surprise viewers. The architecture of Lordran operates in a similar way, with cultural and historic influences taken and combined from across the world. Director Hidetaka Miyazaki explains that *Dark Souls* draws from several real-life buildings and locations in its design. Anor Londo, as the capital of the gods, is inspired by both the exterior form of Milan's cathedral and interior details of the Château de Chambord in France. As we move into the depths of Lordran we encounter architecture such as the Lost Izalith, a vast structure interwoven by tree branches inspired by Angkor Wat in Cambodia. For Miyazaki,

Western buildings are typically used for the rational, elevated cities of the gods because he 'find[s] Oriental designs to be quite chaotic',[11] with Asian and Middle Eastern designs depicted in the lower reaches of the world such as Demon Ruins and Lost Izalith. We might question this, given that one of the most confusing and hostile areas of the game, New Londo Ruins, is based on Mont-Saint-Michel in France – with Miyazaki arguing that the real-world reference provides 'intricate layers of detailing'.[12] Finding other real-life precedents has been a fertile pursuit for the community, and by locating these structural inspirations that underpin the architecture of the game, we can see how it generates surprise through the unexpected combination of different spatial inspirations drawn from across the globe into a new form of *capriccio* space [Fig. 4].

9   L. Jegou, 'Color proportions of an image' tool, geotests.net/couleurs/frequences_en.html#
10 John Macarthur, *The Picturesque: Architecture, Disgust and Other Irregularities* (London & New York: Routledge, 2007), 87.
11 FromSoftware/BANDAI NAMCO, *Dark Souls: Design Works* (Ontario: Udon, 2012), 117.
12 FromSoftware/BANDAI NAMCO, *Dark Souls: Design Works* (Ontario: Udon, 2012), 116.

+ 200%

4

Mapping the real-life inspirations
behind Lordran's architecture
demonstrates how the game uses
a wide and global set of reference
points, surprising the player as they
move between different areas.

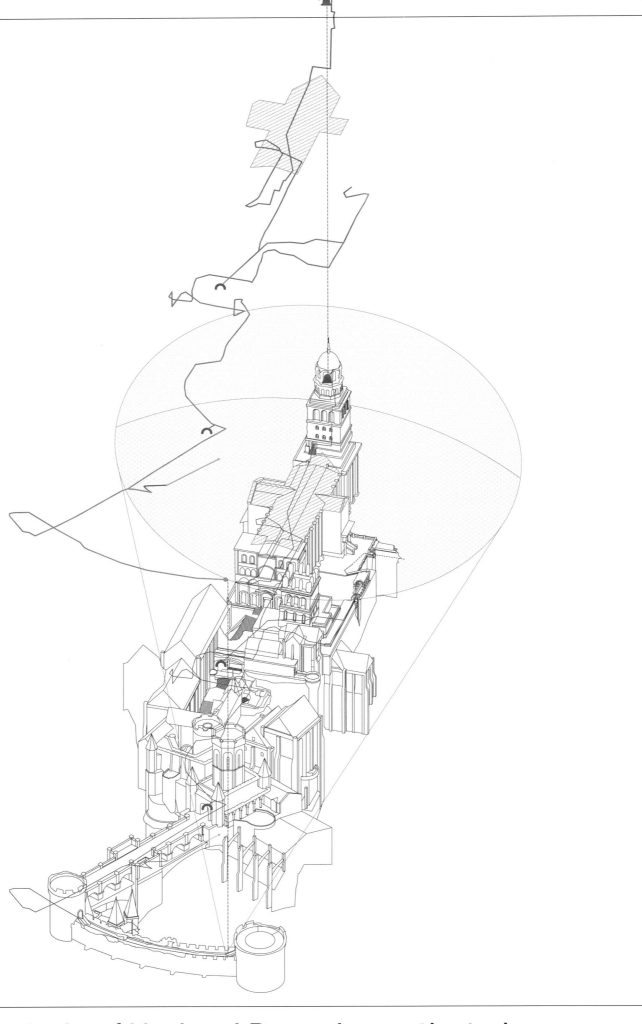

5

Route analysis of Undead Burg shows that players must follow a complex and dangerous path to reach the Bell of Awakening that is significantly longer than the linear distance between points.

3.4   Feet and Eyes

Another key principle of picturesque design was laid out by landscape architect William Shenstone in the mid-18th century, that 'the foot should never travel to [the object] by the same path which the eye has travelled over before'.[13] This concept – that one should never reach a scenic destination in the distance via a direct route – could also serve as a clear summary of *Dark Souls'* approach to spatial design. Players are consistently offered points in the distance that require a tortuous route to reach them. After defeating the Taurus Demon in Undead Burg, players get a view of the Undead Church containing a Bell of Awakening – one of the early objectives of the game. However, even taking the most 'direct' route to reach the bell requires the player to move through a sequence of spaces involving ladder climbing, dodging a fire-breathing dragon (or attacking its tail), unlocking different gates and finding small pathways and staircases that could easily be missed at first glance [Fig. 5]. As the crow flies this distance is roughly 260 m (853 ft ¼ in.), but the intricacies of the designer's route extends it to nearly 1 km (⅝ miles) of navigation.

This approach is even more marked when we reach Anor Londo. While the architecture of Undead Burg is haphazard and tightly knit, our first view of Anor Londo is one of the most picturesque vistas in the game, revealing a sprawling and monumental cathedral at the end of a ceremonial approach. Once more, the route to entering and navigating these spaces is far more convoluted, involving climbing up flying buttresses, across rafters and through bedrooms. Miyazaki calls these 'unexpected pathways' that ultimately enhance the 'satisfaction of arrival' when we reach our destination.[14] This objective is Princess Gwynevere's chamber, found following one of the game's most notorious boss fights with Dragon Slayer Ornstein and Executioner Smough. By analysing a 'direct' path to the objective once again, we can see that even without diversion, we embark on a highly complicated journey through many different ancillary spaces that give us an insight into the workings behind the grand façade of the main building. A linear distance of 450 m (1476 ft 4½ in.) becomes over 1,600 m (5249 ft 4⅛ in.) of meandering circulation, meaning that just like in Undead Burg players must take a route nearly four times longer to reach their destination [Fig. 6].

Much of this relationship between direct view and indirect circulation is enhanced by 'borrowed scenery', or *shakkei*, a term derived from Japanese garden design that describes techniques for incorporating distant views into a design. While the game world is loaded in chunks, low-resolution models and cube-mapped skybox

textures reinforce the impression of an adjacent world beyond our current area. Through meticulous analysis (using bloodstains dropped upon death), the game's community has concluded that they match reasonably well to the actual geometry of the world, emphasizing its continuity.[15] This is preserved through techniques such as 'Level of Detail' models, where several levels of geometric complexity are used at different distances. For example, by looking at models of the Sen's Fortress area, both the high-resolution location itself and when viewed from both Undead Burg and Firelink Shrine, we can see that the building gains visual detail and complexity as we move closer – while in other locations the Fortress is rendered as a low-detail facsimile to preserve the critical viewpoints [Fig. 7]. Such techniques also allow the developers to create the impression of expansive, scenic and sprawling domains with much less explorable geometry. The Ash Lake area, regarded as one of the game's most beautiful domains, has a tiny extent of 'walkable' space, surrounded by concentric rings of low-polygon trees and flat textures depicting a near-infinite flooded forest [Fig. 8].

While Ash Lake is effectively surrounded by scenic views, at other points the developers have framed views to emphasize the visual connection and continuity of the world. The lake itself can be viewed from Tomb of the Giants, a location where players can also catch glimpses of views towards the Demon Ruins. Both are represented as skybox textures, creating a visual connection and borrowing from another central technique of *shakkei* design, *mikiri*, or trimming: the device by which the garden designer limits the borrowed landscape to the features they wish to show.[16] This principle relates to the framing of landscape features (through bushes, walls or other formed openings), and throughout Lordran we can see examples of framed views, even aside from the key vistas we meet. Tomb of the Giants is the most notable occurrence, but we also encounter views framed by the spires of Anor Londo, the ruined walls of Firelink Shrine, or even a last glance out towards the Kiln of the First Flame before we enter our final battle with Lord Gwyn [Fig. 9].

13   William Shenstone, 'Unconnected Thoughts on Gardening', in *The Works in Prose and Verse of William Shenstone Esq. In Two Volumes* (Edinburgh, 1764), 94–110.
14   FromSoftware/BANDAI NAMCO, *Dark Souls: Design Works* (Ontario: Udon, 2012), 116.
15   Illusory Wall, *Dark Souls 1: Distant Views Explained (Part 1)*, illusorywall.tumblr.com/post/132589360859/dark-souls-1-distant-views-explained-part-1
16   Teiji Itoh, *Space & Illusion in the Japanese Garden* (New York, Toyko, Kyoto: Weatherhill/Tankosha, 1988), 31.

Applying route analysis methods to
Anor Londo shows another example
of the game disconnecting scenic
views from actual circulation,
forgoing the large ceremonial
approach and forcing the player
into a complicated journey.

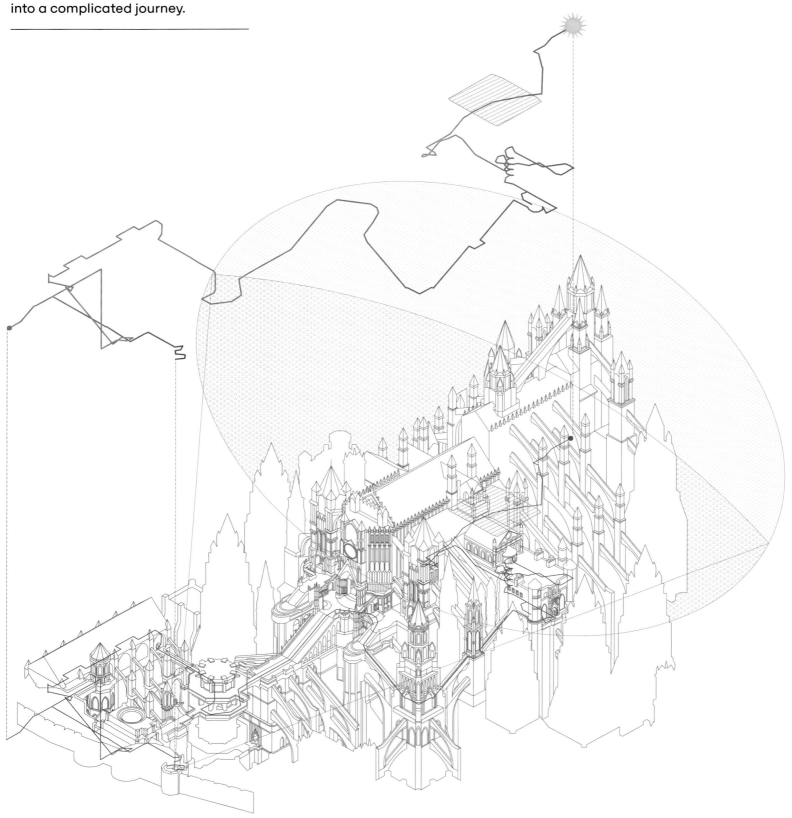

Diagram demonstrating the different 'level of detail' models of Sen's Fortress as it is seen from other locations, enabling it to appear in scenic views from Undead Burg and Firelink Shrine.

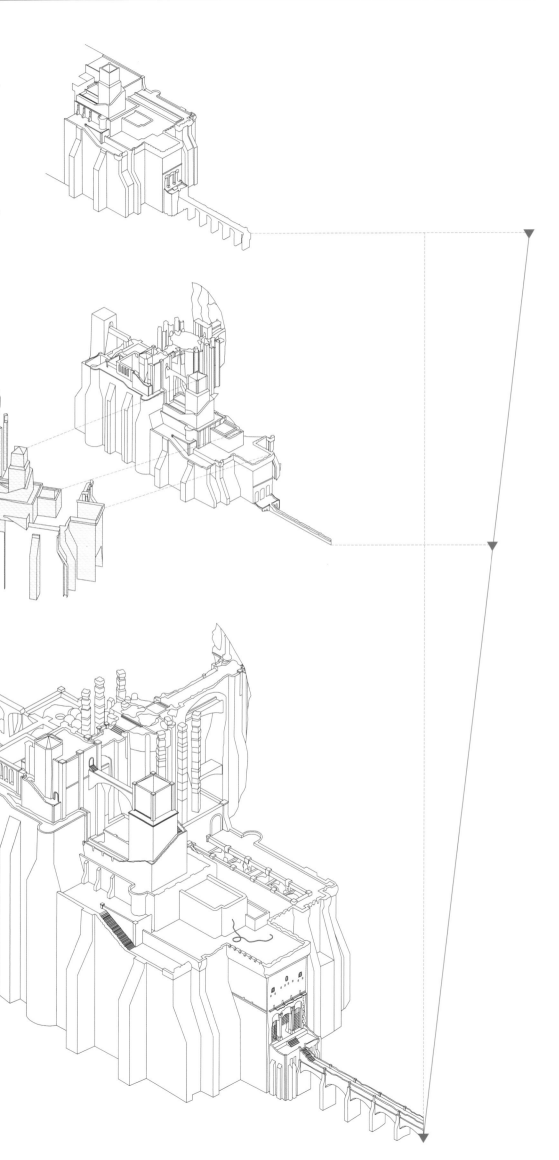

8

Exploded isometric of Ash Lake showing how the small walkable area of the environment is surrounded by rings of simplified geometry and flat skybox imagery suggesting a near-infinite expanse.

9

Framed views encountered in Lordran, demonstrating techniques similar to *mikiri*, used in traditional Japanese garden design to 'borrow landscape'.

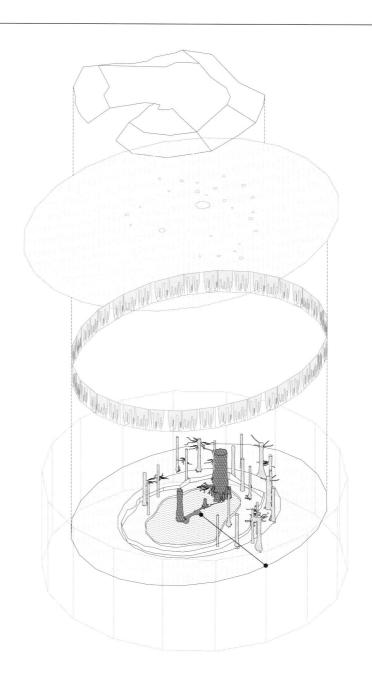

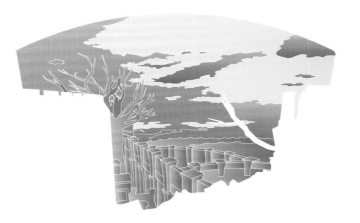

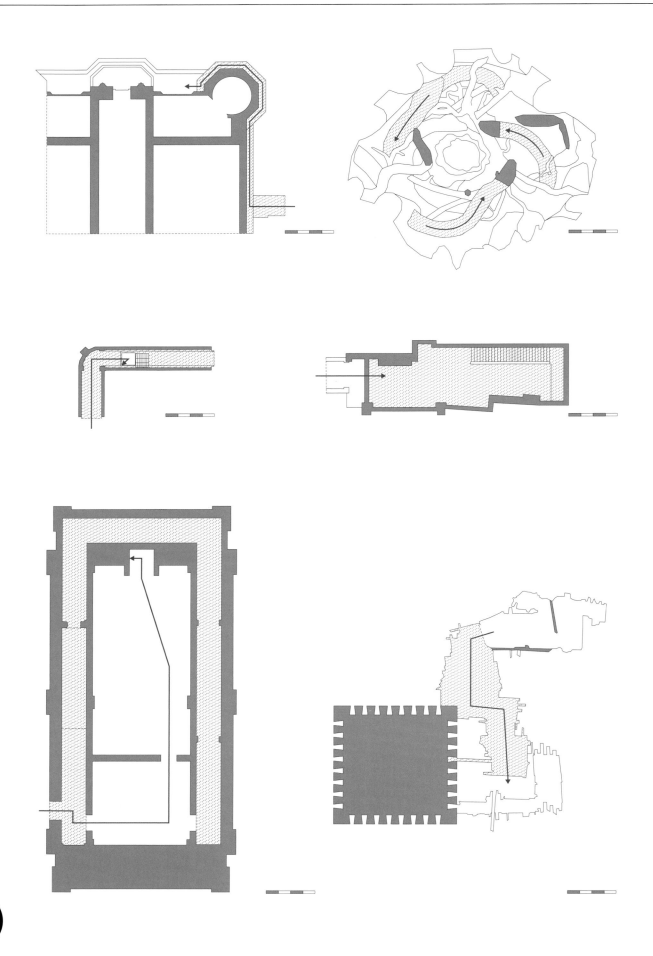

10

Plan fragments showing the small scale of many buildings and environments in Lordran. These 'too-small' spaces can disorient and panic the player, and even prevent them from being able to attack properly, adding to the inhospitable qualities of the world.

3.5   Datum Shifting

This relationship between view and circulation defines another aspect of *Dark Souls*' architectural approach, the destabilizing effect of moving back and forth between spaces that are 'too small' to those that are 'too large'. Players will invariably encounter corridors, rooms and staircases where it might be impossible to even swing a sword freely. Brent Ables observes that 'the spaces of the game impose finitude on the player that moves through those spaces',[17] and this is achieved through highly compressed areas – even when they may appear visually larger. Anor Londo has an infamous ledge reached from a flying buttress, guarded by two archers and under a metre in width, making it easy for a misplaced attack animation or arrow hit to send the player falling to their death. Meanwhile, Undead Parish is home to a boss fight with the Capra Demon, in a space barely bigger than a living room. Here players learn to use the intimate scale of the space to their advantage, healing on a tight staircase that the boss struggles to climb. Across Lordran's architecture, we can see that the 'too small' space is a commonly used design feature [Fig. 10]. The Depths disorients players through narrow corridors with floor traps, while the rickety platforms of Blighttown make it hard for players to predict where the next attack will come from but easy to fall to one's death. In the Great Hollow, quirks from physics that are tied to frame rates mean players on faster computers can even 'slide' from the area's narrow branches to their doom.

In contrast, most boss fights other than the Capra Demon take place in 'too big' spaces, where a giant arena creates an imposing environment that complements the scale of the boss, making player characters quickly appear tiny and insignificant. By mapping all the boss arena floorplans in the game, we can start to identify similarities in their spatial design [Fig. 11]. There are three broad groupings of space: 'architectural', where the form of the building closely defines the battleground; 'rotunda', where the arena takes a very clear circular form; and 'natural', where the fight takes place in some form of environment with a less geometrically defined extent. While there are some crossovers between these categories (such as 'rotunda'-like natural clearings), what is common to most of these spaces is their vast scale. Some areas such as the Abyss do not even have a precisely defined visual edge, with battles taking place in a dark and seemingly infinite void.

In many of these boss-fight spaces the environment can contribute to the success or failure of the player. Often this can be an intentional design, such as the columns in Anor Londo that provide limited cover from the attacks of Ornstein and Smough. However, keen players have also learned new tricks and environmental exploits facilitated by the design of the arenas. By looking at four boss arenas in more detail, we can see how this is encouraged through their design [Fig. 12]. When fighting the Taurus Demon on a rampart in Undead Burg, players can dive into battle head on or take respite by climbing up on to a tower, enabling a diving attack that can significantly weaken the boss. If players stand in the correct position, they can even encourage the boss to unwittingly fall to their death through a gap in the parapet, in a technique called 'cheesing'. Cheesing involves exploiting a glitch or quirk of design to kill a boss with minimum effort. In another example, players battling the Ceaseless Discharge boss, in a large area of the Demon Ruins, can cheese the boss by running all the way back to a fog gate, where the boss will attempt an attack, allowing the player to cut its arm and send it falling into the lava below. While the Bed of Chaos cannot be cheesed so simply, we can also observe areas of the map that are 'safe zones' – here players cannot be hit, so will wait for openings and practise their timing to avoid attacks. Most of these boss arenas also have hazards. Players can fall through the same gap as the Taurus Demon, topple into lava while avoiding the Ceaseless Discharge, or disappear through the floor when trying to dodge the Bed of Chaos. Tension is elevated through the sense that not only the enemy but also the architecture around the player is trying to defeat them.

17   Brent Ables, 'Illumination and Occlusion: Dark Souls Remastered', *Heterotopias*, heterotopiaszine.com/2018/08/23/illumination-occlusion-dark-souls-remastered/.

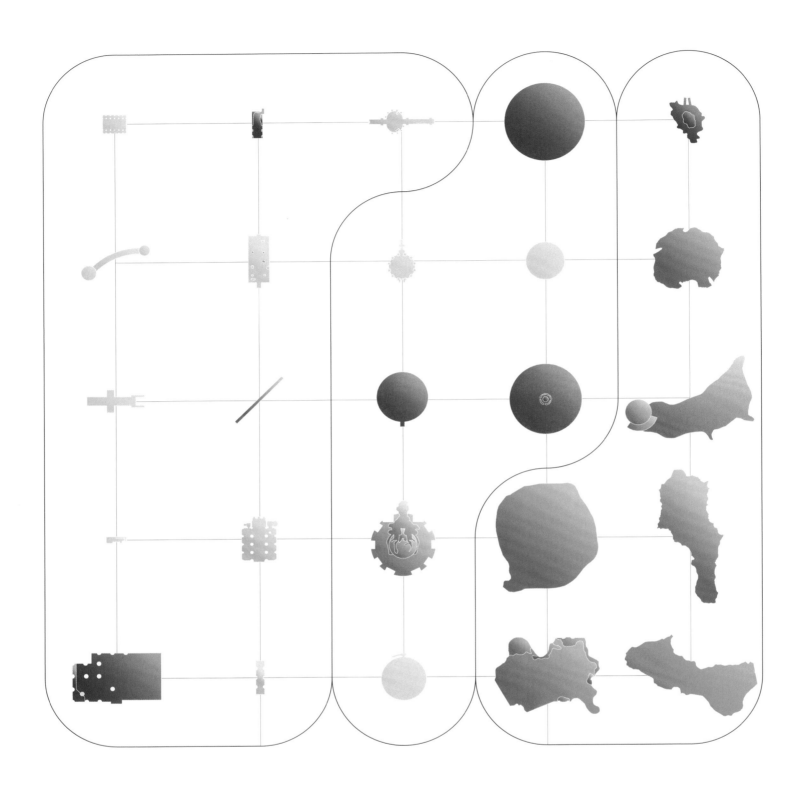

11

Categorizing the different boss arenas in Lordran demonstrates three organizing typologies: 'architectural' spaces within buildings, round 'rotunda' arenas and battles taking place in 'natural' type environments.

☐ Arenas:

11 Architectural
7 Rotunda
7 Natural

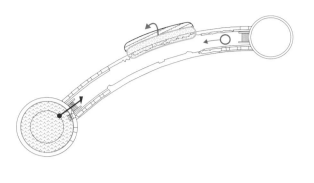

By examining boss arenas in plan we can see how they can both assist and impede the player in their fight, by providing safe zones and 'cheesing' points while also presenting environmental hazards.

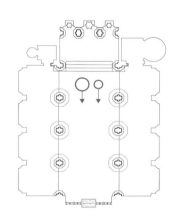

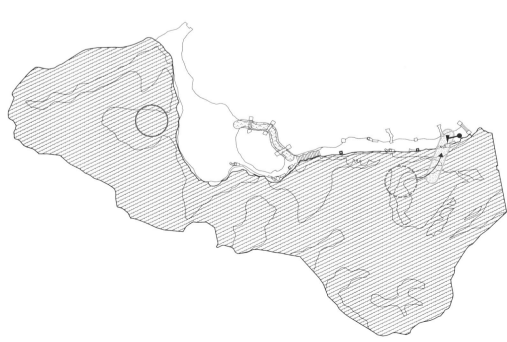

14

Through multiplayer message data we can identify specific spots in Lordran with a high level of social activity, including approaches to boss areas, post-boss bonfires or the ledge where players first meet Solaire of Astoria, the game's most beloved NPC.

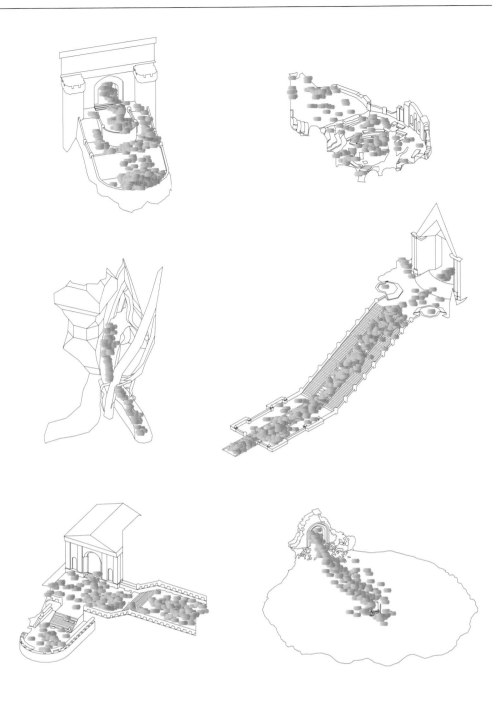

13

Using DriftItem's message data, we can understand the comparable levels of social interaction taking place within the different areas of Lordran. Undead Burg and Anor Londo are the two most popular spots for player interaction and both represent challenging areas.

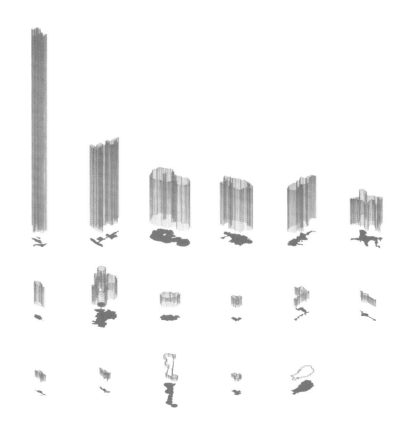

3.6 Collectively Lordran

The social spaces of *Dark Souls* are predominantly formed through oblique communications in the world. Players can observe other users running through their game as ghosts and bloodstains where they may have died. Players can summon and invade other worlds, and even hear others ring the Bell of Awakening, breaking the often-solitary experience of Lordran. Another type of collective communication is the glowing messages players can leave for one another. These might warn of a hazard ahead, or direct someone to a particularly scenic view. Others might encourage players to roll to their death through a gap in the wall, or even interfere with their ability to activate an important mechanism or non-player character (NPC). Some of the most notable studies of these messages were created by a Twitter user called DriftItem,[18] who developed a series of data-scraping tools to obtain multiplayer information from the *Dark Souls* server. Using this database of messaging information, covering three days in 2018,[19] we can overlay around 53,300 unique message points on to Lordran to understand where and how people communicate. This helps us understand the comparative scale of social interactions in each part of the world [Fig. 13]. With nearly 21,000 interactions together, the notoriously punishing early-game areas of Undead Burg and Undead Parish represent the most commented areas of the map, as one might expect, reassuring players that they are not alone in their defeat.

Through DriftItem's data we are also able to outline popular locations for leaving messages [Fig. 14]. A particularly busy area is in Undead Burg, where the players first meet Solaire of Astoria, one of the most famous and beloved NPCs, whose cheerful catchphrase 'Praise the Sun!' is a common message repeated by players (around 3,600 times over three days). Other areas of dense communication typically include moments of trepidation such as the steps towards Anor Londo, or moments of triumph (2,600 instances of 'I did it!') like the messages left by players after the boss Great Grey Wolf Sif. Many players also point out hidden or difficult-to-find pathways such as from Blighttown to The Great Hollow.

If *Dark Souls* 'offers a dynamics of reciprocal one-to-one visibility' where players are 'anonymously separated in their own game worlds, half-visible to each other as ghosts'[20] then messages facilitate a social body of knowledge, or simply a collective spirit, to exist in the world. This knowledge might be helpful, playful or wicked, just like FromSoftware's design of Lordran. But as the popularity of cheerful messages and victorious exclamations show us, overcoming the picturesque, yet dead and ruined landscape of Lordran is a transformative experience for many players. While Lordran is a uniquely unforgiving environment, it is precisely in the lethal beauty of its landscapes and architecture that people find meaning and motivation.

☐ 3 Days in Lordran:

53,300+ Messages
3,600+ 'Praise the Sun'
2,600 'I did it!'

18 DriftItem: twitter.com/DriftItem
19 *Blood Messages*: JSON database by pawREP/ DriftItem, GitHub, github.com/pawREP/Dark-Souls-1-P2P-Data/tree/master/BloodMessages
20 Tom van Nuenen, 'Playing the Panopticon: Procedural Surveillance in Dark Souls', in *Games and Culture*, 2016, vol. 11(5) (New York: Sage), 524.

○ VIDEOGAME ATLAS

Sections

4.1	Landscapes and Logistics
4.2	Taking Measures
4.3	Datascape
4.4	Generic Architecture
4.5	Beaches
4.6	Networking

DEATH STRANDING

Details

Year	2019
Developer	Kojima Productions
Publisher	Sony Interactive Entertainment / 505 Games

Platforms

Microsoft Windows

PlayStation 4   PlayStation 5

In a post-apocalyptic America, social connection is re-established through logistics. The nation's desolate geography is traversed not only by the player making deliveries, but also its non-human architecture, facilities and waystations.

☐ Maps:

70 Orders for Sam
500 Standard Orders

4.1   Landscapes and Logistics

Our contemporary world is increasingly defined by 'non-human' architecture. From automated shipping ports to Amazon's fulfilment warehouses, or sprawling data centres full of servers, structures designed to facilitate the rapid speed of connection required by modern society continue to proliferate. At the same time, we are increasingly mindful of the effects that we humans have on our natural landscape; the scars left on the planet by the activities of the Anthropocene. There are few game environments that tackle the spatial and structural impact of this as much as the American landscape and the United Cities of America (U.C.A.) nation-state depicted in *Death Stranding*, the 2019 game by Kojima Productions [Fig. 1].

The game's story is deeply concerned with connection, both literally and metaphorically. Playing as Sam Porter Bridges, players act as a Porter, a delivery person responsible for shuttling delicate cargo from place to place. Through making increasingly difficult deliveries, Sam establishes a lateral network of connections by joining facilities and cities on to the Chiral Network, repairing a nation destroyed by the *Death Stranding*, a cataclysmic event that leaves creatures called Beached Things (BTs) wandering the Earth, souls unable to return to the land of the dead. Connections are also made between networked players through the sharing of structures and other tools for navigating the landscape, and lead designer Hideo Kojima has framed the game as a new genre – a 'social strand system'.[1]

Like many of Kojima's games, *Death Stranding* has a complex and layered storyline, saturated with symbolic meanings, and this is also true for the environments the player inhabits. In the game Sam will not only traverse America, but will visit Beaches – worlds between the world of the living and what follows death – where time does not pass and which ultimately provide the source of Chiralium that is used to reconnect the nation. Sam will also experience The Seam, a form of purgatory, where as a 'repatriate' he can re-emerge back into the land of the living. Other spaces Sam visits are Strand Fields, Beaches that are sites of collective deaths where souls remain trapped in a repetitive cycle.

Death Stranding's America seems barely similar to its real-world counterpart, instead more closely resembling the landscapes of Iceland. This is not incidental, considering Kojima Productions sent a team to scout locations from the volcanic island, and the game's community have enjoyed making connections between specific Icelandic landforms and those appearing in the game, including the liberal use of Iceland's famous black sands.[2] The landscape is visually sublime (especially combined with the game's soundtrack), with many of the vistas recalling artworks such as Caspar David Friedrich's famous painting *The Wanderer*, a piece that was described by John Gaddis as providing 'a sense of curiosity mixed with awe mixed with a determination to find things out',[3] which may also nicely sum up the player's experience of the game. While the visual appearance of the scenery may be transplanted from elsewhere, the connection between landscape and logistics does remain firmly within the history and ideals of the American landscape and its relationship to technology.

1   Tweet by Hideo Kojima, 5 June, 2019, twitter.com/
    HIDEO_KOJIMA_EN/status/1136074622711975936.
2   YouTube, 'PythonSelkan', 'Death Stranding Locations
    in REAL LIFE! Journey to Iceland (2019)', youtube.com/
    watch?v=3yw81C5ppGY
3   John Lewis Gaddis, *The Landscape of History: How
    Historians Map the Past* (Oxford: Oxford University
    Press, 2002), 15.

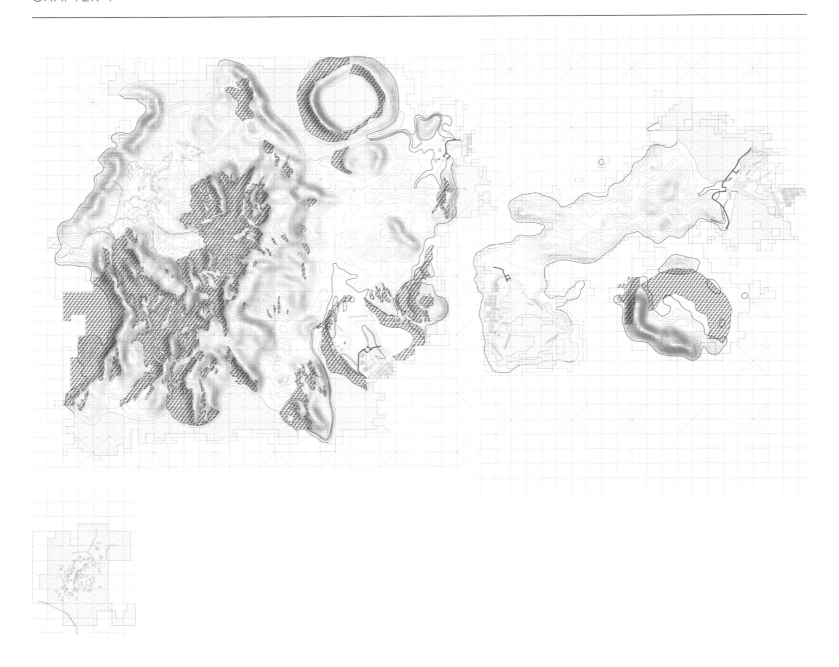

A map of America as shown in the game, with the landscape divided up into three unique areas that align to stages of Sam's coast-to-coast journey.

2

This map compares locations in *Death Stranding*'s Chiral Network map to their real-world location, demonstrating how much the game compresses journeys that would be hundreds of miles in reality.

4.2   Taking Measures

As players journey from coast to coast connecting waystations, it becomes clear that America is compressed and distorted in different ways that are not only visual. Two maps are presented to us as records of the journey – the main map that is used for navigation, and the more symbolic Chiral Network map that is shown after connecting key facilities.

By comparing these maps to each other and the US Geological Survey map of America[4] (data from the USGS was also used in the game), we can start to understand how this compression works. While the Chiral Network map is itself a distortion of the American map, by applying similar deformations to the real map we can trace a comparative path and suggest where key features in the game are located. Capital Knot City, where the game starts, is naturally positioned similarly to Washington, DC. But by the time players have connected the Wind Farm, a linear journey of around 3,000 m (9842½ ft) in-game, the Chiral Network map suggests they have travelled to southern Indiana, some 900 km (559⅙ miles) away [Fig. 2].

The final areas of the game, when Sam reaches Edge Knot City on the coast, are represented on the American map as being located around the Big Sur area of California. In total the linear width of *Death Stranding*'s map is around 12 km (7½ miles), broken into three areas comprising multiple different landscape biomes that cover a journey of some 3,900 km (2423⅓ miles) in reality.

Such literal comparisons can of course be questioned. The Chiral Network map displays a series of craters and fissures in the landscape caused by the Stranding Event, and Sam's journey with Fragile from Port Knot City to Lake Knot City is portrayed as a significant distance, making things hard to define precisely. But in the practical experience of the player, *Death Stranding*'s America is completely compressed and distorted, not only in its use of visual and landscape references from other countries, but also in the way scale and time are manipulated. Despite the compression present in the landscape, the game world is still able to incorporate several different biomes that possess different climates and topography, posing numerous challenges for navigation that can be overcome by means of objects and infrastructure [Fig. 3].

4   United States map obtained using the USGS National Map Viewer, apps.nationalmap.gov/viewer/

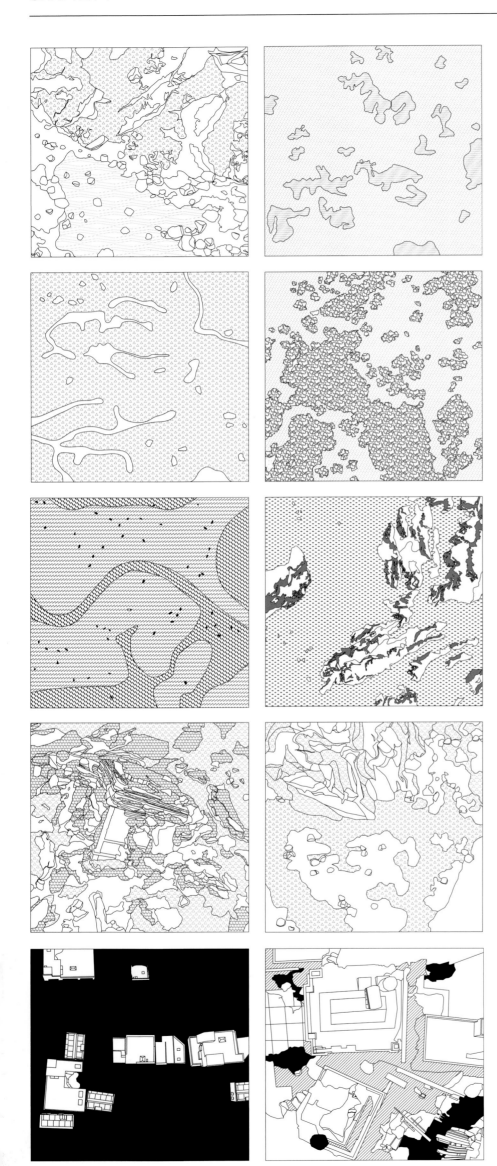

Plan drawings showing samples of the different biomes players encounter within America. These range from Iceland-inspired black sands and hills to later areas of ruined urban space and Strand Objects that rise up from tar.

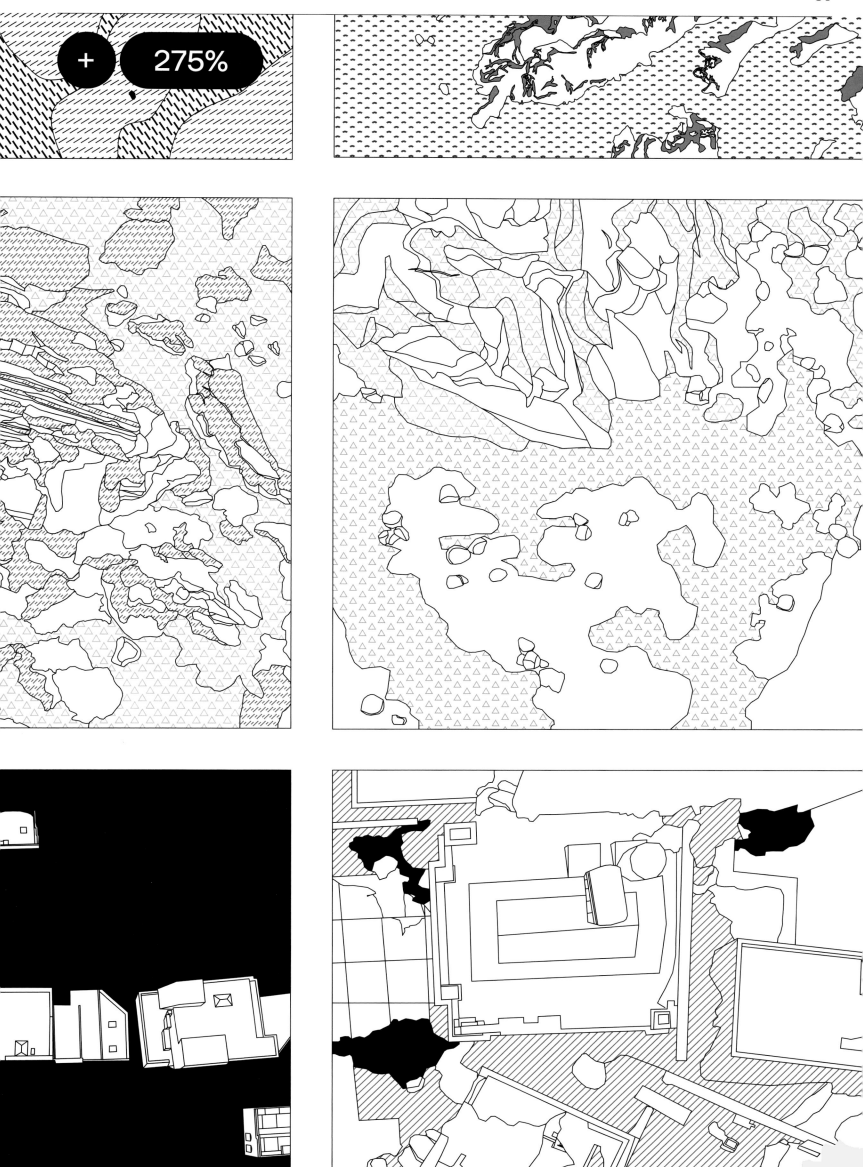

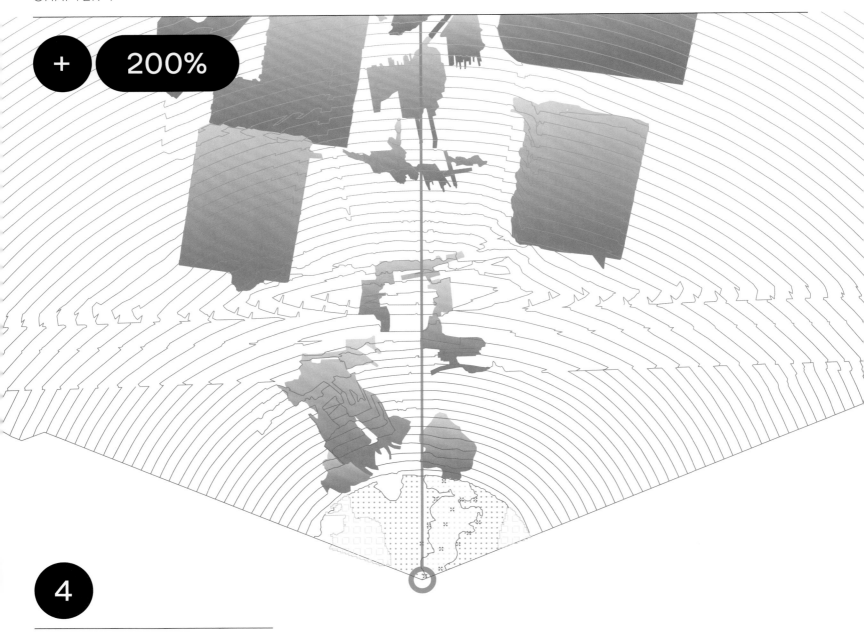

+ **200%**

4

By visualizing an Odradek scan
from above we can see that the
scanner fires out a series of contour
waves across the landscape in an
approximately 135-degree cone.

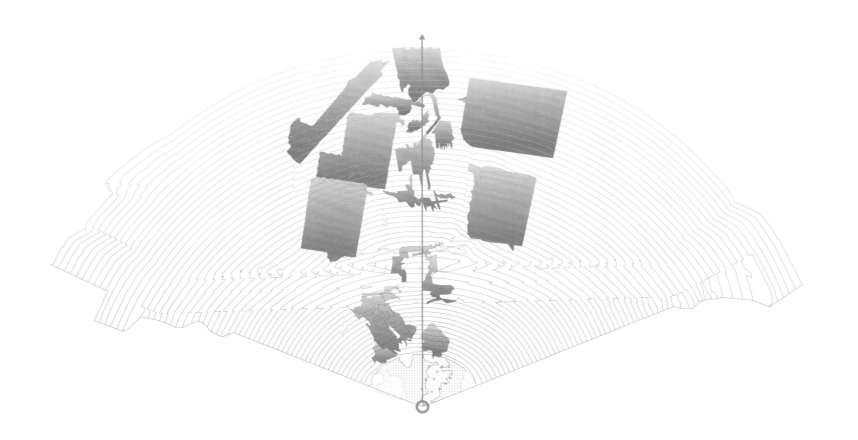

4.3 Datascape

Navigating through *Death Stranding*'s world requires an intimate knowledge of the ground beneath the player's feet. The load that Sam is carrying affects his ability to balance, and while carrying large amounts the player must constantly adjust to the landscape through fine-tuning movements. To assist in route-planning and assessing the environment, the Odradek Terrain Scanner is a device that Sam can use to obtain information on the surrounding ground conditions, status of cargo tags and marks left by other players. Upon activation of the scanner with a button press, it fires a wave that reveals data through a set of coded graphics that are imposed on to the environment in a roughly 135-degree cone from the camera direction of the player [Fig. 4].

While the visual form of *Death Stranding*'s landscapes remains sublime, the Odradek enables players to quantify it as a datascape, to examine closely what the logistical impact of each movement might be. Through tools to move the camera away from Sam, we can witness the full extent of the Odradek's sightlines, observing how a conical set of contours are applied on to the terrain before the graphic markers are placed. This process also suggests an analytical protocol taking place – rather than a LiDAR 3D scanner as used in the real world today, which returns a set of points containing colour information back to the device, the Odradek can send complex sets of information about the ground conditions back to Sam so the player can properly plan their movements. BTs appear more ethereally rendered by the Odradek, and cannot be reduced (or enhanced) into a set of data points in the same way.

This is integrated with Sam's cufflink interface, used for the planning of more complex routes, allowing the player to tilt the map to understand the elevation of a given journey. As players progress, they also unlock the ability to see weather patterns on the map, facilitating the planning of routes that bypass areas of Timefall, associated with BT presence and damage to cargo. Players can project thirty (real-time) minutes into the future, with rainfall density and wind directions indicated on a 45-degree grid overlaid on the landscape.

While all this visual information is given to the player to aid them, as with any videogame there are many layers of information and processing taking place without being explicitly displayed. As detailed by Eric Johnson, one of the game's AI programmers, the game relies heavily on complex implementations of 'navmeshes' (navigation meshes) – sets of information that allow non-player characters (NPCs) to traverse the world.[5] As Johnson describes, America is divided up into 12.5-m2 parcels that are processed in a bubble around characters as they move through the world. Characters such as MULES or other Porters move using this system, detecting 'high cost' areas such as rocky terrain or rivers and avoiding them where possible. Connecting the world together and enabling more long-distance movement is an invisible network of 'roads' that these characters can use to navigate, and a system of some 2,000 hand-placed 'jump links' where characters can climb or descend terrain. These invisible networks are separate from those that the player can build, but they similarly come to define the American landscape as one of technological connection, where, as Johnson says, 'in general the whole world is alive and in motion'.[6]

This means that while the visual qualities of the scenery are seemingly Icelandic, the act of measuring and quantifying ties *Death Stranding* closely back to an American conception of landscape. In his influential book *Taking Measures Across the American Landscape*, landscape architect James Corner discusses the paradoxical nature of the American landscape, as both 'efficient and wasteful' and 'brutal and spectacular'.[7] For Corner, the precision of modern infrastructure and the measurements required to realize it mean that 'some of the most banal measures in the modern landscape (roads, transmission lines, and survey lines, for example) actually provide a "hyper-reality" of exhilarating and emancipating opportunity'.[8] It is through such measures that players start to reconnect America, whether that is by imposing 'survey lines' through the game's route-planning function, or collaborating to build roads, power stations and other structures.

5 Eric Johnson, '"Death Stranding": An AI Postmortem', GDC AI Summit, GDCVault, gdcvault.com/play/1027144/AI-Summit-Death-Stranding-An.
6 Ibid.
7 James Corner, *Taking Measures Across the American Landscape* (New Haven & London: Yale University Press, 1996), 25.
8 Ibid., 26.

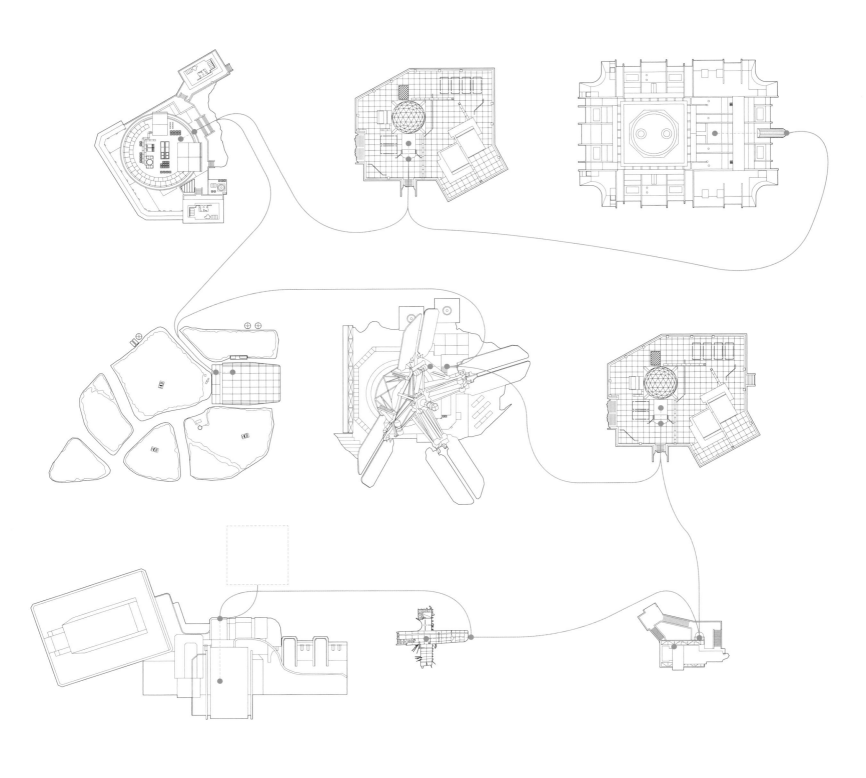

5

Plans of key structures encountered by Sam during his coast-to-coast journey. These buildings tend towards 'non-human' architecture such as infrastructural facilities, automated farms and communications relays.

4.4   Generic Architecture

If the landscape and its data support connection and quantification, then the buildings and human-made places that Sam visits serve to emphasize that this is a world given over to logistics. As players establish the network through deliveries, they repeatedly encounter the same type and form of building. The main facilities that define the journey are somewhat more unique, from a hospital containing the President's Oval Office to a crematorium and an industrialized farm, although studying them in roof plan still reveals repeated architectural motifs [Fig. 5]. By contrast, other structures such as prepper shelters dotted around the landscape are defined through a kit-of-parts architecture, suggesting that they are buildings that could be ordered, flat-packed and delivered to a location. There are many examples of architectural systems that were designed for prefabrication, such as pre-sawn timber houses sold by the Sears catalogue in America, and more advanced systems such as Jean Prouvé's 1950s Maison Tropicale system.[9] In both cases, prefabrication was used as a way of quickly delivering buildings and infrastructure to the frontier, in much the same as *Death Stranding*'s human communities reoccupy the post-*Stranding* landscape.

What remains consistent is the player's engagement with architecture, operating at the level of entryways, terminals and interfaces, with deeper exploration confined to cinematic cutscenes. Each engagement with a building reinforces the non-human and generic nature of *Death Stranding*'s architectural language. Such buildings – like real-world data or fulfilment centres – are, as architect Liam Young argues, 'the precursors of a new aesthetic and formal movement, a technological sublime'.[10] The marvellous landscapes are complemented (or completed) by the comparative facelessness of the architecture. Despite this, Distribution Centers serve as key markers in the landscape and story; an architectural form resembling a ship that is duplicated across the map. Each centre comes to be defined more by its surrounding territory and the connections this brings, with centres further out into the wilderness showing more signs of weathering and degradation, wearing their distance from the network on their façades [Fig. 6].

Interactions with the Distribution Center as a space are limited to the terminal, which emerges from the floor, and the elevator that descends into it. Players observe lines of shelving disappearing into a foggy basement, but their attention is always focused on a particular and narrow set of features [Fig. 7]. This reinforces the importance of surfaces in *Death Stranding*, particularly the ground or floor beneath Sam's feet. Distribution Centers are not the only buildings that use the floor as their primary spatial interface; in fact, nearly every architectural space Sam encounters uses the floor-embedded terminal as a way for the player to interact with the network. These floor interfaces vary between different buildings but still use repeated features [Fig. 8]. The prevalence of markings and guides also defines these as spaces of logistics, for vehicles or people to be directed in efficient ways, in contrast to the rolling landscapes beyond and the invisible territories of BTs. As architectural theorist Keller Easterling has argued, 'the floor is now arguably the most important architectural surface', where it 'becomes the brains of an intelligent navigation system'.[11] This is the reality of today's non-human architecture, which we see reimagined in Sam's all-too-human story.

9   Jean Prouvé, *Jean Prouvé: the Tropical House* (Paris: Editions du Centre Pompidou, 2011).
10 Liam Young, 'Neo-Machine: Architecture Without People', in *Architectural Design: Machine Landscapes: Architectures of the Post-Anthropocene* (Oxford: Wiley, 2019), 13.
11 Keller Easterling, 'Floor.dwg', in *Cabinet*, Issue 47, *Logistics* (New York: Cabinet, 2012), 98.

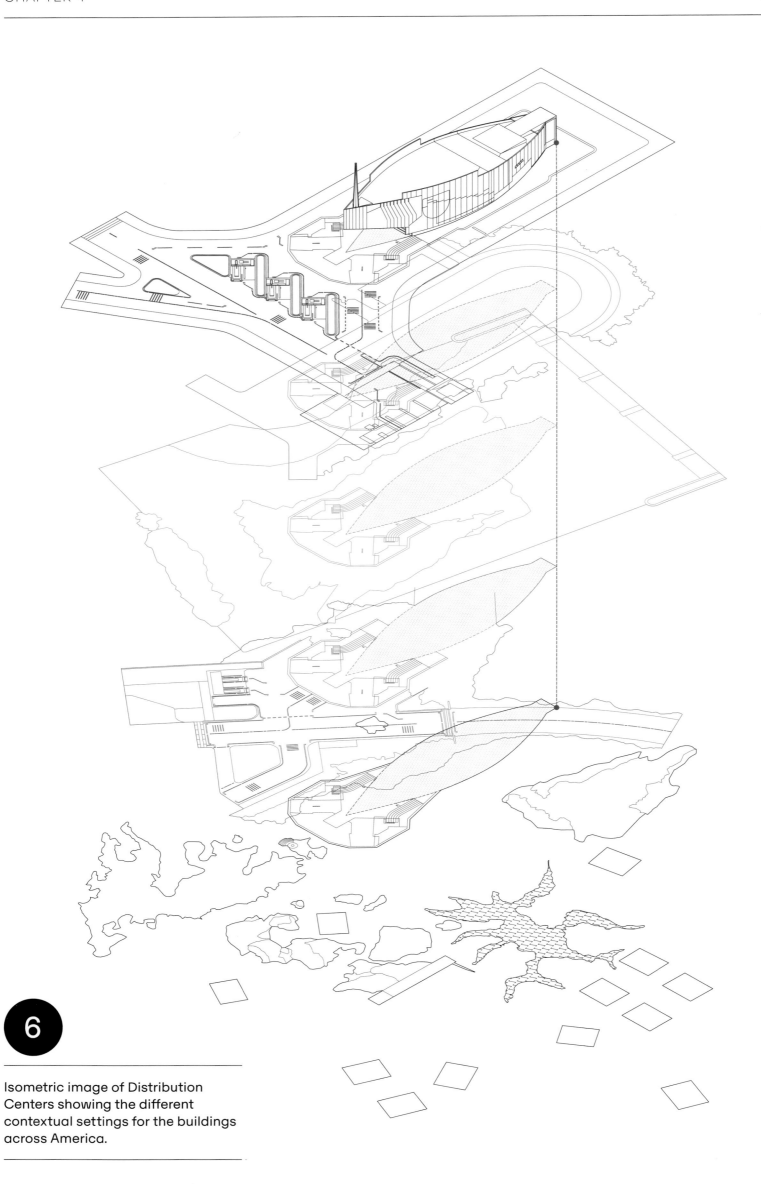

6

Isometric image of Distribution Centers showing the different contextual settings for the buildings across America.

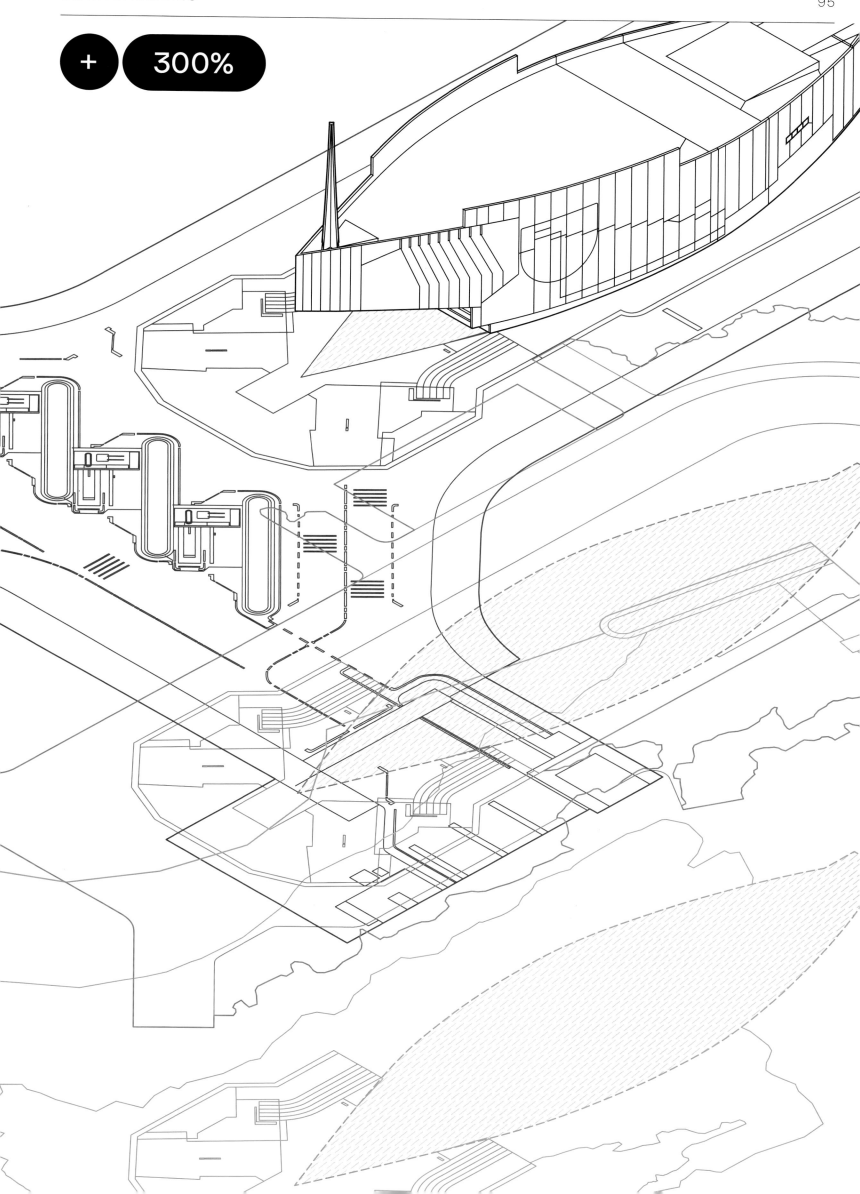

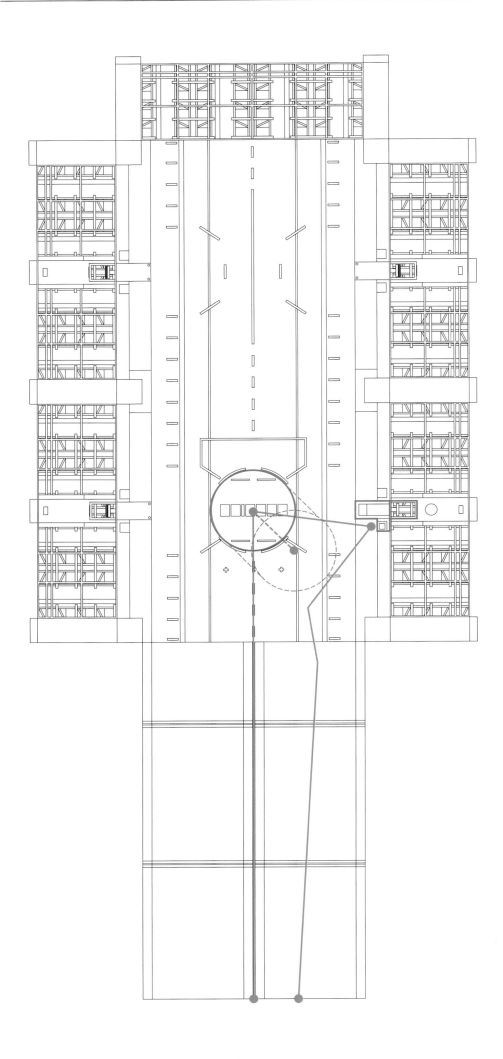

Unfolded interior elevation of a Distribution Center showing the limited spaces that Sam interacts with, and the lines of shelving disappearing off into the distance.

Floor typology elevations demonstrating how similar interfaces and markings are used across many different buildings in the game, contributing to the importance of the floor in *Death Stranding*'s architecture.

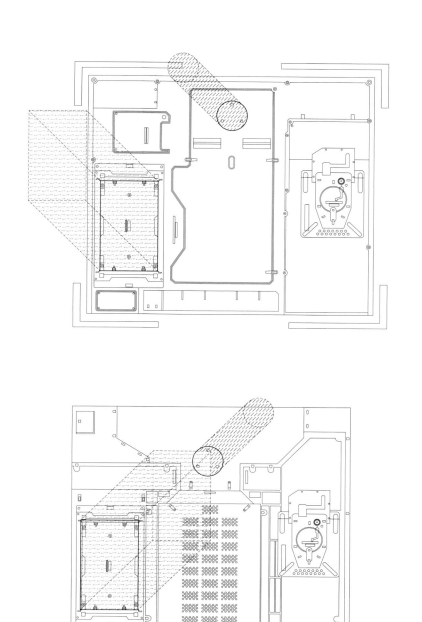

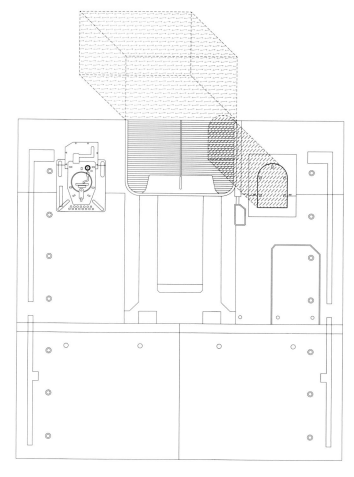

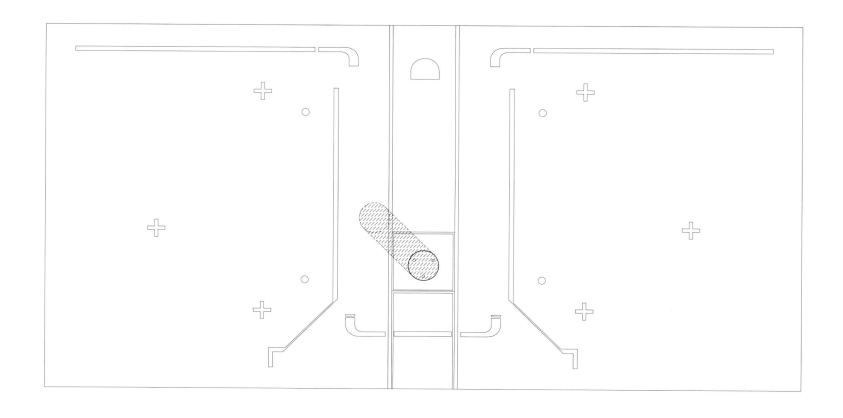

These interfaces continue to be found in the many prepper shelters that Sam encounters in the American landscape. While, as discussed, these are based around what is clearly a kit-of-parts structure, it is not clear what subterranean facilities below were excavated, or how [Fig. 9]. Different shelters have certain minor customizations to provide at least some sense of individual identity to their identikit forms.

This generic architecture is strongly asserted at Mountain Knot City, where a city containing 84,000 people is represented through several small container-like structures arranged around a Tar Pit. This suggests a city of people living a subterranean existence, but also reframes urban space around this language of the non-human – there are no windows and no signs of life to be found. Through a population density map, we can see that in the fiction of the game, urban environments still contain most of the population [Fig. 10], but the built elements in the landscape have the effect of inverting that condition in the mind of the player – we barely ever get any indication of society's presence, beyond a few low-resolution skyscrapers as backdrops to industrial facilities.

While *Death Stranding*'s auxiliary buildings tend towards the generic and infrastructural, this approach continues at a smaller scale with the structures players can build within the world, creating connections with others online through a system of likes (likes being another manifestation of an American landscape, but a social one).

Structures are made using the Portable Chiral Constructor, and are seemingly 3D-printed in place. Although these are fictional technologies, 3D-printing systems using computers to control either the deposition or solidification of building materials on-site are increasingly being used to fabricate real buildings. In *Death Stranding*'s frontier these structures serve several purposes, including speeding up connections between places, offering respite from Timefall and providing power to vehicles. This set of structures is reminiscent [Fig. 11] of what British architectural historian Reyner Banham called 'gizmos', small mass-produced units that could be placed into a site to increase its potential for human habitation where 'because practically every new, incomprehensible or hostile situation encountered by the growing American Nation was conquered, in practice, by handy gizmos of one sort or another, the grown Nation has tended to assume that all hostile situations will be solved by gadgets'.[12] Through the deployment of these various devices to the landscape, along with smaller objects such as ladders and ropes, players are able to tame the natural environment and work together to increase connectivity between players.

Isometric image showing Prepper shelter variations. While the external envelope might change very slightly, the entranceway and interior space remain the same in each structure.

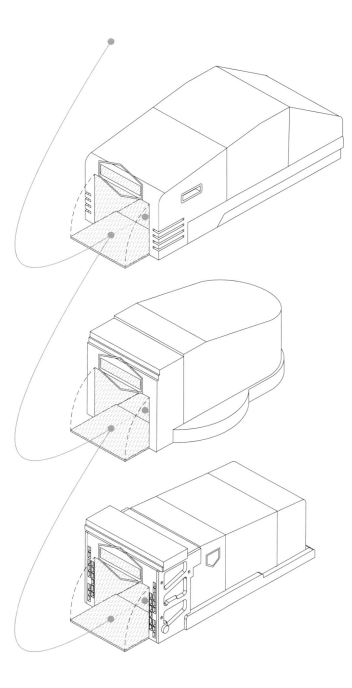

12   Reyner Banham, *Design by Choice* (London: Academy
     Editions, 1981), 111.

 U.C.A:

08 Cities
315,000 Citizens

10

Population density map of America showing that *Death Stranding*'s population is still concentrated in cities, but this is never encountered by the player.

11

A library of user-made structures produced by Chiral 3D printing. These prefab elements allow players to collaborate across the network to reconnect America.

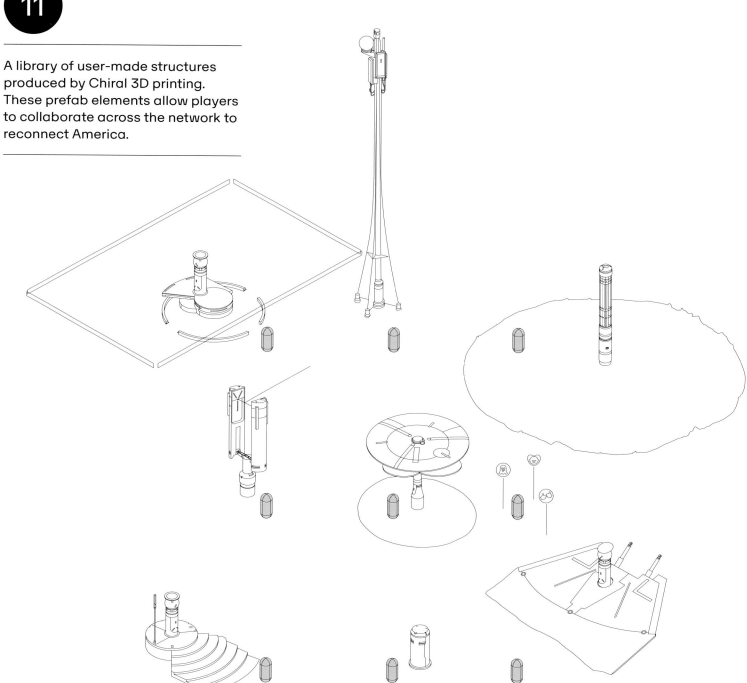

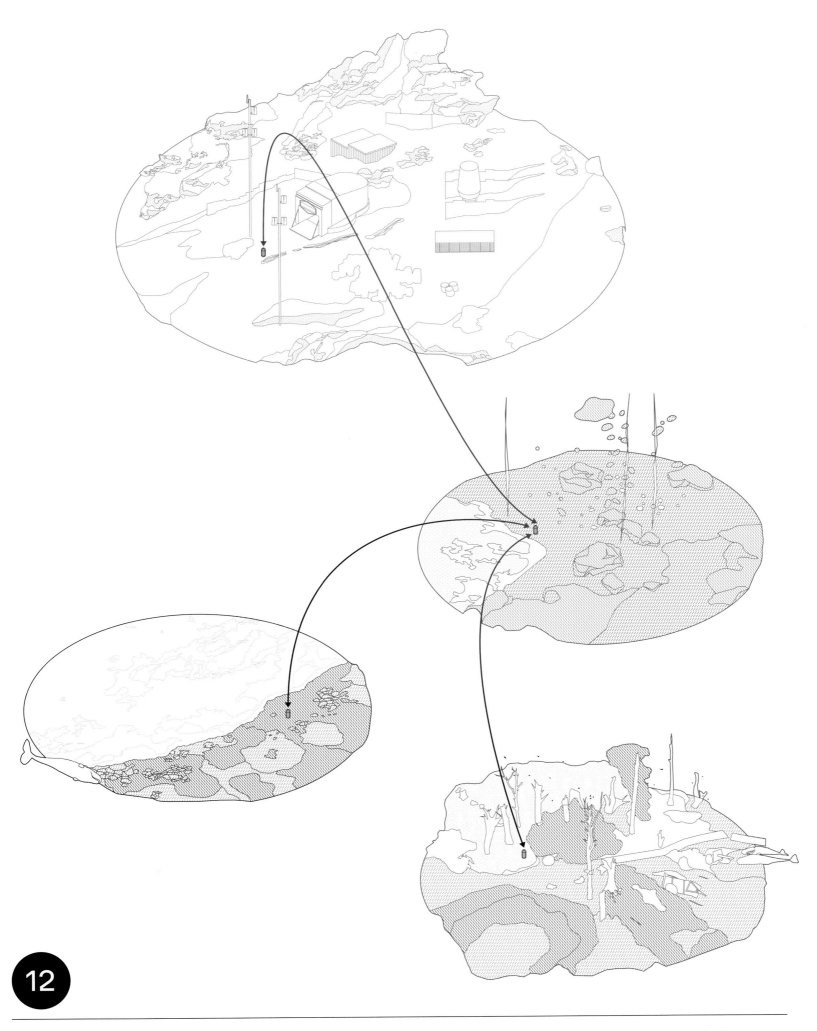

12

Isometric diagram showing the notional relationship between America, The Beach, Strand Fields and The Seam based on Sam's journey through the game.

4.5   Beaches

Aside from the horizontal movements Sam makes across the American landscapes, there is another form of movement intrinsic to *Death Stranding*'s world – the transition from the physical world to the Beach and back again. Beaches are defined as the space between the worlds of the living and the dead that is unique to each individual soul. The BTs that Sam encounters on his journeys represent souls that were unable to pass through the Beach into the land of the dead and remain stranded in the physical world. Most Beaches players encounter are literally that, sections of empty coastline where black sands meet the sea, strewn with the bodies of stranded whales.

Beaches are reached through a zone known as The Seam, which is an environment equivalent to purgatory. When players die, they will enter The Seam, with the landscape appearing flooded and Sam's body floating in the ether. Like the physical world, this is a networked environment, with players able to see where other players have died. As Sam is a repatriate he can return to the land of the living from The Seam, avoiding the transition to the world of the dead and meaning that the player's experiences of Beaches are predominantly found through narrative cutscenes and other mission levels separate from the main open-world environment.

By visualizing this relationship we can see the transitions that Sam makes during the game, from the collective space of the American landscape and The Seam, where the traces of other players can be encountered, through to individual Beaches and finally Strand Fields, special types of Beach that host more conventional third-person combat missions. These Beaches represent moments when many people die in a short period and are symbolized by historical battlefields encompassing both world wars and the Vietnam War. At these points the design of the environment becomes both more architectural and linear, with Sam fighting in bombed-out churches and sneaking between thatched huts [Fig. 12].

4.6   Networking

After *Death Stranding*'s story has been completed, Sam and the player are returned to America, where there are still deliveries to be made and connections to maintain. Across the course of the game, the player will have forged many paths, linked many nodes, ventured into hostile territory and accessed the support of others through shared deliveries, ersatz infrastructure and helpful hints left glowing in the landscape. The map that this playthrough might produce is a network of all those points of interest and the connections between

them. Yet ultimately, as Ulises Ali Mejias argues, such an emphasis on the network as an organizational structure can become 'nodocentric',[13] privileging only the connection between two points and not the (potentially disruptive and noisy) reality that sits between them. And it is the reality of the unforgiving landscape that will be remembered. While Sam dutifully connects the world, players will not forget the romantic beauty of the American/Icelandic hybrid and the hours of concentrated navigation required to complete those links.

13   Ulises Ali Mejias, *Off the Network* (Minneapolis & London: University of Minnesota Press, 2013), 60.

○ VIDEOGAME ATLAS

DWARF FORTRESS

SLAVES TO ARMOK: GOD OF BLOOD, CHAPTER II: DWARF FORTRESS

Details

Year	2006
Developer	Bay 12 Games
Publisher	Bay 12 Games
	Kitfox Games

Platforms

Microsoft Windows

Linux   macOS

As a procedural environment rendered entirely in symbols, *Dwarf Fortress* encourages players to imagine the world that exists in the visual gaps, drawing out the rich societies and histories created by the game.

☐ Maps:

66,049 Regions
38.65Bn Tiles
1050 Year History

5.1   Procedural Histories

Of all the most complex and sophisticated game worlds, the most detailed and intimidating is quite possibly that of *Dwarf Fortress*. Defining the world is made very difficult by the fact that the game is predicated on a sprawling procedural system that generates not only a global environment, but also the societies that inhabit it, their histories and culture, the cities and structures they build, and even the individual psychology of every inhabitant. Developer Tarn Adams describes this as 'the idea that you can be playing a game without a story, but a story will arise as you follow the different threads and pieces of information that are presented to you'.[1]

The game is primarily focused on the design and construction of dwarven fortresses, with players constructing elaborate fortifications to defend themselves and their society from a hostile world. As with world generation, there are almost infinite possibilities for players to achieve this, and just as many ways to fail, with the game providing deep systems for construction, farming and industry, alongside procedures for preserving the cultural and mental wellbeing of the dwarf community. These fortresses can often become huge and complex endeavours, and involve many of the considerations associated with a real-world piece of architecture, such as the efficient circulation of space, the creation of pleasant internal environments and the conscious use of locally obtainable building materials.

In a notable example of this procedural complexity, a *PC Gamer* article based on an interview with Adams detailed how cats in the game were getting drunk while grooming themselves having entered dwarven taverns and getting spilt alcohol on their feet. The amount of alcohol ingested compared to their tiny body mass would then make the cats vomit and die in the tavern.[2] The space of a drinking establishment becomes a manifestation of what Martinez-Garcia terms 'systemic uncertainty' in the game, where 'players can never be sure of exactly how exactly and how realistically the modelled world operates, only that it does'.[3]

Dwarf Fortress also offers an Adventure mode where the player can explore the environment in a more traditional role-playing game (RPG) format, and Legends mode, where the geography, history and lore of the world can be exported into a series of database files and maps that can subsequently be explored on other software. With one such world generated by the game, 'Ospazsmata, The Windy Realm', we can see the map represented as a vast series of tiles, within which continents, oceans and other landscape features can be understood. The global scale of this world is vast – based on the 'large' template in the game's generation system, Ospazsmata is 257 world map tiles wide, a real-world distance of some 500 km (310⅔ miles) [Fig. 1]. But this world is also dense with many intricate systems.

1   YouTube, *Noclip – Video Game Documentaries*, '*Dwarf Fortress* Creator Explains its Complexity & Origins | Noclip Interview', youtube.com/watch?v=VAhHkJQ3KgY.

2   Wes Fenlon, 'How cats get drunk in *Dwarf Fortress*, and why its creators haven't figured out time travel (yet)', *PC Gamer*, pcgamer.com/uk/how-cats-get-drunk-in-dwarf-fortress-and-why-its-creators-havent-figured-out-time-travel-yet/.

3   Mario Martinez-Garza, 'For !!SCIENCE!!', in *International Journal of Gaming and Computer-Mediated Simulations*, 7(2), April-June 2015, 46–64.

A map of a world generated by *Dwarf Fortress*, entitled 'Ospazsmata, The Windy Realm'. Here we can see the IBM Codepage 437 tileset used to symbolize the prevailing landscape conditions of each grid square.

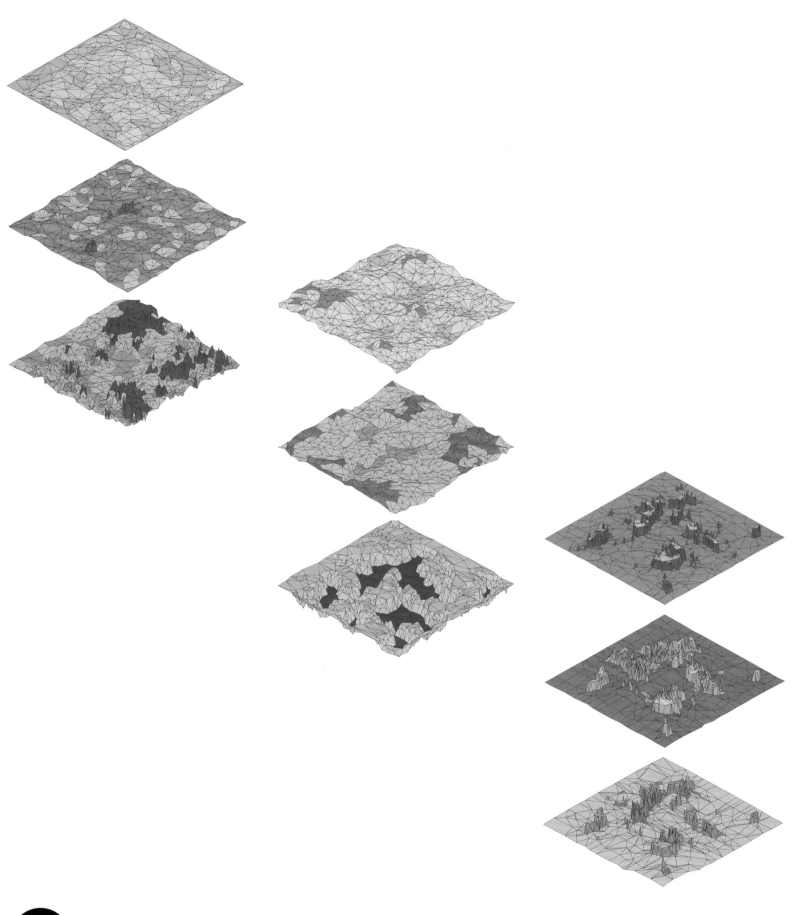

2

By visualizing all the map data produced by the game's database of information, we can see the different parameters that come to define the structure of a generated world.

5.2   A Database World

These maps allow us to build a more complete understanding of the environment, but also demonstrate what aspects of the world define *Dwarf Fortress* as a game experience through a visual landscape of unique data sets. The maps we can create from the game include cartographies we might expect to find in reality, relating to vertical elevation or weather, but also the distribution of evil and the relationship between different noble houses [Fig. 2].

The desire for players to understand such complex worlds has led to the generation of many community tools that allow for all these intricate strands of history and geography to be visualized and organized.[4] Legends Viewer allows players to import database files from their game worlds and display them in multiple different ways. In visualizing Ospazsmata, these tools offer us an understanding of how the environment was formed through different forces, political relationships and conflicts, just like our real world [Fig. 3]. At the same time, despite all these tools for visualization, this history is not necessarily a narrative one in the traditional sense. Instead, a *Dwarf Fortress* world history ties much more closely to the aesthetic of a database, because it is one. Ospazsmata's largest (and ongoing) war, the War of Spikes, is described through 594 entries in Legends Viewer's event log, transcribing each individual death, the killer and the location. We can see the battle sites and understand that thirty-nine pillagings took place in total, while also reflecting on the fact that this was one of twenty-one different wars the world has witnessed.

In many ways, the complexity of *Dwarf Fortress*'s simulated world is emblematic of computation itself. The world is created through an algorithm, and this produces a vast database of information that requires software to sort it into an intelligible set of meanings. Media theorist Lev Manovich argues that 'the database supports a

range of cultural forms that range from direct translation (i.e., a database stays a database) to a form whose logic is the opposite of the logic of the material form itself – a narrative'.[5] Beyond the (literally) blow-by-blow accounts of battles represented in the database, the narrative is something generated by players themselves, with the rich lore and stories that people generate through engaging with such a deep simulation.

Yet we can also see the simulation's database generate other forms of information that are far more spatial, and in turn generate new stories. While creating towns and cities in the world, *Dwarf Fortress* also produces maps that are effectively architectural plans of these settlements. Ospazsmata's largest generated human town, Amazedbrush, is home to 1,340 humans and one dwarf. It possesses a keep, a market and three taverns among around 200 buildings that make up the town. All buildings are rectangular in shape and follow the cardinal grid, meaning that they create stepped frontages towards any diagonal roads, of which Amazedbrush possesses multiple. Although the town has a castle, we do not see the layers of walls that we might expect in a typical medieval town. The keep, the Bastion of Tactics, appears well protected by walls but the rest of Amazedbrush opens out on to farmland [Fig. 4]. Other settlement plans generated include Dark Fortresses, examples of goblin architecture, where a vast central building is surrounded by a complex network of trenches and guard towers. In this regard, goblin design appears to be much more aggressive and oriented towards militaristic design, with surveillance, protected thoroughfares and no-man's land surrounding the area [Fig. 5].

☐ Amazedbrush:

1 Dwarf
1,340 Humans
200 Buildings

4   Py LNP's *Lazy Newb Pack* provides a launcher that integrates mods and visualization tools into the *Dwarf Fortress* experience.
5   Lev Manovich, 'Database as a Symbolic Form', manovich.net/content/04-projects/022-database-as-a-symbolic-form/19_article_1998.pdf

3

Dwarf Fortress generates different civilizations and cultures that can be understood through the connections and territories they come to occupy in the world, and the relationships they build between one another.

4

Isometric map of a human town named 'Amazedbrush' shows buildings aligned on a cardinal grid within a patchwork of farmland, and a keep overlooking the surrounding area.

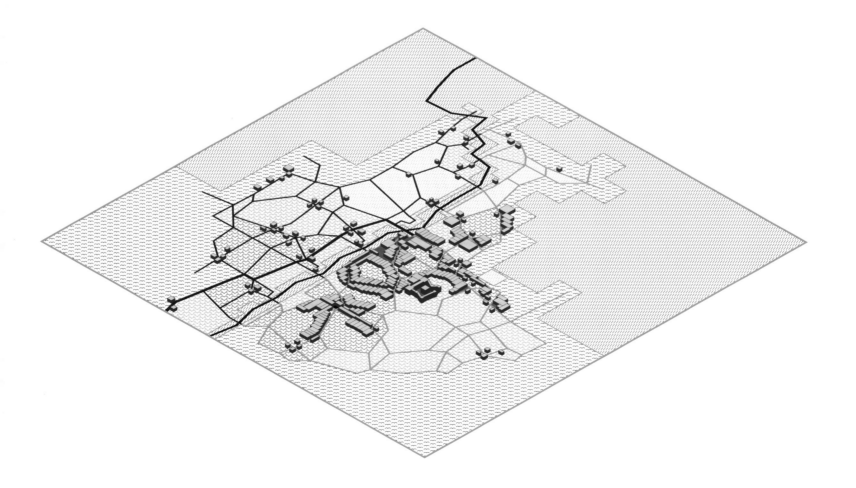

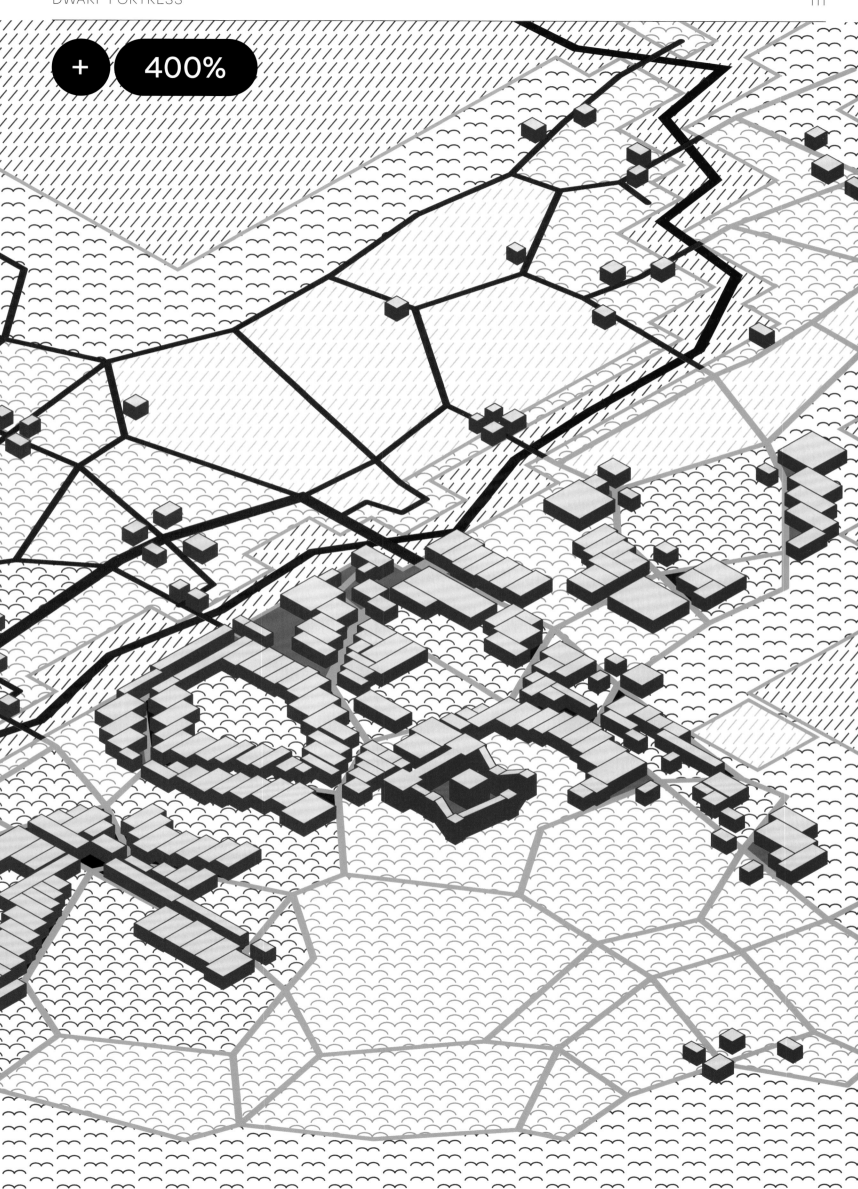

5

The goblin architecture of a Dark Fortress is far more militaristic than human architecture – with a central tower surrounded by smaller watchtowers and accessed via deep trenches.

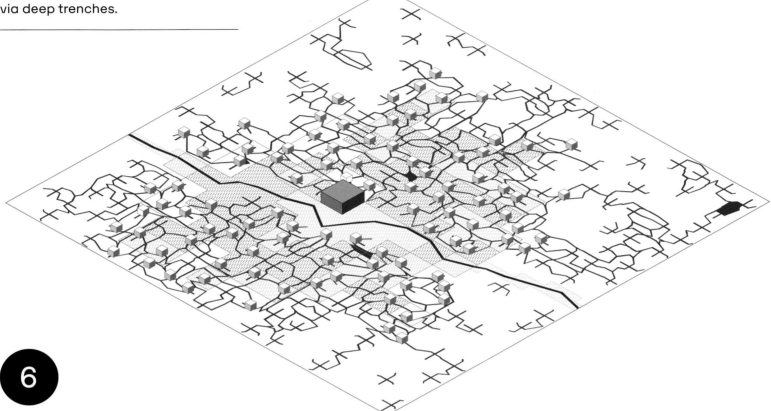

6

Based on an abstracted map generated by the game, this isometric drawing shows the rough outline of a dwarven fortress, demonstrating how dwarves closely integrate living and industrial spaces.

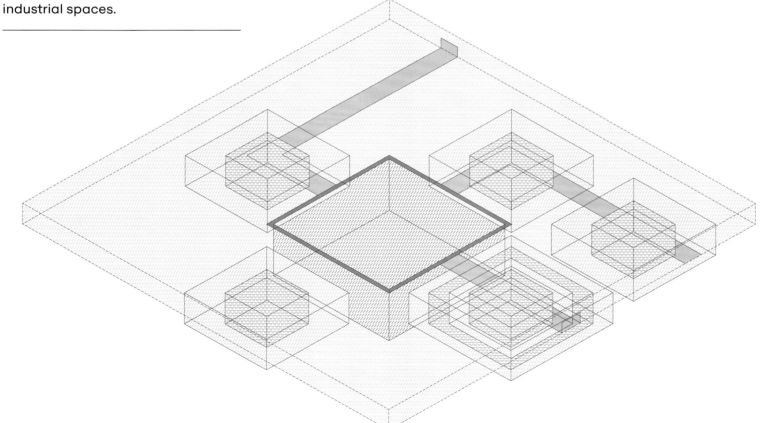

We can also see sets of far more abstract plans representing other dwarven fortresses and structures such as Mountain Halls, which are settlements buried deep under mountains. While these simple geometric plans do not convey the complexity of the space one might encounter while visiting in Adventure mode, they do demonstrate one of the key spatial relationships in dwarven design, which is the close proximity of living and industrial stacks [Fig. 6]. In the fortress 'Coalslaughter' (population 398) we can see how residential and industrial areas alternate, establishing a relationship between spaces for resting and spaces for productivity as a key facet of fortress design that players will need to overcome. The Mountain Hall 'Axechasm' (population 174) has the exact same extents as 'Amazedbrush', but is significantly less dense, although it still shows some of the dwarven stack design elements, interconnected by vast tunnels [Fig. 7].

In all these cases, information retrieved from the vast database that is a *Dwarf Fortress* world is then re-encoded into other types of informational form, whether that is a step-by-step history or an architectural plan. While the game relies on visual symbols that are hard to read without an in-depth understanding of their meaning, *Dwarf Fortress* continues to be expanded and clarified through community tools to give 'lazy newbs' the ability to comprehend and engage with its worlds.

☐ Settlements:

222 Dwarven
158 Elven
48 Goblin
122 Human

A Mountain Hall represents a series of carved chambers at the scale of a town, but far less dense, containing only a hundred or so 'deep dwarves'.

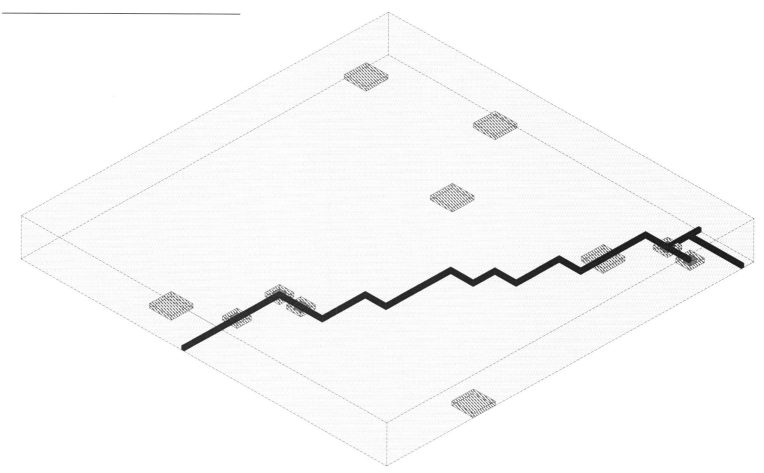

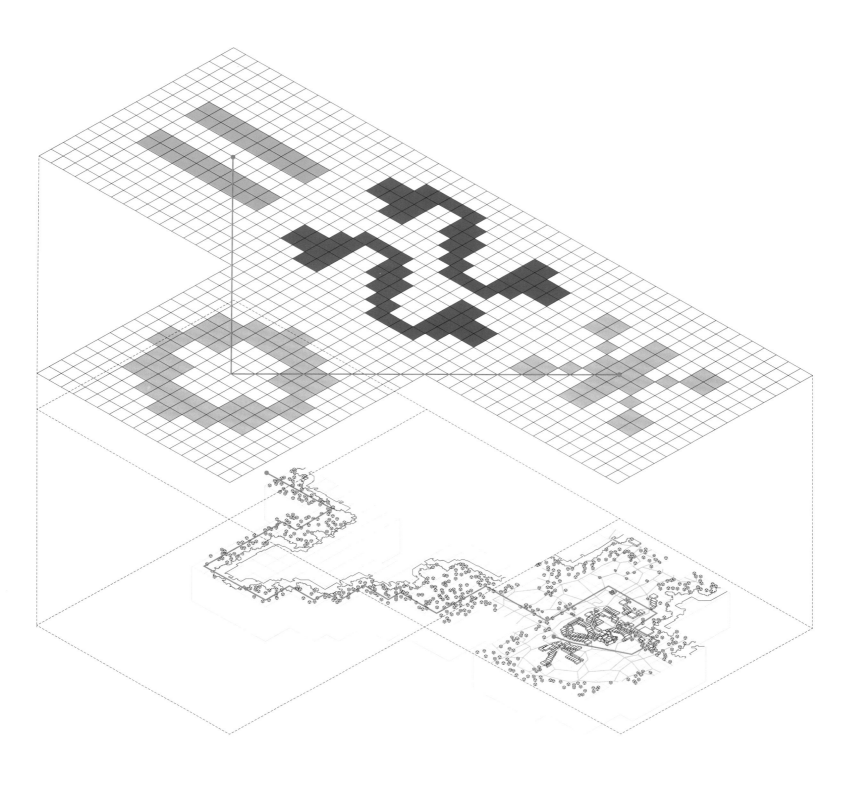

8

A journey between three symbolic world map tiles
is actually part of a much more complex landscape,
demonstrating the way *Dwarf Fortress*'s characters
hold multiple layers of information within them.

5.3 Visual Encoding

One of the most visually striking qualities of *Dwarf Fortress* is its use of text characters rather than graphics to represent the world. The game uses the IBM Codepage 437 character set as the tileset for the game, which comprises 256 characters including those used in ASCII, and other characters for line drawing and symbolic representation.

This means that the world of the game, and everything contained within it, is encoded into a highly symbolic language. Because *Dwarf Fortress* represents the complexity of many systems in great detail using a limited number of characters, these tiles are often used contextually and may take on many different meanings at different points within the game. For example, the character ~ can represent such varied elements as a dirt road, a ploughed field, a smear of blood or a conger eel. Its meaning can range between a likeness to the shape of the character itself, and the first letter of its subject matter. As a result, the game requires intense participation from the player by means of their visual imagination.

Considering that so much of *Dwarf Fortress* concerns the creation and maintenance of in-game architecture, it is somewhat fitting that the player is tending to such a symbolic representation of space. The history of architectural drawing runs alongside the development of codifications and symbols to communicate specific technical messages to a contractor. Today many CAD and 3D modelling programs employ systems of 'blocks' – repetitive drawn elements that can be used and reused across projects.

This symbolic language is also strongly reminiscent of cartographic techniques applied in the real world, where icons, lines and hatches assume a value that is tied to an index of meanings. As Mark Monmonier argues in *How to Lie with Maps*, 'the value of a map depends on how well its generalized geometry and generalized content reflect a chosen aspect of reality'.[6] *Dwarf Fortress*'s basic maps appear impenetrable to an outsider, but like an architectural drawing they are full of details and meanings for players who have expertise in reading them. This symbolic designation is more clearly seen if we track a brief journey between two human settlements carried out in Adventure mode using the Isoworld tool to generate imagery as we move [Fig. 8]. Here we can see that the three symbolic tiles found on the world map actually represent a far more complex world found on ground level. Each of these tiles contains 768x768 smaller-scaled tiles, which represent the units with which the player will design and build their fortress. As we can see from the journey, this means there is a great deal of spatial complexity that is reduced down to a single region map tile that symbolizes the prevailing landscape condition.

A single character contains many spatial and social meanings within it, and these are applied recursively. Like a fractal design, we can see the same symbol repeated again and again at many different scales, although crucially, its meaning is changed at each different level.

One way in which communities have tried to make this language more intelligible is to design new graphic tilesets for the game. These graphic appliqués are used to emphasize different qualities of the *Dwarf Fortress* experience. Most tilesets continue the base game's relationship between forward-facing 2D depictions of objects or characters, with a top-down 2D view of built elements such as walls. However, some tilesets depict elements like columns in forward-facing oblique, allowing the player to see the illusion of thickness and depth in their structures. This way of representing a built structure actually has its history in fortress design; the cavalier oblique technique of drawing (also common to many other 2D games) was first developed to communicate the thickness of fortification walls clearly while still showing their entire façade to the viewer.[7]

Beyond this there are also several tools for visualizing the world in three dimensions, in both isometric (Isoworld, Stonesense) and full 3D (Armok Vision). In Armok Vision, connecting *Dwarf Fortress* to the *Unity* game engine enables players to explore their constructions in a first-person mode that bears a striking resemblance to *Minecraft*.[8]

6   Mark Monmonier, *How to Lie with Maps* (Chicago and London: The University of Chicago Press, 1991), 25.

7   Massimo Scolari references 'soldierly perspective' as a term of oblique drawing developed by a France's 'Superintendent of Fortresses' – an appropriate description of a *Dwarf Fortress* player – in *Oblique Drawing* (Cambridge, MA & London: MIT Press, 2012), 6.

8   Youtube, Nookrium, 'Armok Vision – 3D & First Person *Dwarf Fortress*', youtube.com/watch?v=K7XoPbYRLqo.

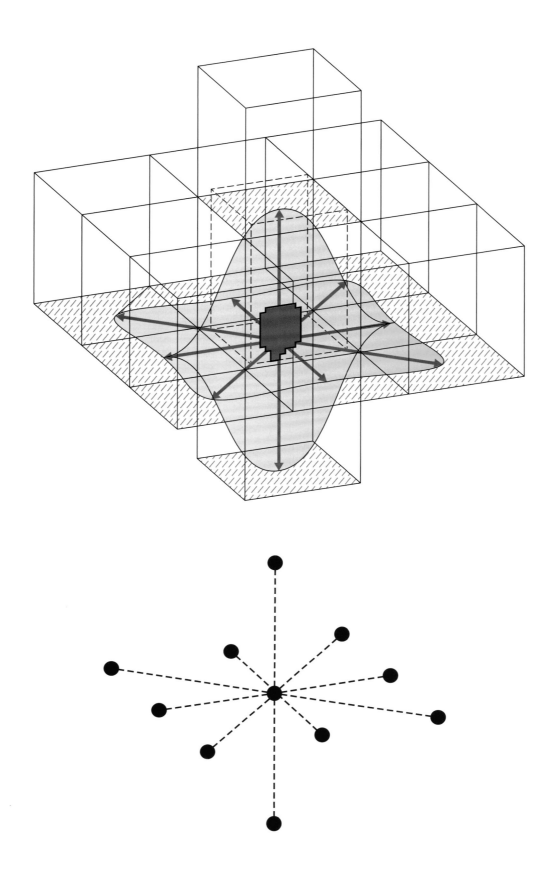

9

An isometric study of dwarf mobility, demonstrating how dwarves can move vertically and diagonally at the same time as in cardinal directions. This movement has a significant impact on how players plan spaces.

5.4   Space Planning

The act of planning a fortress is similar to architectural design. However, the logic of the game's grid-based system allows for players to design building layouts that would be impossible in reality.

Central to this is the dwarves themselves, who possess the ability to move on a lateral grid, up and down stairs and, crucially, diagonally. While dwarves move consistently in the cardinal directions, they can move the distance to a diagonal grid space in exactly the same time as it takes to move one space laterally. While moving diagonally, dwarves can slip through the gap between two walls meeting at their corner. By using stairs or ladders, dwarves are also able to move between 3-m (9-ft-10-⅛-in.) floors (called z-levels) at the same speed it takes them to move 2–2.4 m (6 ft 6¾ in.–7 ft 10½ in.) horizontally [Fig. 9].[9] This unusual proficiency in vertical and diagonal movement has been utilized by players to create fortress layouts with high levels of efficiency that can seem bizarre when compared to real-world ways of thinking about spatial design.

The design of bedrooms is a good example of this. As explained in a detailed design guide,[10] dwarves prize privacy in their resting spaces, alongside the provision of storage for their personal items. By looking at community-created floorplans, we can see the different ways in which players achieve this [Fig. 10]. More conventional plans work around 3x1 tile bedroom spaces that are laid out around a central stairwell to minimize the walking distance for dwarves to reach accommodation. Such designs can be scaled up and down across one floor of the fortress. However, other configurations seek to exploit the systems of the game more clearly in their layout. A design for a 'self-contained apartment' complex employs openings in the ceiling or floor to access bedroom spaces vertically by ladders from a lobby sandwiched between accommodation units. This design responds to dwarf happiness penalties applied to spaces that have holes in the wall (required for a door) by removing doors entirely from the design. A diagonal bedroom design exploits how dwarves may move between two diagonally placed wall corners by removing the need for doors or ladders. If we read this as an architectural plan, the space is jarring, and makes no sense without access, but within the systems of the game it is very efficiently designed. The final, arguably most extreme, form of exploit is to simply designate multiple bedroom spaces over the top of one another in a technique called 'overlapping bedroom'. Here, every dwarf sees a large open-plan space containing many bunks as being their own personal bedroom and can receive the happiness benefit of this while the player retains the benefit of high-density communal sleeping areas.

Another key aspect of space planning a fortress comes in the layout of traps, where the design of the building can provide various forms of security devices. The game's community have developed many novel ways of dealing with large numbers of enemies. Here again we can see interesting exploits of the character movement and physics systems, including how enemies will path themselves while attacking fortresses [Fig. 11]. Architectural trap designs include 'crosshair traps' that catch enemies within the corners of four walls, containing them on top of a trap tile which they cannot escape from. The careful placement of trap tiles can also allow for friendly caravans to still make deliveries to the fortress by turning back on themselves, while the straight-line movement of enemies sees them caught up in the lines of defences. Water is also used as a security device in designs that allow players to flush large amounts of stored water through a structure to either trap invaders in a closed room and drown them, or use the force of the water to push enemies off narrow pathways into chasms below. Each of these designs shows ingenuity in exploiting the game mechanics to create defendable structures – and just like in the real world, these security measures run from the overt language of the heavy wall through to more subtle protective borders.

9   *Dwarf Fortress* Wiki, *DF2014:Tile*, dwarffortresswiki.org/index.php/DF2014:Tile
10   *Dwarf Fortress* Wiki, *DF2014:Bedroom design*, dwarffortresswiki.org/index.php/DF2014:Bedroom_design

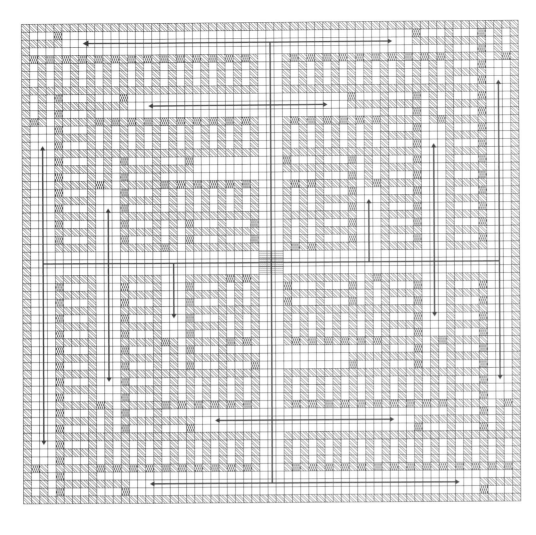

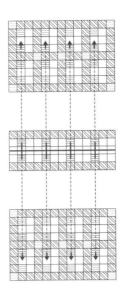

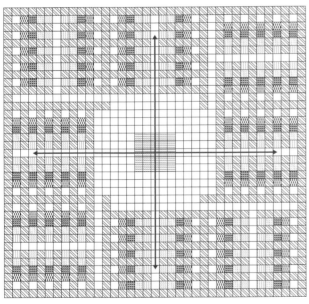

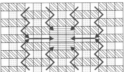

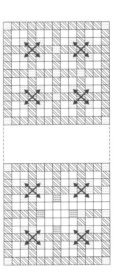

10

Plans of different dwarf bedroom layouts made by the community, designed to maximize the efficiency of movement. Some of these designs emphasize the dwarves' ability to move through diagonal intersections of walls and make quick vertical movements.

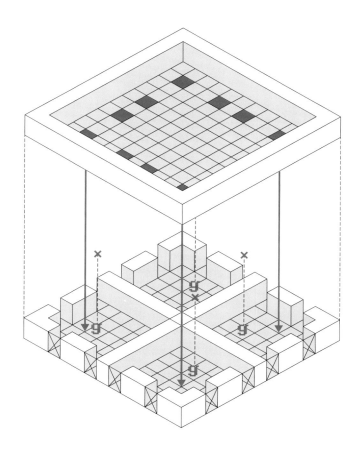

Isometric diagrams showing trap designs invented by the community that make use of pathfinding and physics, utilizing the architecture as a security measure against invaders.

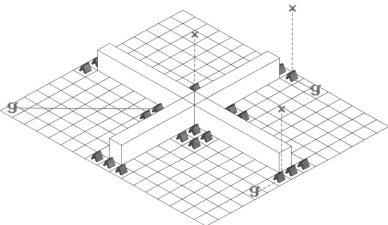

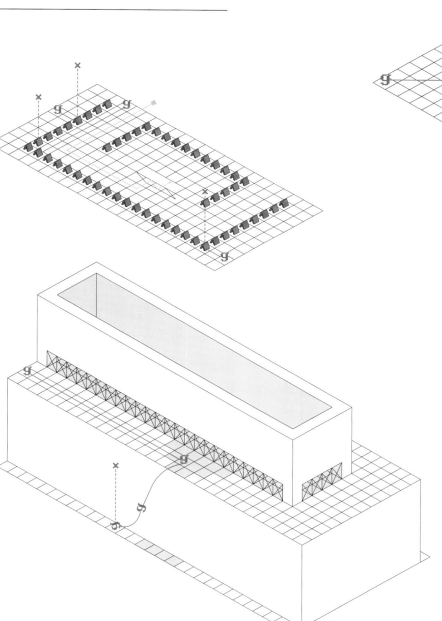

12

Wireframe through a dwarven fortress, revealing the depths it reaches far below the ground, and how the circular design is defined by a set of stair cores that allow for high levels of vertical mobility.

5.5   Megaprojects

While bedrooms or traps allow specific types of space planning to be applied in the service of a more efficient and safer fortress, they are one small part of the design process, especially when we consider fortresses that can be classed as Megaprojects. This title is reserved for highly complex constructions that often incorporate specialist and unique engineering feats in their design.

If we look at a fortress such as 'Earthenjaws' in the world 'Aluramul' created by the user 1hNWPEyVxhCtpYSrZRca,[11] we can see an example of a fortress that is designed on a radial plan, with a central core running the entire depth of the structure, surrounded by four other sub-cores providing easy access for dwarves to move vertically through the building. As we move from the ground to subterranean levels, we see how the circular plan of the fortress is applied at different scales, depending on the utility and access needs of that part of the facility. At certain points cave systems intersect the fortress, connecting to the central stair core and presumably allowing pathways out to mining opportunities. In all, 'Earthenjaws' possesses fifty-seven floors (roughly 170 m (557 ft 8⅞ in.) in depth), with the stair core continuing for another sixty-five levels to allow for future development [Fig. 12].

Using websites such as the DF Map Archive, we can gather more evidence of the scale of Megaproject undertaken by the community.[12] Looking at the top-rated fortresses on the site we can also see the idiosyncratic touch of their designers, just as we would when looking at an architectural plan. There are huge fortresses that take a cellular approach to design, those that stick rigorously to a structural grid system, and even fortresses built into a bridge between two continents. This is reminiscent of the Medieval Old London Bridge, part of a city built on to a thoroughfare across the water, resonating between historical forms of building and the designs conjured up by the *Dwarf Fortress* community, surely taking many weeks or months to complete.

Dwarf Fortress presents a giant procedural history for players to engage with. With its heavily symbolic visual style and seemingly infinite database of factoids and events, the world of *Dwarf Fortress* is ultimately fully formed by the imagination of the player. In the words of Tarn Adams, 'your own mind is a story-building engine'.[13] In the 1960s, the architect-engineer-scientist Buckminster Fuller proposed the World Game, where the entire world would be simulated by computers and world citizens would gather together to prototype the future of our planet's civilization. Through the complexity of *Dwarf Fortress*'s simulation, perhaps Fuller's grand idea has been realized, but with dwarves rather than humans, rendered in IBM Codepage and with an ultimately hopeless end to society, because, as the game reminds us, 'losing is fun'.

11   Fortress design downloaded from *Dwarf Fortress File Depot*, uploaded by user '1hNWPEyVxhCtpYSrZRca' on 2 March 2020.
12   *DF Map Archive*, mkv25.net/dfma/
13   YouTube, *Noclip – Video Game Documentaries*, '*Dwarf Fortress* Creator Explains its Complexity & Origins | Noclip Interview', youtube.com/watch?v=VAhHkJQ3KgY
14   R. Buckminster Fuller, *The World Game: Integrative Resource Utilization Planning Tool* (Carbondale, IL: World Resources Inventory).

☐ Fortress:

57 Floors
170 m (558 ft) Depth
122 m (400 ft) Diameter

Sections

FINAL FANTASY VII

Details

Year	1997 (Original) 2020 (*Remake*)
Developer	Square Enix
Publisher	Square, Square Enix, Sony Computer Entertainment, Kitfox Games

Platforms

PlayStation: 1/4/Portable · iOS

Xbox One · Nintendo Switch

Android · Microsoft Windows

Remake: · PlayStation: 4/5

The dystopian 'rotting pizza' of Midgar appears in two games made decades apart. It is a city that emphasizes technology – both in the Mako infrastructure underpinning its design, and in the evolution of the game tools used to create it.

☐ Maps:

9 Sectors
9 Reactors
3 Radial Zones

6.1   The City and the City

It is not a stretch to say that the circular form of Midgar, seen from above with the towering Shinra Building at its heart, is one of the most iconic urban forms in videogames. The opening shots of the original *Final Fantasy VII* and its two-decades newer *Remake* both begin focused on Aerith Gainsborough, one of the game's main characters, before zooming all the way through streets and districts to present the city in all its foreboding – and round – glory.

Both games tell the story of Cloud Strife, a mercenary soldier who finds himself helping an eco-terrorist organization named AVALANCHE. This group, led by Barret Wallace and Cloud's childhood friend Tifa Lockhart, is trying to prevent the destruction of the planet by the ruling Shinra Electric Power Company, who power Midgar through the removal and processing of Mako energy, the life force of the planet itself. In a complex and layered story, Cloud and his companions encounter Aerith, one of the last remaining Cetra (Ancients), and battle with Sephiroth, a former member of SOLDIER, an elite group of Mako-enhanced warriors, who seeks to obtain the power of a god.

Cloud's group will eventually incorporate many other characters as they travel the world, but Midgar remains a central point in the story, and a place that is returned to at the end of the game. The city's radial form, with its high surrounding walls and clearly defined spatial hierarchy between a central monument, overworlds and under-plate slums, is both iconic as a game setting and closely connected to historic forms of utopian (and dystopian) architecture. It clearly represents the worst excesses of Shinra's strip-mining of the world's resources, by elevating what is essentially a giant piece of Mako infrastructure into an urban framework [Fig. 1].

While Midgar only formed a small portion of the original game, the *Remake* takes place entirely within this city, meaning that while well-known areas of the first game such as the Sector 7 Slums and the Shinra Building can be compared between the two games, there are other new areas of the city that reveal more about its unique operations. By tracking the routes through Midgar taken by both versions of the game, we can see how the newer game diverges from the original path, allowing us to experience new areas that add depth to our understanding of the city. Yet what is interesting in comparing the two games is not only the formal or narrative changes that the city has undergone in twenty-three years, but also how these are closely linked to the technologies used in creating the game environment and making it playable.

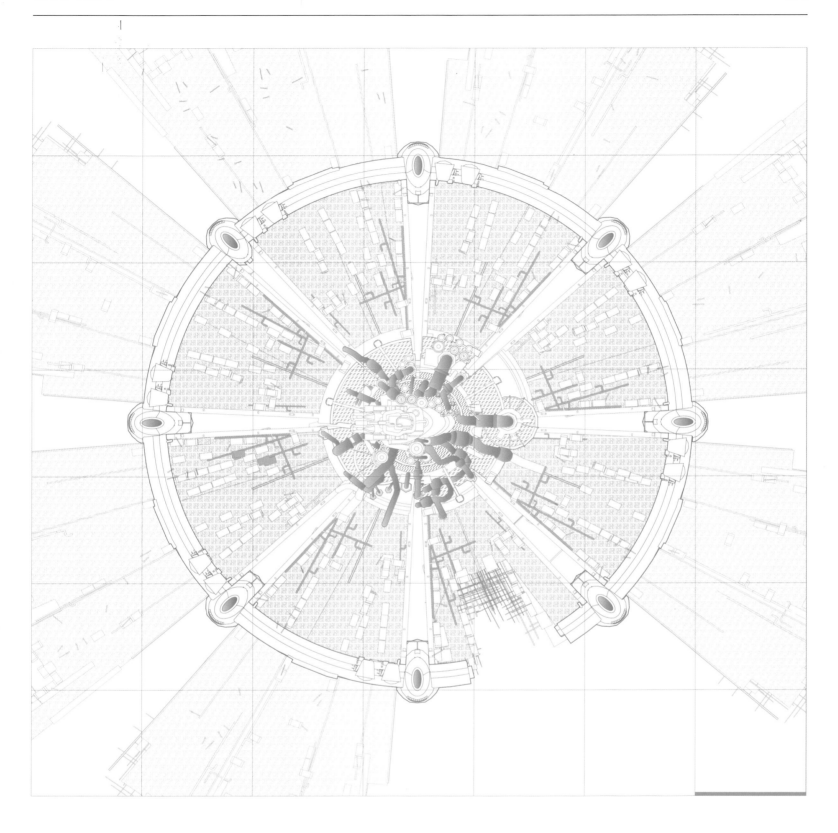

1

Map of Midgar showing the city extents within the inner ring of Mako reactors and the 'rotting pizza' divided up into different sectors. The lines of Mako infrastructure run out from the Shinra Building into the city beyond.

+ 450%

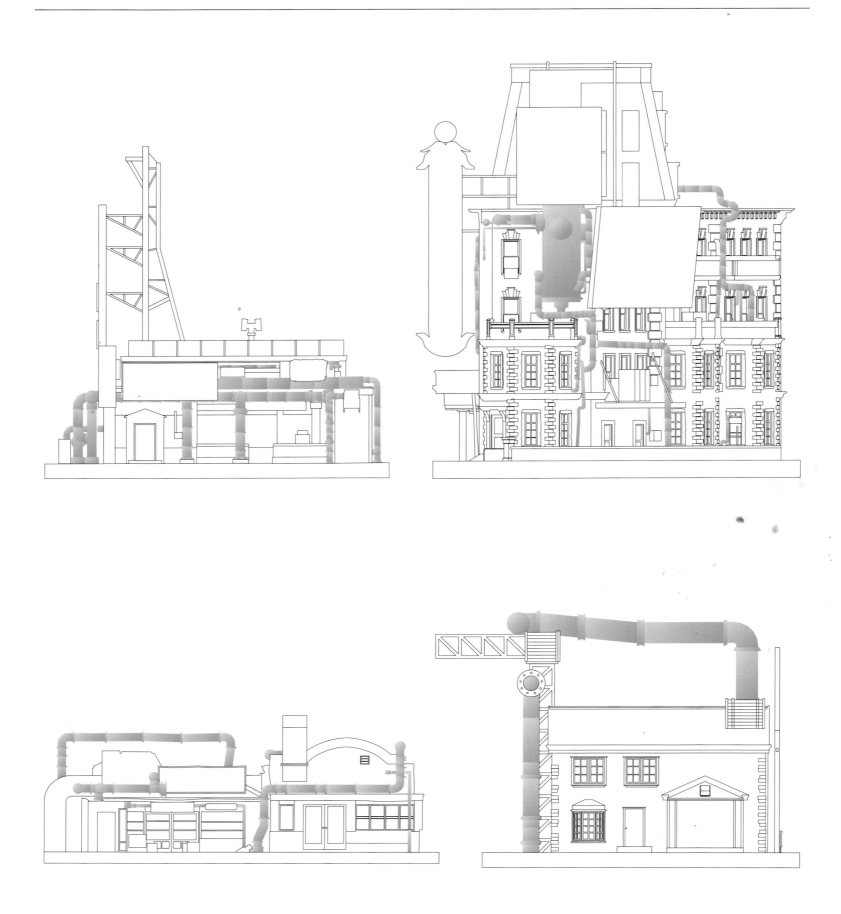

2

Elevational studies of buildings within Midgar showing how the pipework and infrastructure of Mako penetrates different types of structure across the neighbourhoods of the city.

6.2   Mako and the Megastructure

The form of Midgar as a giant plate, with the city growing out radially from a central point, is highly symbolic of its role as the dystopian capital of the world. Circular cities are common in the history of utopian fiction and design. For example, the 17th-century *City of Truth* published by Ambroise and Jérôme Drouart recreates a 15th-century poem as a giant circular city with a large structure at the centre, divided into five portions by roads radiating out to the edge of the city, just like Midgar.[1] In the 1970s the Italian architect Paolo Soleri proposed a series of giant self-contained cities called *arcologies* that often took radial forms.[2] Yet, far from these idealistic structures, Midgar, held together by the tendrils of Mako infrastructure, is described by characters as 'the rotting pizza'.

Through its encapsulated form and close integration of technology, Midgar is closely related to megastructural architecture of the past. It is particularly easy to see a resemblance to certain projects emerging from the Metabolist movement in architecture that developed in postwar Japan, such as Kiyonori Kikutake's Marine City. However, the Metabolists were aligned with the idea, as described by Kisho Kurokawa, that 'technology is an extension of humanity', where 'design and technology should denote human vitality'.[3] In Midgar, we can clearly see that such vitality is reserved for the upper layer of the city with the slums demonstrating the underbelly to an urban metabolism of Mako. The spirit of the city is very different.

Throughout a player's time in Midgar, they are never far away from understanding the reliance on a nervous system of Mako power. Mako, the planet's lifestream, is being steadily removed to power Midgar, and the precarity of the city's relationship with its destructive requirements is present in the architecture that players encounter across the city. Even ordinary buildings, seen across different sectors in the *Remake*, clearly show us how Mako infrastructure has penetrated every level of the city [Fig. 2]. With their quasi-industrial language they could remind us of Naoya Hatakeyama's photographs of Japanese limework buildings, where pitched-roof shacks are skewered by huge runs of pipework.[4]

As players journey into the structure of the plates that hold the upper city above the slums, we come to understand that this extends to powering an artificial sky, illuminating the towns below. Interestingly, the type of light used in the game has also been considered specifically, with the developers seeking to recreate the type of mercury vapour lighting common in Japan, giving the city a Tokyo-like hue even if its architecture references other cities.[5]

The building that ties the Mako megastructure of Midgar together is the hulking Shinra Building, the physical and political centre of the city. The building itself plays a key role in both versions of the game, with Cloud and his team climbing their way to the top of the huge structure. Although the Shinra Building is clearly designed to be monumental, it is also utilitarian, punctured by the tendrils it sends out to the city to carry Mako energy. Its sheer scale turns it into an 'automonument',[6] a term coined by Dutch architect Rem Koolhaas to describe a building that becomes monumental purely due to its size in relation to other structures. In its basic form, the Shinra Building is the heart of the city, dealing in the flow of Mako and the flow of political influence. This is turned on its head later in the original version of the game (we are yet to find out its role in the *Remake*). Near the end of the story, a giant cannon named Sister Ray is transported from a town called Junon and mounted on to the Shinra Building to fight the Diamond Weapon, a huge creature created to defend the planet. As the cannon fires, it sucks all the energy from Midgar, plunging it into darkness. Here we see the city-as-infrastructure completely subservient to the Shinra Building and its weaponry. Ironically at this point, the 'automonumentality' of the building is also subverted by the presence of the even larger cannon, turning the whole city into merely a giant battery [Fig. 3].

1   Bartolommeo Del Bene, *Civitas veri sive morvm*, 1609, obtained from archive.org/details/civitasverisivem01delb/page/n11/mode/2up
2   Paolo Soleri, *Visionary Cities: The Arcology of Paolo Soleri* (New York: Praeger, 1991).
3   Kisho Kurokawa, *Metabolism in Architecture* (London: Studio Vista, 1977), 27.
4   Naoya Hatakeyama, *Lime Works* (Tokyo: Amus Arts Press, 2002).
5   Simone de Rochefort, 'The real architecture behind FF7 *Remake*'s Midgar', *Polygon*, polygon.com/videos/2021/4/12/22380031/final-fantasy-7-*Remake*-midgar-architecture.
6   Rem Koolhaas, *Delirious New York: A Retroactive Manifesto* (New York: The Monacelli Press, 1994), 100.

3

Isometric study of the Shinra
Building showing how the building
originally functions as a centrepoint
to Midgar, with huge mako pipes
running in and out before becoming
a subservient structure, used to hold
up the giant Sister Ray cannon.

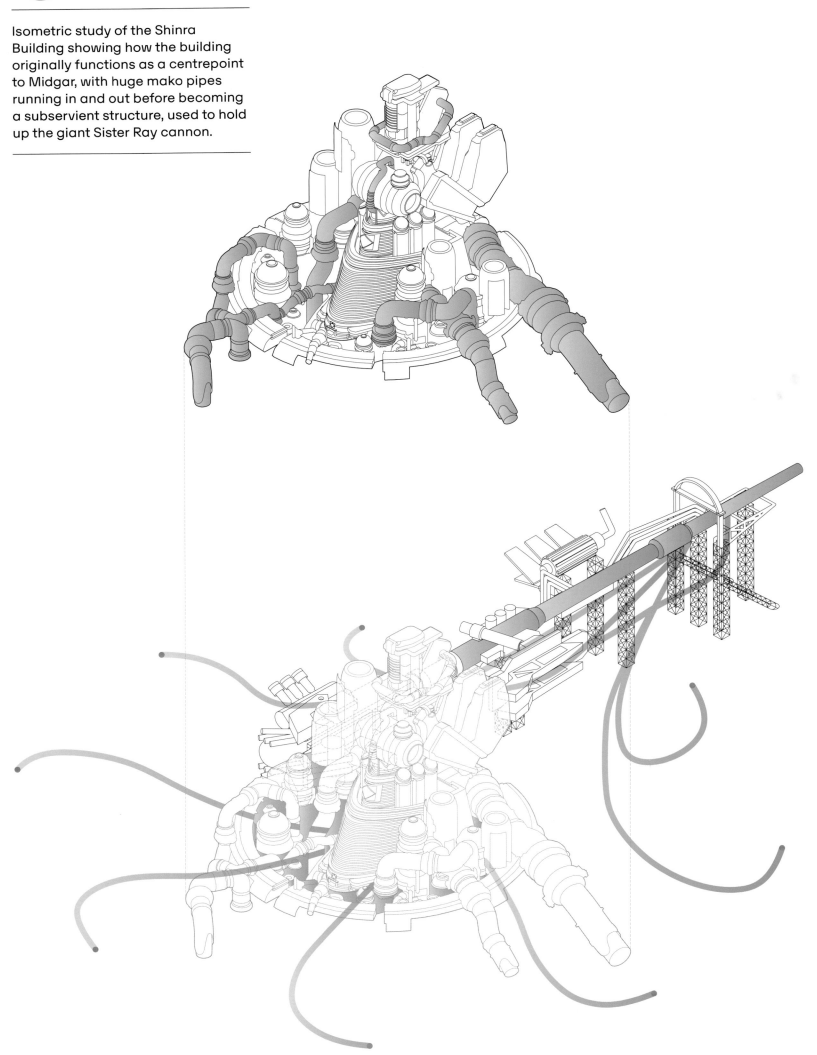

+ 450%

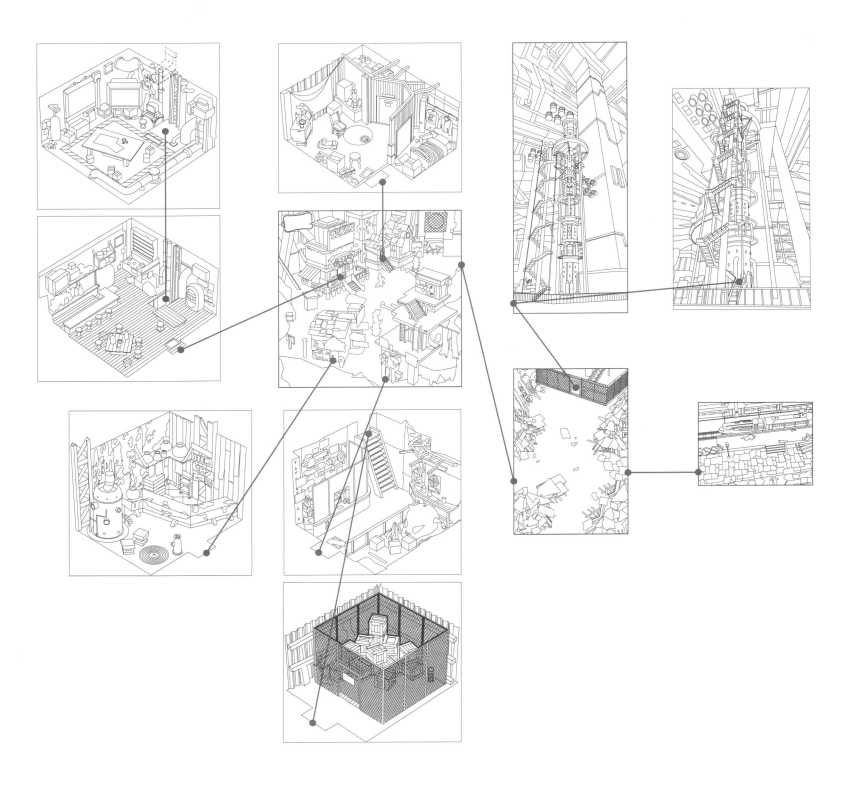

4

Various flat 'field maps' that make up Sector 7 in the original game. By placing these together we can see how the district is made up of a series of discrete spaces connected by camera transitions.

6.3   Field to Field

Aside from the look and feel of the city, the two-decade gap between recreations of Midgar has fundamentally changed the way the architecture is experienced. While the *Remake* has a more conventional structure expected of contemporary third-person games, the original version of Midgar was seen through an innovative combination of 2D and 3D representations.

To create a cinematic experience on early 3D technology, the developers of the original games used what have come to be known as 'field maps' to structure the game world. A field map was a pre-rendered 2D background, upon which 3D characters would move and interact. Invisible to the player was a 3D model called a 'walkmesh', which defined where the player could move, aligned with the viewpoint of the background to produce a convincing feeling of three-dimensional space. Each field map represents a different viewpoint, and Midgar itself is made of many of these maps. The Sector 7 Slums for example, is comprised of eleven field maps that illustrate both exterior and interior scenes [Fig. 4]. As such, the Sector can only really be understood as a series of fragmented viewpoints that are tied together into a city within our imagination. Larger field maps could scroll horizontally and vertically, while smaller ones were static. By extracting the walkmeshes from each of these scenes, we can build a clearer picture of the actual geometry that defines Sector 7 within the game, which is in fact a series of horizonal or angled surfaces with no walls. Any sense of architectural enclosure is achieved by placing different parts of the rendered view in front of or behind the walkmesh to give the effect of characters moving behind objects [Fig. 5].

As the player moves through Midgar they are encountering a large set of discrete maps, each of which contains unique information about battles and interactions. As a whole, *Final Fantasy VII* uses around 684 field maps to describe the world (excluding a number of 'black maps' and other development maps), of which Midgar is comprised of around 160. By drawing all these fields together we can build up an alternative mapping of Midgar, which demonstrates the way we really understand the city, beyond the iconic circular form seen from above [Fig. 6]. Within this large set of field maps,

there are multiple different camera angles used, allowing the world to be shown in distinct ways. As players journey through the Shinra Building, the game reverts to a top-down aerial view that lets the player navigate through the hallways of the facility. The interiors of shops and other small spaces are typically presented in a near-isometric view, while one-point perspective is often used in tunnel-like spaces.

In contrast, the *Remake* uses a series of larger sector maps that expand the scale of the playable world. Gaps that were once jumps between fragmented scenes are now integrated into a continuous space, although the new game still relies on loading screens rather than one seamless urban environment. The original game's designs, built around the cartoon proportions of the low-polygon figures, has been flattened and spread out into an environment scaled to more typical human proportions. Drawing an overview of the Sector 7 Slums from a similar angle to the original game allows us to understand how the complexity of the area has been increased, while still retaining key elements such as the Seventh Heaven bar and local shops [Fig. 7]. Yet even in the new game with its increased fidelity, we can sometimes miss the variety of camera angles used in the first game, which made every single moment cinematic. In terms of navigation, just as the original game maps are actually a series of polygonal walkmeshes defining where we can move, the graphic iconography of the minimap in the *Remake* gives us a clear message as to the spatial constraints present in the new environments. The design of each map, split into different sectors, only draws the interior edge of space, giving us no clue as to the material or structure of buildings, treating the edge of a pile of rubble in the same way as a high-security wall [Fig. 8]. The design of each map highlights only the explorable space and, like Giambattista Nolli's famous 18th-century map of Rome,[7] this means that the gaps and thoroughfares between buildings become the primary focus of the environment.

7   Nolli's 1748 map *La Nuova Topografia di Roma* used dark shading for buildings (called poche), helping to define the space *between* buildings rather than the buildings themselves.

☐ Field Maps:

168 Midgar
704 Total

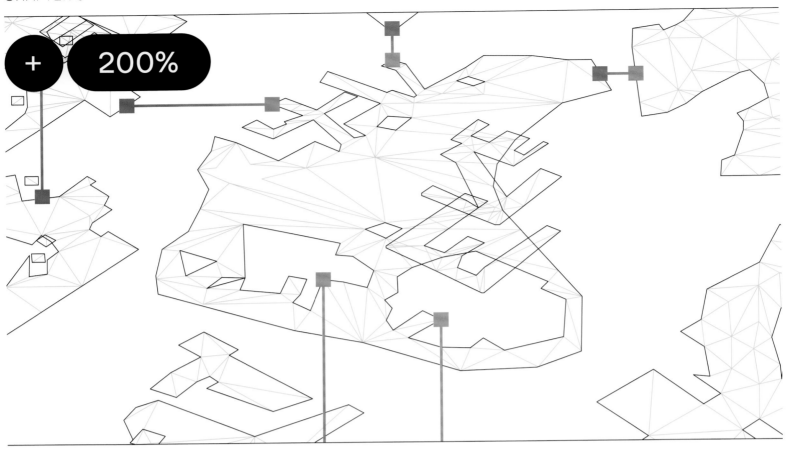

+ **200%**

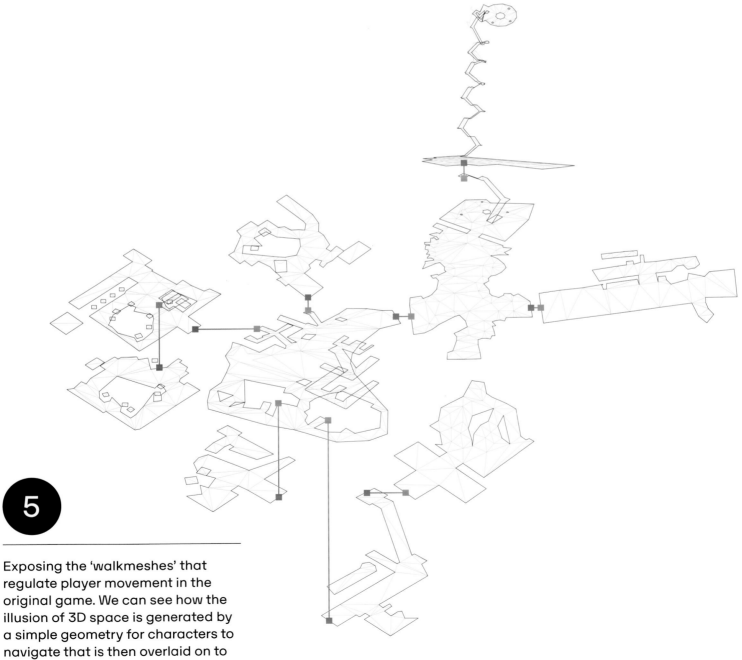

5

Exposing the 'walkmeshes' that regulate player movement in the original game. We can see how the illusion of 3D space is generated by a simple geometry for characters to navigate that is then overlaid on to the field map backgrounds.

Collecting and transcribing every
field map from the original *Final
Fantasy VII* to build an alternative
mapping of Midgar from the way we
actually encounter it in the game.

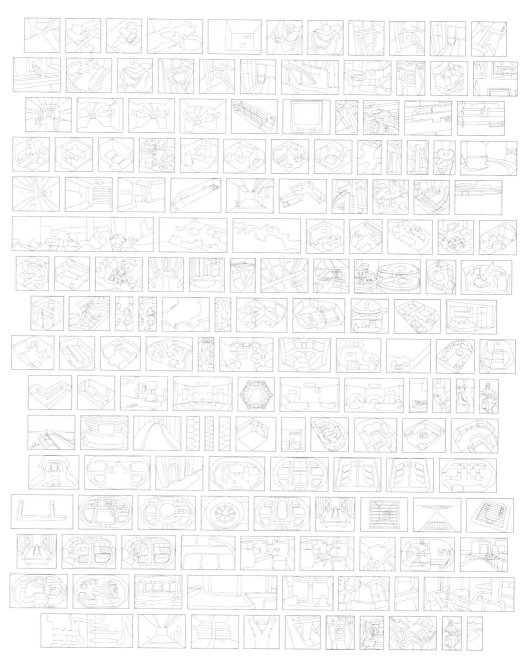

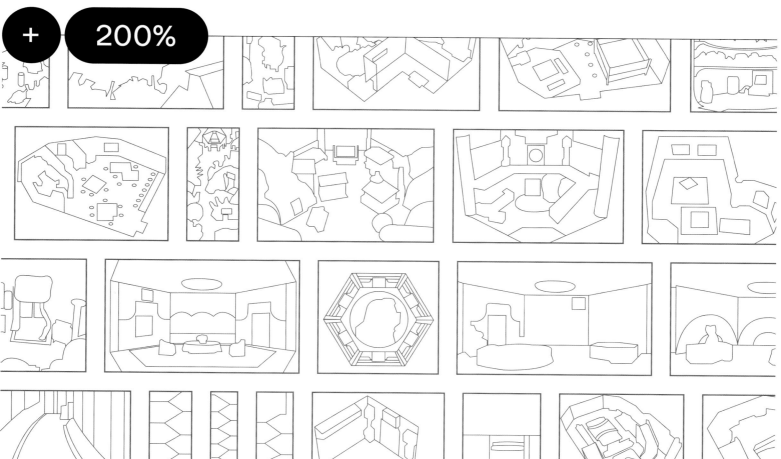

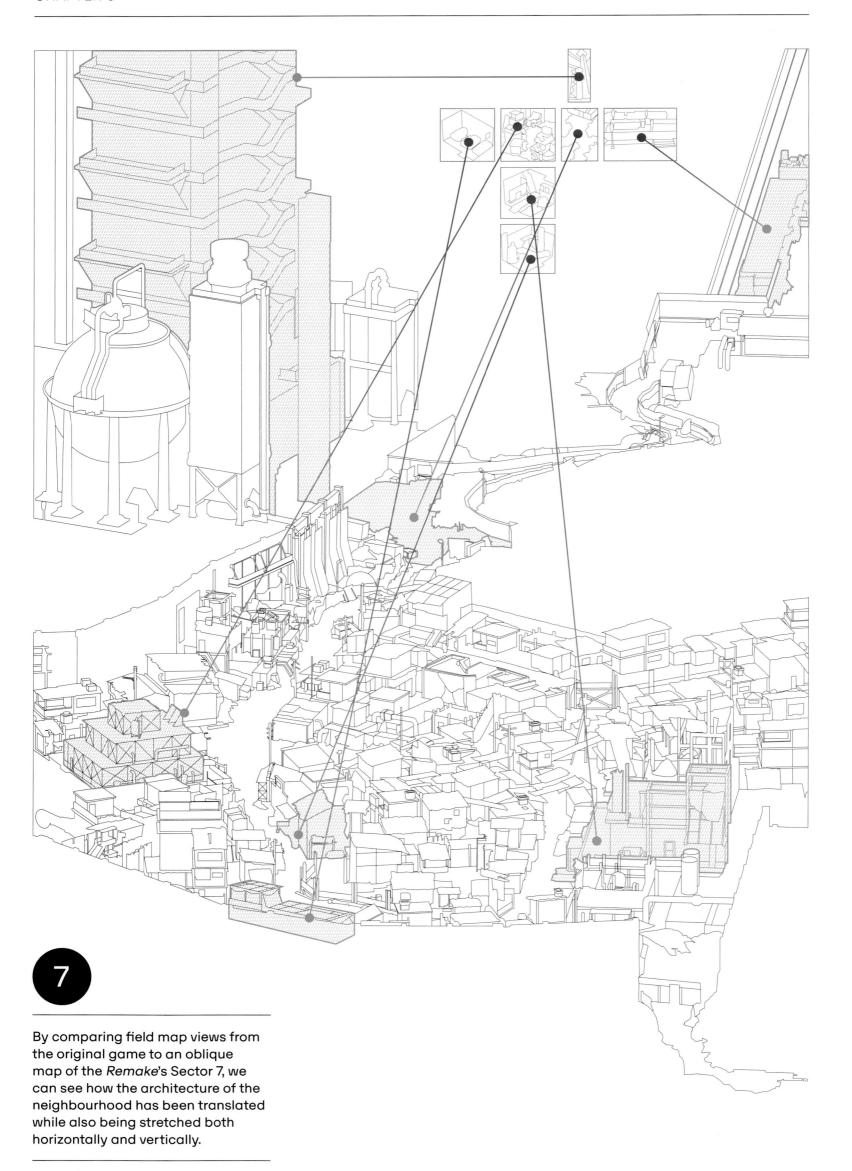

7

By comparing field map views from the original game to an oblique map of the *Remake*'s Sector 7, we can see how the architecture of the neighbourhood has been translated while also being stretched both horizontally and vertically.

+ **250%**

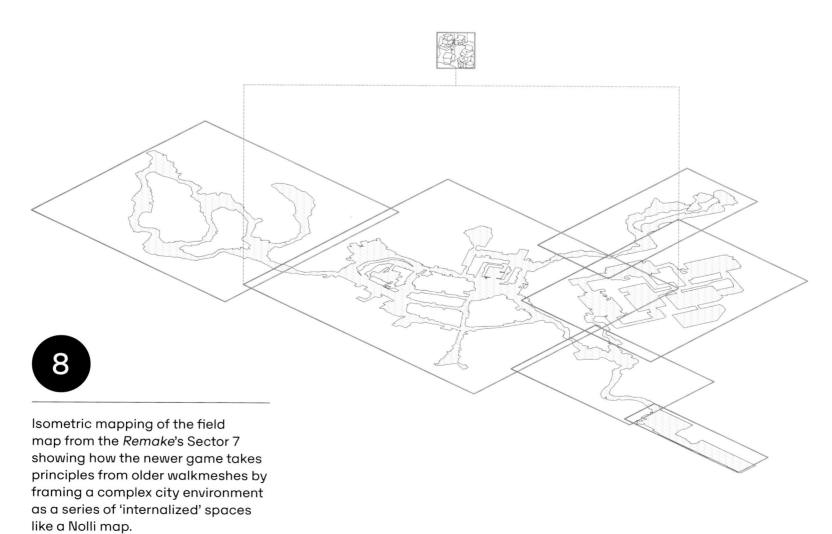

8

Isometric mapping of the field map from the *Remake*'s Sector 7 showing how the newer game takes principles from older walkmeshes by framing a complex city environment as a series of 'internalized' spaces like a Nolli map.

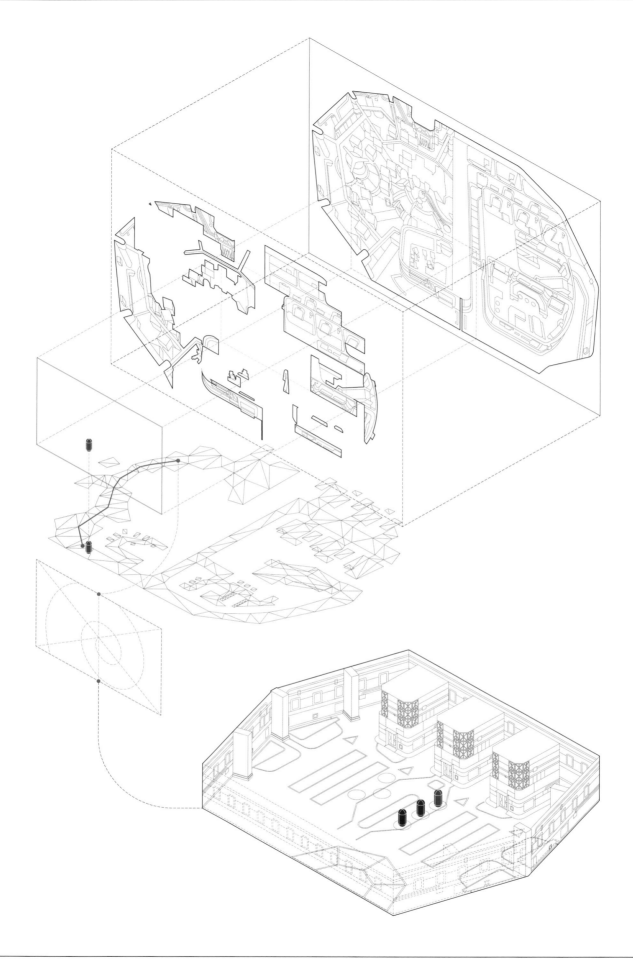

9

Dissecting the transition from field map space to battle map space in the original *Final Fantasy VII*. Here we can see how a randomized encounter moves the player to a full 3D space for battles, where character models also assume more detailed forms.

6.4   One Small Step

The original *Final Fantasy VII*'s field maps were also key to another core structure of the original game that is altered in the *Remake* – the presence of random encounters that trigger battle scenes. Each field map possesses a numerical value that defines the possibility of having a random encounter with an enemy, and if triggered this produces a screen transition, transporting the player to a battle map. These maps are fully 3D modelled and use higher-resolution character models than the field map, but they are also spatial archetypes – the same battle map will be used on multiple field maps. For example, several different encounters in the Shinra Building taking place on different field maps will take the player to the same battle arena. As such, the typical experience of Midgar is not only defined by the field map but by repeated journeys back and forth to battle map spaces [Fig. 9].

As outlined in several deep-dive explorations by the game's speed running community, the chance of having an encounter is defined by a step counter that records all steps taken by the player during a playthrough of the game.[8] By comparing the step counter to a defined value, a 'battle check' is performed that calculates when an encounter will occur. Skilled players can manipulate this due to the difference between walking and running through the world.[9] A walking step covers one-quarter of the distance of a running step, but a battle check will take place on each step, so four walking steps produces four checks rather than one check for a running step of the same distance. Because these checks are not linear, and rely on comparisons to specific values, speed runners have exploited ways of moving between walking and running that are more mechanically efficient at moving across a field map than running alone.

In contrast, the *Remake* version of Midgar can be structured at a more human scale, relying on the design of contained spaces to create natural battlegrounds. Yet by mapping a journey through the newly expanded Sector 5 Slums, we can see that while the full 3D environment allows the designers to dispense with the old remote battlefield spaces, they still employ demarcated areas where encounters will happen. Here there are four battlegrounds in which players fight powerful enemies, and each of these is clearly separated from the main routes of the map. Two of these areas are gated, making the transition to the battle zone even clearer. But this also holds true for smaller encounters, where enemies are either seen lying in wait, or pop out from behind scenery. In each case, as we can see from the map, there are enlarged spaces providing enough floor area for combat to take place. These spatial settings, combined with a revised Active Time Battle system, enable the *Remake* to embody the spirit of the original game in a more fully realized 3D world.

□ Battle Check:

x = Danger
y = Enemy Lure
r = Random (0.255)
Battle if (x*y)/256>r

8   YouTube, 'FF7 Random Battle Mechanics Guide' by user 'XeroKynos', youtube.com/watch?v=g36-lzRCb68. Further details on battle mechanics can be found in Terence Fergusson's *The FF7 Enemy Mechanics v.1.11,* a huge 135,000-word document originally posted to GameFAQs and now only accessible via the Wayback Machine: web.archive.org/web/20200208031538/ gamefaqs.gamespot.com/ps/197341-final-fantasy-vii/ faqs/31903

9   This drawing is a translation of a Battle Check diagram produced by YouTube user 'XeroKynos' in the video referenced above.

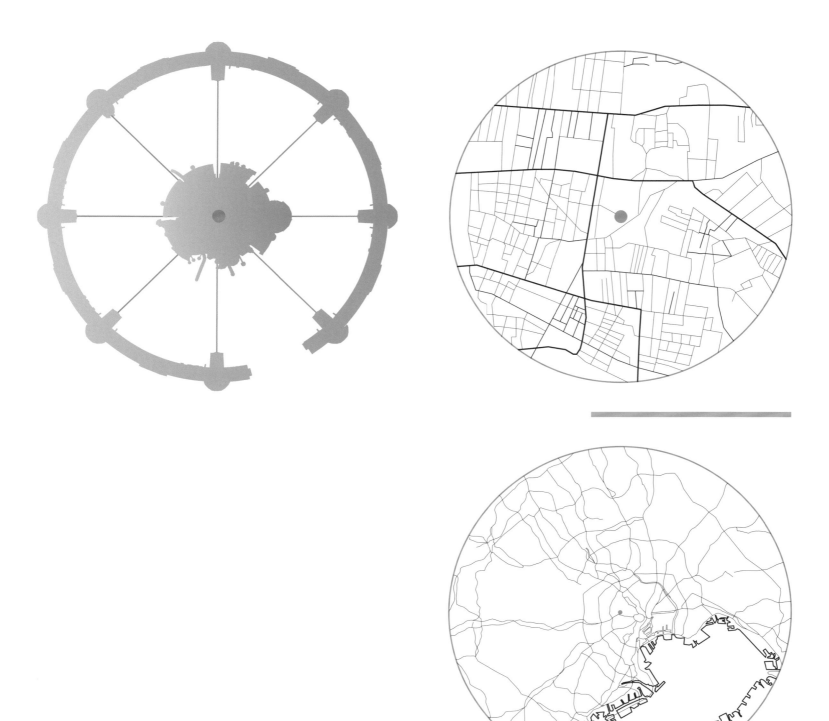

10

Comparing different sizes of Midgar as described in the game, showing how the city could be the size of a few blocks in Shinjuku, Tokyo, or stretch all the way out of the city to Yokohama depending on which data source we use.

6.5   Shifting the Scales

While the general physical form of Midgar is well established across both the original game and its *Remake*, understanding the precise dimensions of the city is somewhat more complex. This is because both games make conflicting statements about the dimensions of Midgar, contradicting the scale of the architecture that we see on our screens.

During a mission in the original game, AVALANCHE member Jessie Raspberry shows Cloud a 3D map of the city on a digital screen in a train carriage. Jessie explains that the upper plates are suspended 50 m (164 ft ½ in.) (roughly thirteen storeys) above ground, and that the onscreen digital model of Midgar is at the scale of 1:10000. The game shows the screen panning and zooming into the model, and a very rough estimate from this sequence suggests the inner city would have a diameter of 5 km (3 miles). These indicated dimensions do not appear to tally with the low height stated by Jessie.

In the *Remake*, a loading screen explicitly states that the upper plates are now 300 m (984 ft 3 in.) above ground. This generally tallies with the height of the pillar structures that players can observe in the Sector 7 Slums, rising far above the town below. By analysing the in-game map to find the proportions of the city, this would suggest that the inner ring of Midgar is only around 1,750 m (5741 ft 5⅝ in.) in diameter. This aligns more closely with a scale model of Midgar built to celebrate the *Advent Children* animated film.

However, later in the *Remake*, when players return to the Shinra Building from the first game, Cloud, Tifa and Barret are shown into a gallery containing a room-sized scale model of Midgar. This model is also described as being at a scale of 1:10000. Based on its scale compared to the characters, the model of the central portion of Midgar is roughly 6 m (19 ft 8¼ in.) wide, meaning that the implied diameter of the city within the ringed walls would be some 60 km (37¼ miles). The *Remake*'s developers have described the 'structural contradictions' of the first game, and how they obtained a sense of scale for the city by looking out from the top of their offices in Shinjuku, Tokyo.[10] The city as represented in the Shinra model is equivalent to drawing a circle centred on Shinjuku all the way to Yokohama. Tokyo's urban area is over 3,900 km^2, and in comparison, Midgar at this scale is 3,600 km^2, but significantly denser. Yet, seen as a 1,750-m (5741-ft-5⅝-in.) diameter plate in comparison, at this scale Midgar would only occupy a very small slice of Tokyo. By overlaying these together, we can gain a deeper understanding of the conflicting scales presented to us by the game [Fig. 10].

☐ Midgar:

1.75–5 km (1–3 miles) Wide 50–300 m (164–984 ft) High

10 Naoki Hamaguchi, 'The Architects of Midgar: how we rebuilt FINAL FANTASY VII REMAKE's City of Mako', Square Enix, square-enix-games.com/en_GB/news/final-fantasy-vii-remake-designing-midgar.

11 Studio Bentstuff / Digital Hearts, *Final Fantasy VII Remake Material Ultimania* (El Segundo: Square Enix Books, 2022), 255.

12 United Nations, 'Population of capital cities and cities of 100,000 or more inhabitants: latest available year, 1996–2015', in *Demographic Yearbook 2015*, unstats.un.org/unsd/demographic-social/products/dyb/documents/dyb2015/table08.pdf.

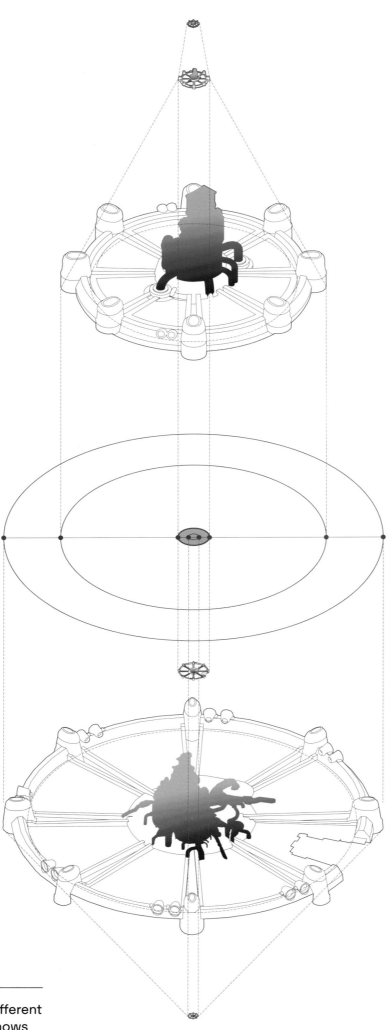

11

Scale comparison using the different
suggested scales of Midgar shows
how difficult it is to accurately
dimension the city, with some
suggested sizes many times larger
than others.

This would have an even bigger impact on the Shinra Building, which would rise to around 14 km (8¾ miles) above the plates in the Shinra model scale. Despite this unimaginable height, both versions of the game reference the top floor of the building as the seventieth. Even accounting for floor-to-ceiling height discrepancies and double-height spaces, the gap is unsurmountable. The safest conclusion may be that the 1:10000 scale model is a misrepresentation of the city; a piece of propaganda to promote Shinra's power.

In early 2022, with the release of the *Final Fantasy VII Remake Material Ultimania* book, we were given the clearest indication of Midgar's scale through a dimensional map showing the city to be around 5 km (3 miles) in diameter, mirroring the estimate from the first game[11]. If we consider the population density of the world's busiest cities, such as the 'city proper' of Manila defined by UN data from 2015[12], this would suggest that a central city with a 5 km diameter could house over 1 million inhabitants at a density achieved in real-world cities, validating the smaller-scaled versions of the city. In visually comparing all the different scales of Midgar, we can see how both the information given to us by the game and scales investigated by the community, alongside analytical drawings are ultimately unable to draw a complete conclusion.

At a smaller level we can also see changes in scale within pieces of iconic architecture from the game, as they make the transition from the original game's cartoony proportions to the *Remake*. This has been discussed with Sector 7, but there is also evidence of this change in one of the game's most iconic buildings. Aerith's house in Sector 5 is integral to the game's narrative, with the designers translating some of the essential features of the house into its new version. Notable elements that stand out are the triangular windows, and the hexagonal tower behind the main frontage of the house, although in the *Remake* it now has a larger overhanging roof [Fig. 12]. As there is presumably less issue with objects and plants covering the player's path compared to the original static camera, the surrounding areas are now brought in closer to the house to integrate it with Aerith's flowerbeds.

Although Aerith's house, surrounded by flowers, represents a rare moment of respite in a picturesque landscape, as with many such dystopic cities, the fate of Midgar appears to be tragic. This quality is carried across two different games released twenty-three years apart using very different technologies. The rotting pizza, with its unsustainable thirst for Mako and rigidly enforced social hierarchy, traps a society within its walls and allows it to fester. While this is the case in the first game, with the *Remake* and its branching storyline, pushed by the whispers of fate, perhaps Midgar might be heading in a different, more positive direction. Only time will tell.

Architectural study of Aerith's house. We can pick out key details and iconography that has been translated from the original game to the *Remake*, understanding how technological advances have allowed the building to become more complex and accurately human-scaled while retaining key symbolic elements.

○ VIDEOGAME ATLAS

Sections

FORTNITE

Details

Year	2017
Developer	Epic Games
Publisher	Epic Games

Platforms

(PlayStation: 4/5) (macOS)

(Xbox: One/Series X/S) (iOS)

(Android) (Microsoft Windows)

(Nintendo Switch)

The island of *Fortnite* is one of the most consistently revised environments in gaming: terraformed, flooded and overturned by its creators while being perpetually reshaped by its players.

☐ Maps:

1 Island
2+ Chapters
18+ Seasons

7.1   Landscapes of Lore

Played by more than 250 million users worldwide, *Fortnite* can be seen as one of the most significant games in recent history, reaching a vast audience through its ever-changing narrative structure and media tie-ins. Set on an island, its landform is designed to receive players skydiving from a school bus at different locations, both natural and urban. As shown in this state (Chapter 2, Season 7), parcels of land are divided by rivers and interconnected by roads that lead to the most urban areas, with forest, coastline and mountain biomes occupying different ends of the island [Fig. 1]. In its Battle Royale format, this sets the scene for players to begin searching for loot to defend themselves from other players, in the hope of become the last player standing. The map has evolved incrementally since the game's inception, taking two primary forms across Chapter 1 and Chapter 2, with smaller evolutions between each season. By overlaying these different island forms we can start to understand how the world has been tweaked around the evolving narratives of the game. In Chapter 1, the landmass of the island was intersected by a primary river running north to south, connected to an inland lake. In the following chapter, tributaries were formed around a central sub-island, dividing the overall landmass into smaller parcels [Fig. 2]. This shift coincided with players being able to utilize the bodies of water for swimming, rather than being constrained by the water as was previously the case. Between the chapters, the terrain became more extreme, diversifying much of the vast and green landscape into a series of more complex micro-environments.

After increasing the player occupancy to 100 players in the Battle Royale mode, the desire for players to find 'high ground' within the map led Epic Games to create further built-up urban areas and extreme topographies that include snow-capped mountain ranges and showcase the after-effects of catastrophic events. Alongside this, denser woodlands, murky waters, swamps and larger areas of agricultural land further intensified the map with more diverse themes, evolving the named locations and introducing new points of interest (POIs). Through these changes, *Fortnite*'s island ceased to read like one continuous parkland, and developed into a series of smaller, interconnected zones, each with a unique setting and environmental storytelling.

The evolution of the landscape has also taken on extreme forms, such as the flooding of the map in Chapter 2. This was triggered by the collapse of the Wall of Water (a water-based storm event) in the previous season. With more surface area submerged by water and less land for players to distribute themselves across, the world became more crowded as players concentrated themselves on the areas above sea level. As the flooding subsided, new parts of the map emerged, as the island transformed itself following the natural disaster [Fig. 3]. Alenda Chang describes the occurrence of environmental collapse in videogames as falling into 'graphical spectacle of environmental modelling'.[1] While *Fortnite* uses disaster, threat and collapse as part of its lore, the ongoing structure of its narrative is that players work through these challenges to overcome them as the seasons progress. Like many other multiplayer games, the 'meta' (the optimal strategy for winning at any given time) of *Fortnite* is constantly changing, and the redesign of the world is a large and defining part of this.

This state of constant progression and repair takes place at a smaller scale within the island as various buildings, features and locations continue to transform. One of the most evolutionary examples is a warehouse location named Dusty Depot, destroyed by a meteor that hovered over the island in the previous season. The warehouses were subsequently replaced by Dusty Divot, a crash site undergoing excavation over time. The buildings and landscape within the crater went through several changes, from barren to overgrown, and this ultimately led to a full reinstatement of Dusty Depot [Fig. 4]. The colours of the warehouses were switched around, leading players to question whether this was an intentional alteration or a developer error. Despite the vastness of the map, players remain captivated by these small and detailed shifts, sequestered within seasons and across chapters as the island continues to change.

1   Alenda Y. Chang, *Playing Nature: Ecology in Video Games* (Minneapolis: University of Minnesota Press, 2019), 232.
2   Mark J. P. Wolf, *Building Imaginary Worlds: The Theory and History of Subcreation* (Routledge: New York, 2012), 158.

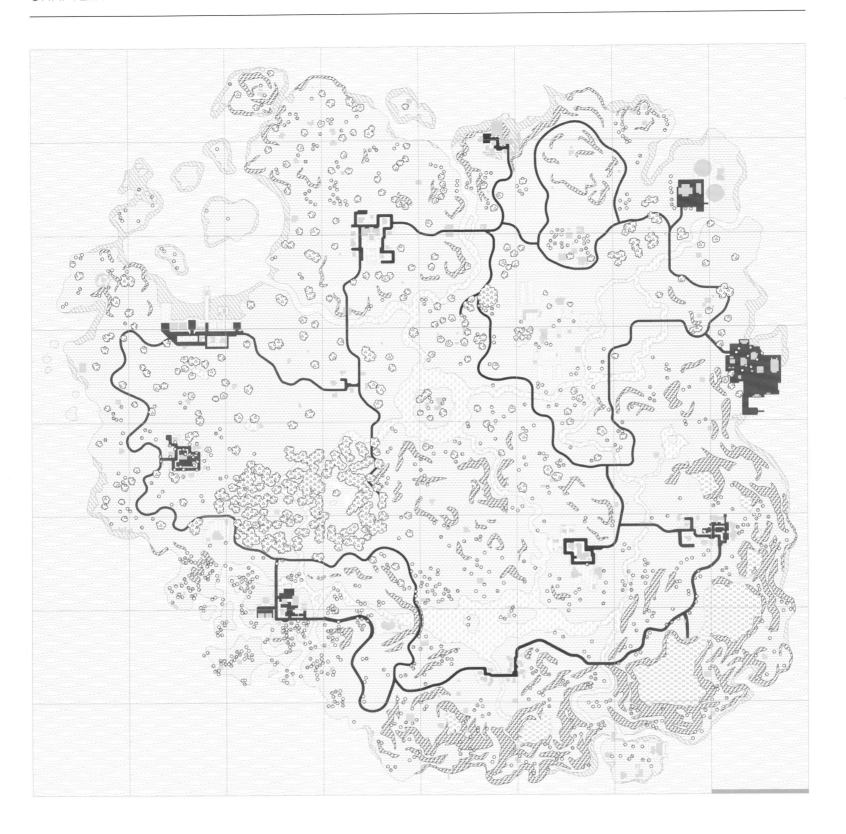

1

Playable extents of the Chapter 2, Season 7 map, showing how landscape, infrastructure and named locations are distributed and connected across the island.

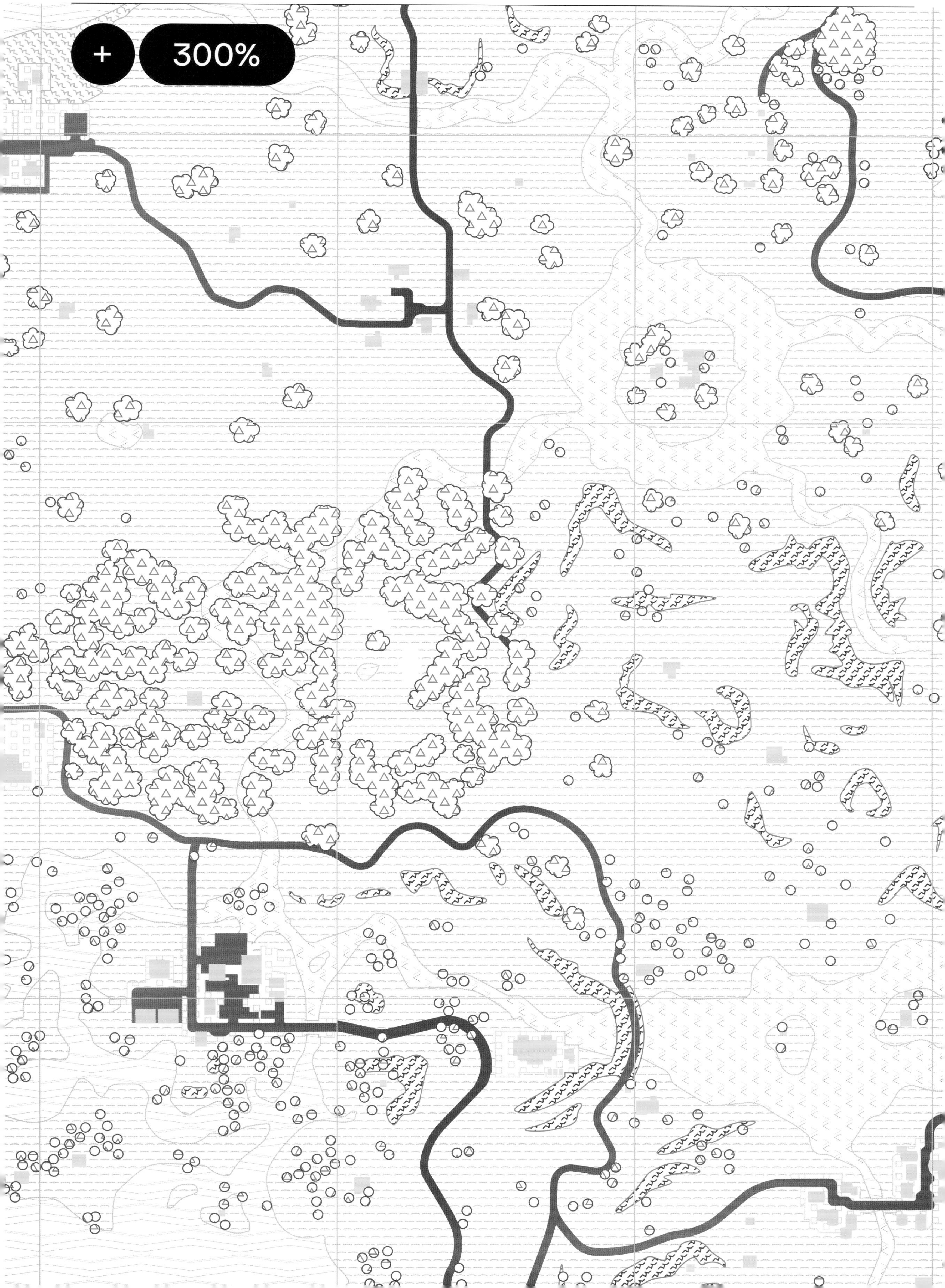
+
300%

Overlaying Chapter 1 and
Chapter 2 maps to understand
how the island has changed in size,
character and morphology.

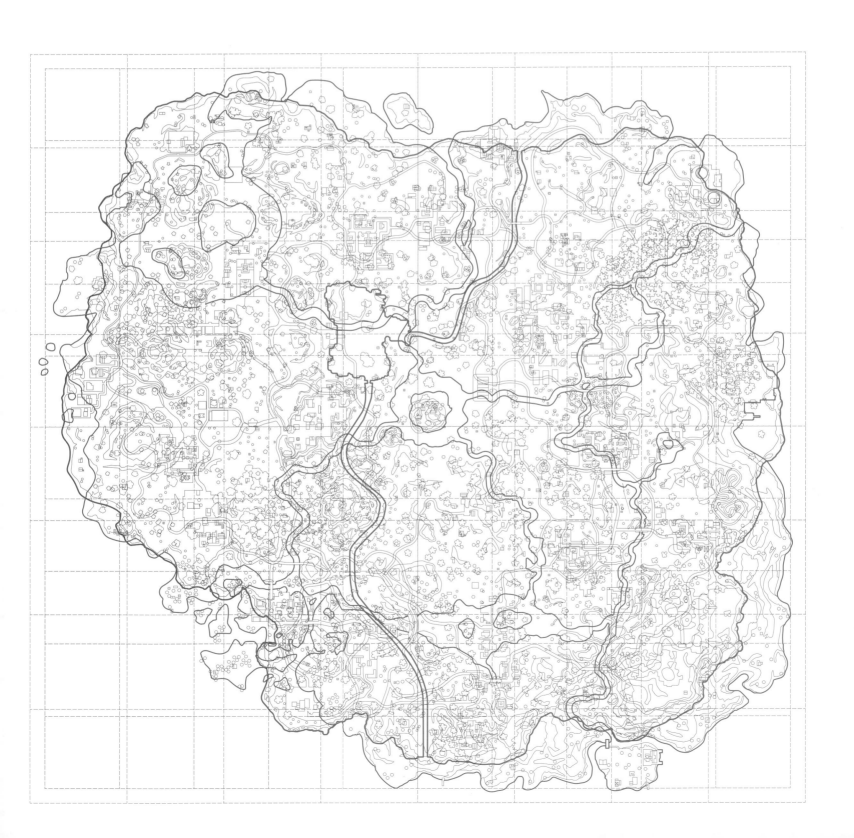

+ 350%

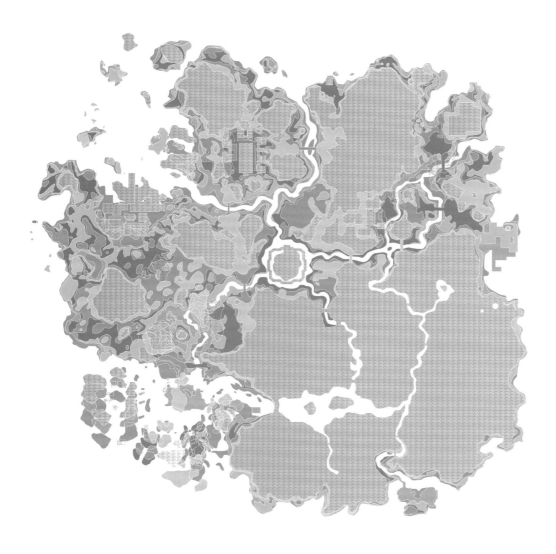

Floodplain maps of the island when it became submerged by water in Chapter 2, emerging incrementally across subsequent seasons. These are overlaid to show how players gained more access to land as the island resurfaced.

The evolution of Dusty Divot, a point of interest that was destroyed and repaired as a result of the evolving narratives across the game, allowing us to track its physical changes.

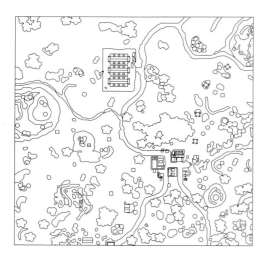

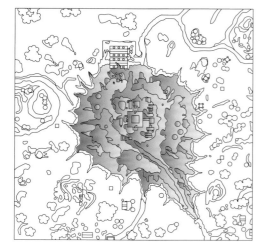

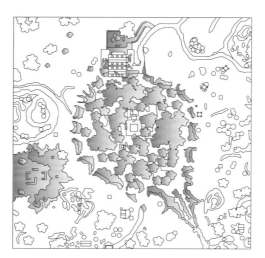

Biome map showing woodland,
jungle, snow, desert and grass plain
environments positioned within the
same island in Season 1.

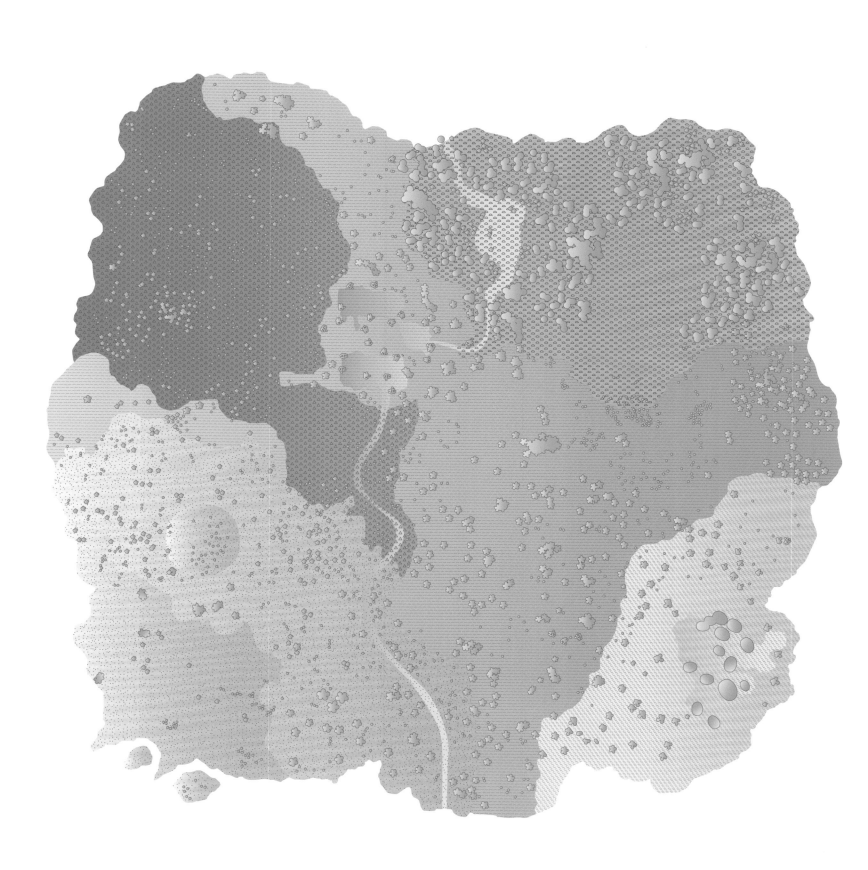

6

The utilitarian language of porta-potties, dumpsters and haystacks operating as hiding spaces, giving them an elevated status within the game.

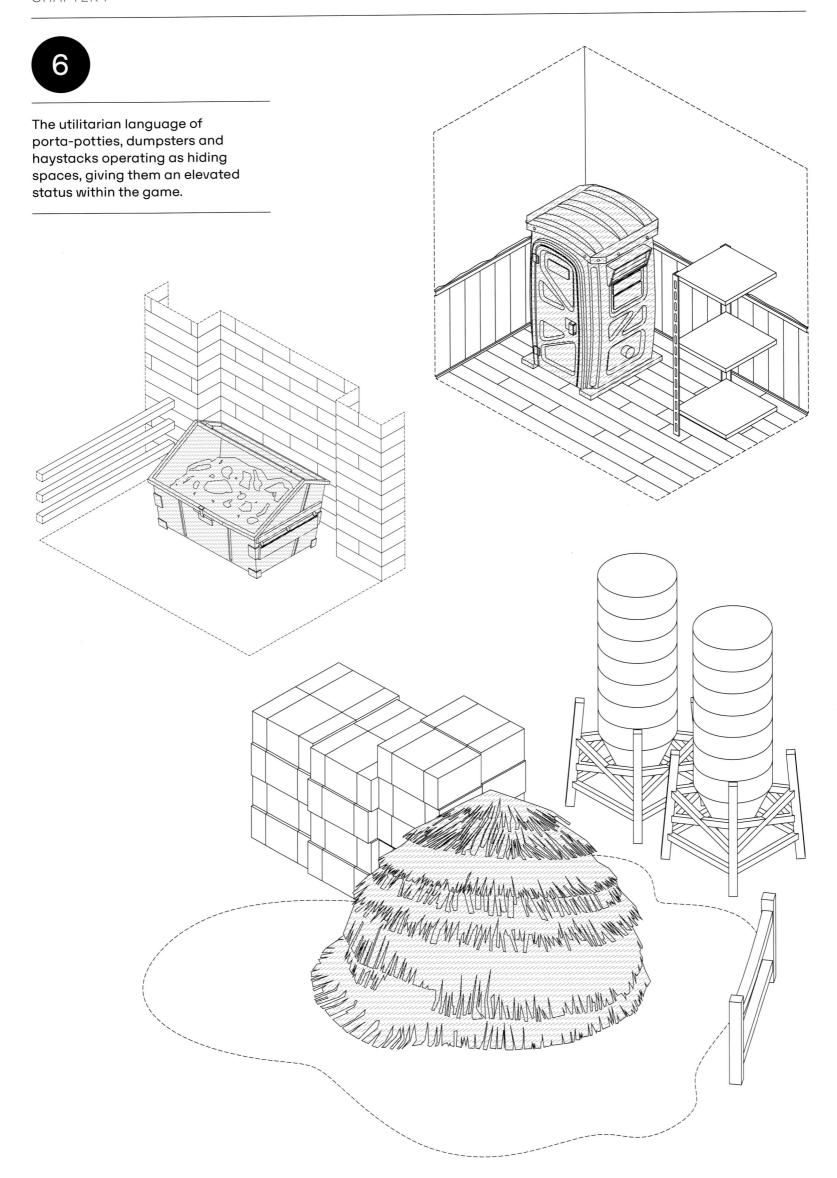

Arguably the most distinct collection of biomes assembled within one season was experienced in the latter seasons of Chapter 1, where the map consolidated arid desert, tropical jungle and snow climates interconnected by more neutral grass plains. Traversing through one to another, the player becomes attuned to the particularities of these local zones as they utilize each unique geography for their own pursuits. Much like moving through a theme park, changes in the atmosphere, density, colour and sound can be noticed when the player enters a new biome [Fig. 5]. As Wolf writes, 'whereas regions of Earth usually have large areas of fairly homogeneous terrain, many fictional maps will contain a wide variety of geographical features in close proximity'.[2] These compressions of space are characteristically enhanced for the player to encourage a variety of experiences and associations through their exploration of the map.

The removal and introduction of different biomes is driven by an overarching theme for each season. Straddling different time periods, narratives and fictions, the map adapts itself to accommodate the season's theme as an overlay on to the island. Shifting between narratives that include medieval, space, superheroes and secret agents, new visual languages are created to embed these into the island. This enables *Fortnite* to host external references through events, spaces and skins, keeping the player spending and engaged. Although the 'last player standing' objective defines the overall gameplay, these new narratives translate into spaces within the game, typically framed around missions that individuals and teams can perform in the battle area, and contributing to *Fortnite*'s ongoing lore. This might involve racing a Ferrari around the roads or getting instructions from Ryan Reynolds as part of a film tie-in. In both cases, these transmedia elements encourage players to undertake tasks that see them engage with the world in different ways compared to combat and building. An example of this can be seen with the porta-potty, an in-game object previously operating as a hiding place. Following a map alteration to accommodate a secret agent theme, several porta-potties became entry points

to a network of secret tunnels, leading to non-player character (NPC) encounters and potentially some rare loot. By merging all these reference points together, the developers are using *Fortnite* as a testing ground for, as they describe, 'an entertainment experience of the future'.[3]

This spatial relationship reinforces the game's business model, allowing alterations to be made to existing landscape features made without having to rip up the world and start again from scratch. As such, we can see multiple references brought together in one space that do not normally coexist, meaning that *Fortnite*'s world becomes a postmodern combination of symbols and images that sit outside their normal narrative meaning.

The map then operates as a realm for both active and passive gameplay to take place. Edging towards the eye of the storm, players utilize natural geographical features such as undulating terrain, rocks, rivers and trees to camouflage themselves within the landscape. Alongside this, hiding places in the form of dumpsters, haystacks and the aforementioned porta-potties can be activated to take cover from enemies out of plain sight [Fig. 6]. *Fortnite* calls on the language of these seemingly common, utilitarian objects to give players leverage over one another, meaning that their in-game capabilities provide different affordances[4] to those in reality. One might go out of one's way to avoid using a real-world porta-potty, yet in the game there is nothing to smell or see, only a safe space in which to hide.

3   Donald Mustard, 'Fortnite's experimental story is an
    attempt to create "the entertainment experience of
    the future"', theverge.com/22338403/fortnite-story-
    narrative-interview-donald-mustard-epic-games.
4   See James Gibson's theory of affordances: James
    Gibson, *The Ecological Approach to Visual Perception*
    (Boston: Houghton Mifflin, 1979), 127.

7

Mapping the phases of the dynamic
storm event over the course of
the game, and its effect on player
movement and population. As the
storm shrinks, so does the level
of inhabitation.

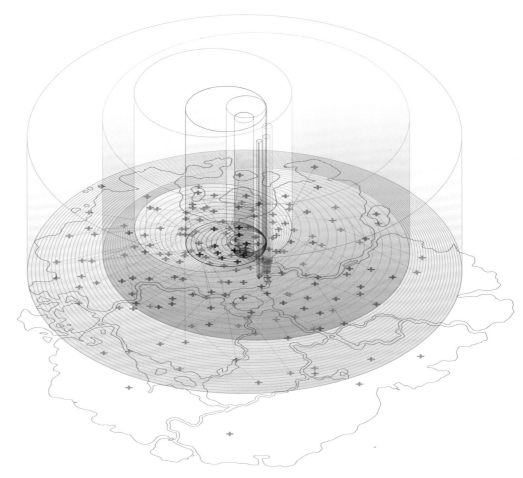

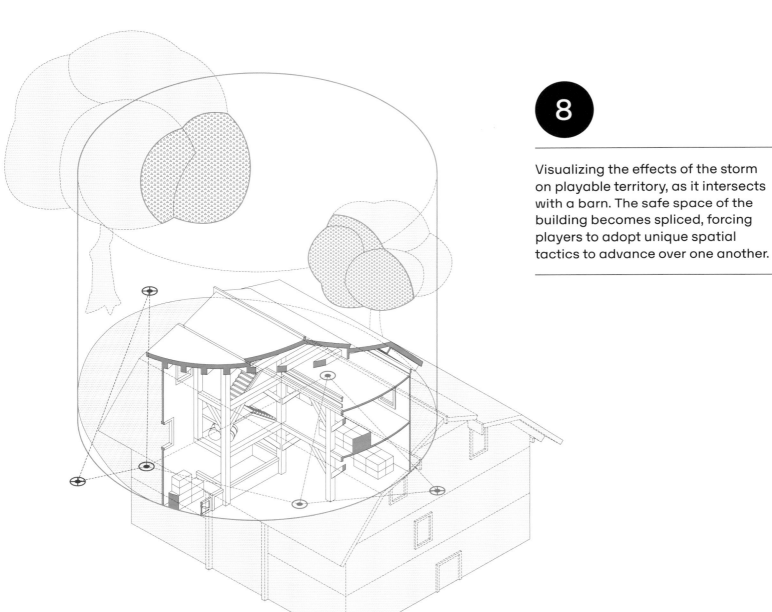

8

Visualizing the effects of the storm
on playable territory, as it intersects
with a barn. The safe space of the
building becomes spliced, forcing
players to adopt unique spatial
tactics to advance over one another.

7.2   Storm Space

The existence of the contracting 'safe zone' during battle is defined by the forces of the dynamic storm event that takes place during every game. Appearing as a purple zone on the map, the player is allotted a decreasing amount of time before the storm periodically shrinks and alters its territory. The storm 'walls' become more visible – as a blue illuminated vertical barrier that sweeps over and across buildings, roads, players and terrain. As the player moves towards the eye of the storm, the weather and atmosphere become brighter, offering them a clearer view of the enclosing world. This zone becomes a magnet for players, drawing them closer together from opposite ends of the island. This tends to combine with a decrease in population over the course of the game, as players eliminate one another during battle or get caught in the storm, where their health plummets. As the game progresses, the storm becomes more aggressive, causing greater damage as it gets smaller and more mobile, decreasing the chances of survival as it shrinks to its climax [Fig. 7].

In the early phases of the game, the storm 'waits' before it shrinks again, offering the player a forecast as a chance to move towards its next projection, which, depending on your initial landing position, can often be located on the opposite side of the island. While it is possible to outrun the storm in its early stages, the increasing speed at which it shrinks often requires the player to use other transportation techniques such as cars, speedboats, launchpads and ziplines to move closer to the safe zone. This correlation between size, speed and damage becomes increasingly important, as the player must negotiate between obtaining an optimum position, suffering damage from the storm or running headlong into battle.

Where the storm chooses to stop at each stage is seemingly random, creating interesting spatial consequences for the player. If the storm ring intersects the middle of the building, the space within it becomes fractured, as doors and stairs may no longer fall within the safe zone [Fig. 8]. Players are required to respond to these situations creatively by breaking through walls or roofs to escape or track down approaching players. This impresses the force of the environment on the player, causing them to make decisions with different consequences each time.

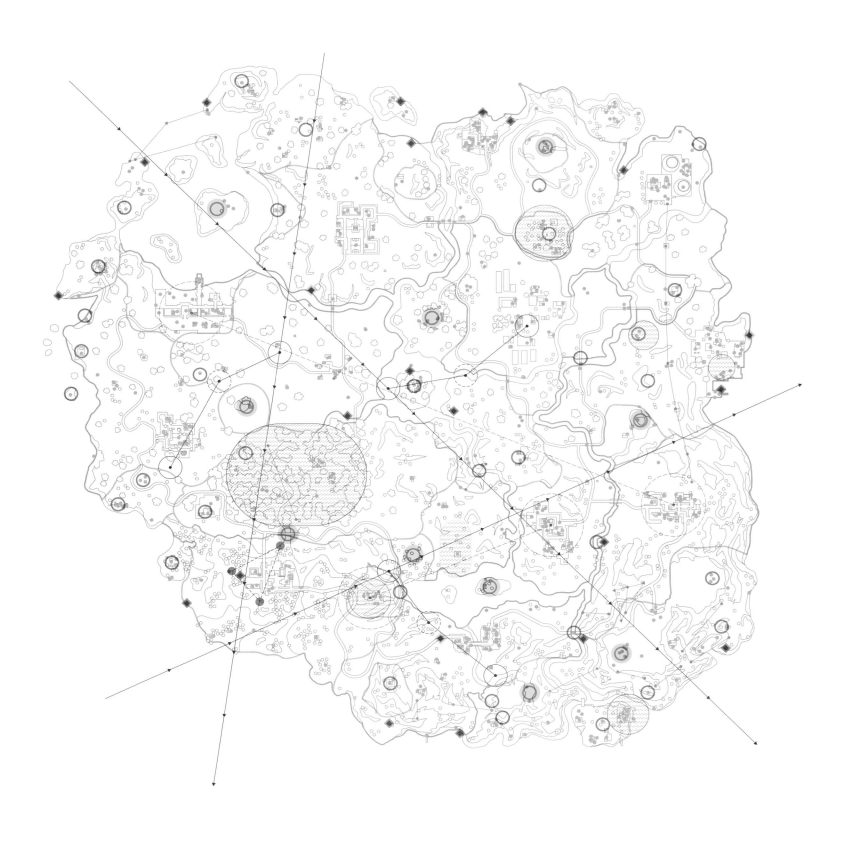

9

Mapping the available resources across the island, from supplies to loot locations, points of interest and various methods of transportation.

7.3 Architecture of Defence

Fortnite's building system is heavily tied to the distribution of world resources across the map. The island is rife with these at the start of the game, most densely clustered around the various named locations. These are sought out by players during the game, as they obtain items to enhance their performance and strengthen their chances of survival. Within the Battle Royale structure, batches of quests are also set for the player, which encourage them to interact with the world and its narrative in different ways. These range from playful to resourceful, from dancing around campfires, to answering payphones, driving vehicles, visiting POIs and interacting with NPCs for further rewards, inciting the player to engage with the map differently each time [Fig. 9].

By harvesting wood, stone and metal, the player learns how and where these materials populate the map by associating them with specific biomes, vernaculars and building typologies. While wood and stone can be sourced from natural features such as trees and rocks, metal is extracted from manufactured objects such as cars and shipping containers. Walls and floors of existing buildings contain all three world resources, inviting the player to destroy the base map to facilitate their own structures. Looking closely at the architecture that is generated by the player, its visual style appears patchy, imperfect and nailed together from bricks, panels and material cuts of different sizes. This is not the work of a craftsperson or an artisan, but is rather constructed at speed from a variety of resources, with the most basic of tools. At the same time, this patchwork nature reminds us that materials are being reclaimed and redeployed in the construction of contemporary buildings in reality, such as Amateur Architecture Studio's Ningbo History Museum in China, whose distinctive façade is largely composed of materials collected from the surrounding area.[5]

In *Fortnite*, building techniques can be utilized to attain high ground in combat, but also to access parts of the map that do not have direct contact from the ground. By getting on to the roof of a building without having to search for its staircase or leaving a fortress without locating a door, additions to existing buildings also provide an alternative to destroying them (which makes more noise). However, both these techniques leave the player vulnerable to others discovering their position through the visible alterations being made to the existing map. As the components used by players are visually different to those of the pre-built structures, even a single wall left behind is a clue that other players can use to track where opponents have been.

During combat, the player utilizes the three given materials – wood, brick and metal – to create spaces for protection. In its basic form, the player can create a full enclosure around them using walls, floors and roofs, and in addition, ramps and stairs, to hide, heal, or revive. When building a protective structure, the player must choose materials by their strength and build rate. With a starting 'health' score, each material has a defensive value that increases with time. As the material gains its health, it remains translucent, making it possible to spot the player's location during building [Fig. 10]. Rather than make any aesthetic judgments of the composition of materials, the player negotiates between speed and strength to either increase their level of protection or build more rapidly. Skilled players can make these decisions quickly; through practice and by observing built structures within the battle area, it is possible to identify different patterns of play through the materials and forms used.

☐ Items:

15 Named Locations
52 Landmarks

5   Benedict Hobson, 'Wang Shu's Ningbo History
     Museum built from the remains of demolished villages'
     accessed 10/06/21, dezeen.com/2016/08/18/video-
     interview-wang-shu-amateur-architecture-studio-
     ningbo-history-museum-movie/

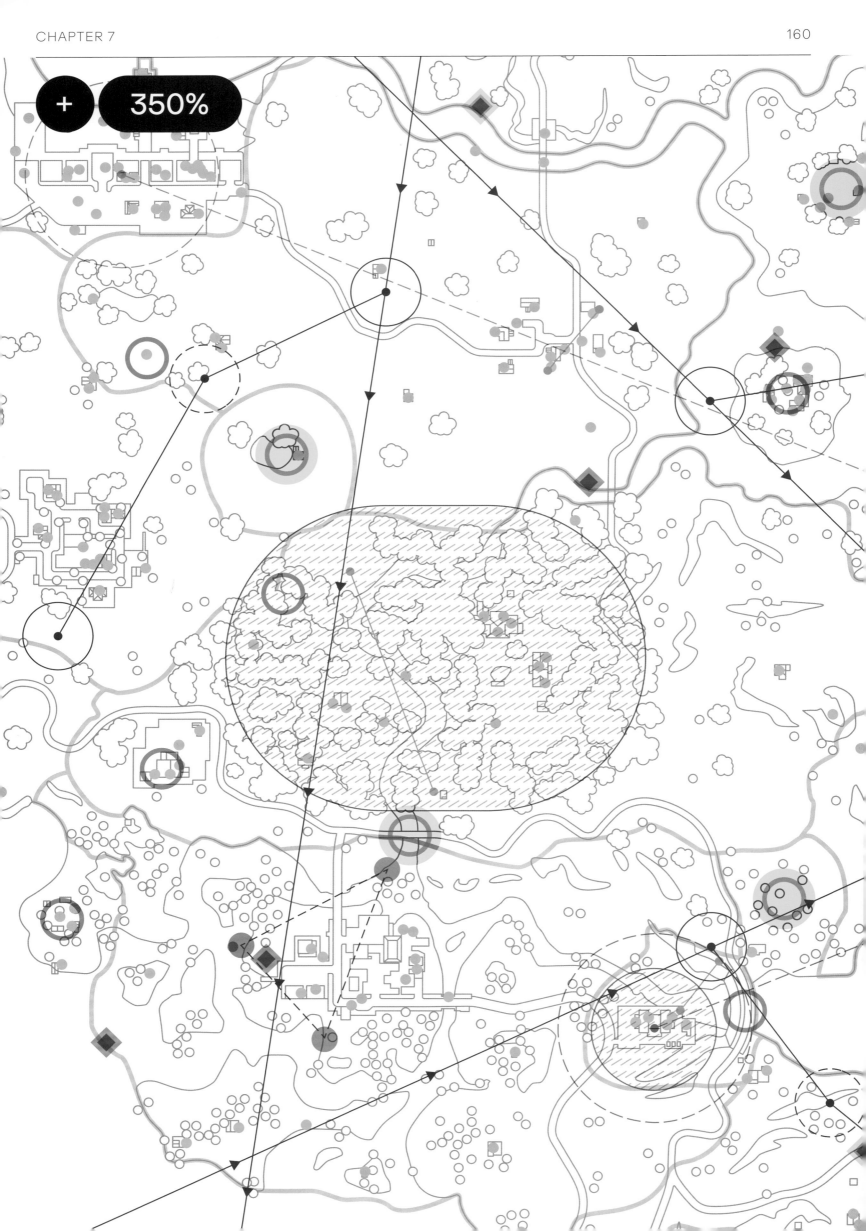

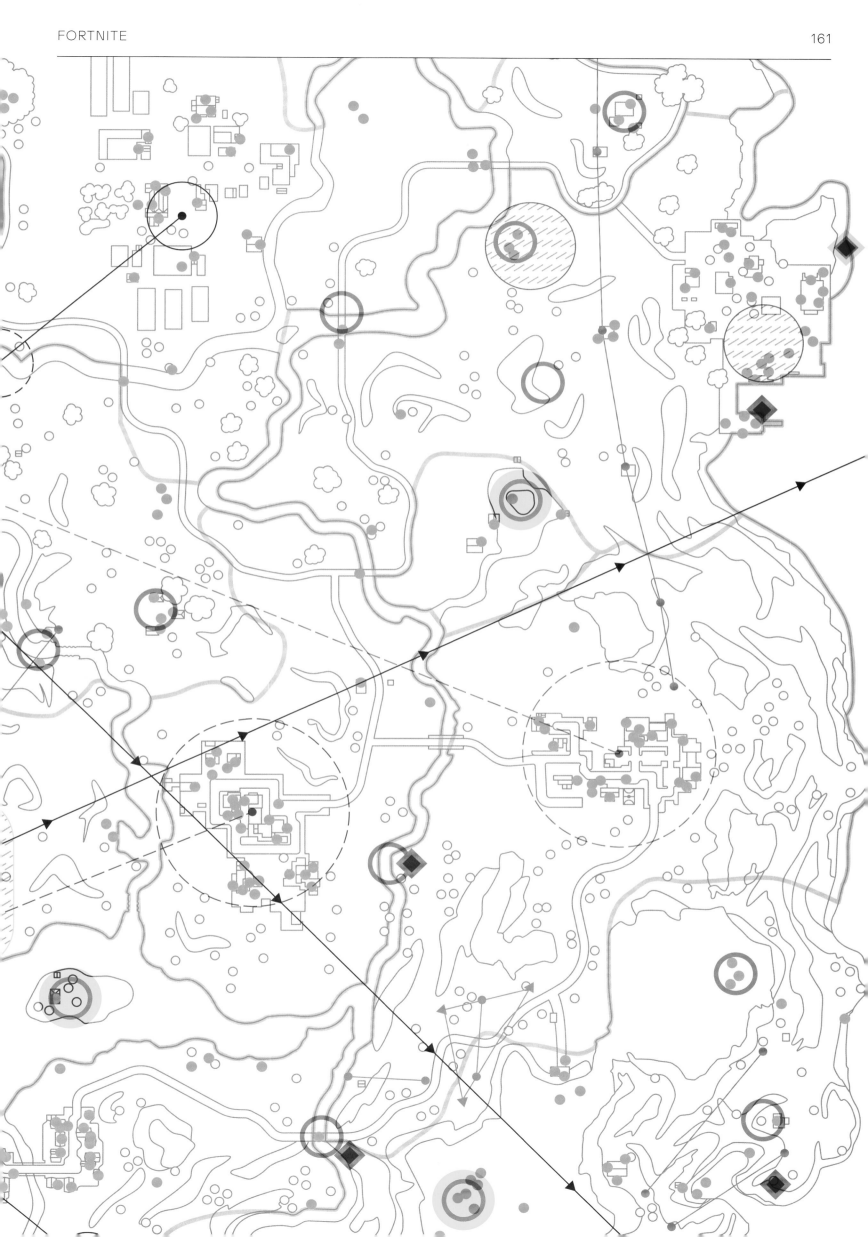

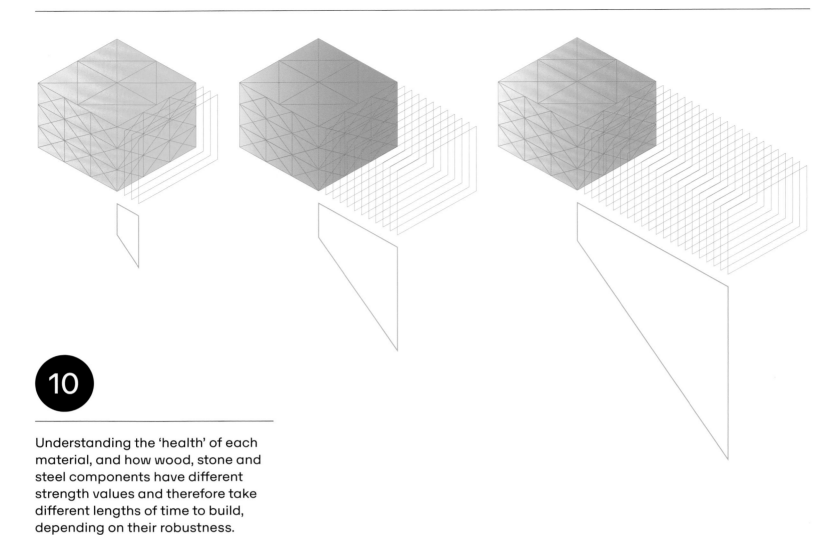

10

Understanding the 'health' of each material, and how wood, stone and steel components have different strength values and therefore take different lengths of time to build, depending on their robustness.

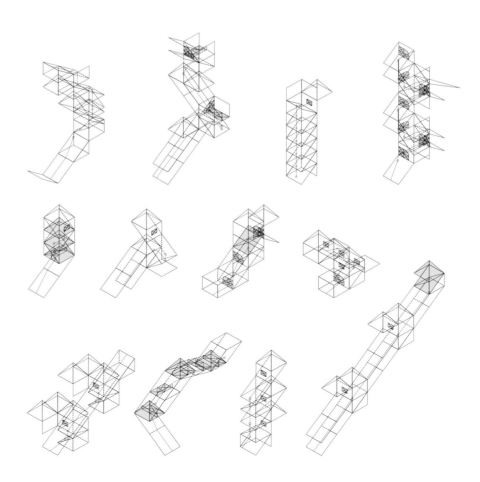

11

The architecture of 'retakes' – spatial set pieces deployed by players to attain high ground over one another. The player uses a complex choreography of moving, building and editing as they ascend, leaving a spatial trail behind them as a unique form of protection.

Playing with both speed and height, players have developed techniques to protect themselves and gain high ground over their opponent. These are known as 'retakes', or a combination of different moves that result in intricate defensible structures. Many of these require the player to both build and edit as they progress through the retake, utilizing the full capacity of *Fortnite*'s building system to establish a dynamic response to other players' actions. Timing and positioning are critical here, as well as the choreography of button pressing and clicking from the player, all contributing to the consistency and success of the retake. These result in a collection of unusual architectural typologies all built around the movement of the player, leaving a spatial trail of their movement behind them [Fig. 11].

One of the most popular retakes is to perform a '90' variation – a tower structure that is constructed by the player moving vertically while rotating in 90-degree increments. Depending on the angle of attack, the movement of the player and placement of the building components, different tower forms to manifest. These unique variations result in forms that are linear, cranked, boxy and irregular, playing on rotation and repetition to grow taller. Providing the ability to take cover

instantaneously, these towers place less pressure on strategic positioning of players within the landscape, encouraging a more direct journey into the storm's eye where the implementation of this architecture can be used to full effect [Fig. 12]. With a smaller safe zone, and less surface area to play on, players take to the skies where an infinite zone of vertical airspace becomes their primary source of protection.

While players do not always encounter one another, they are able to witness their former actions. The creation of player-built structures within the world leaves traces of inhabitation and signals a presence to others. Open loot boxes, discarded weapons and fractured walls also emphasize these trails. At the end of the game, everything is removed and reset, creating a new and completely unique set of spatial clues each time.

Analysing the different methods for '90s' – a building technique with varying complexities and spatial forms for advancing vertically at speed.

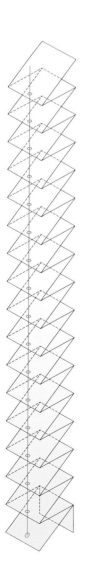
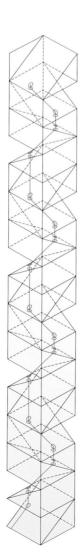
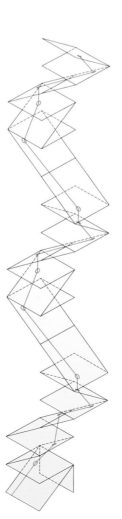
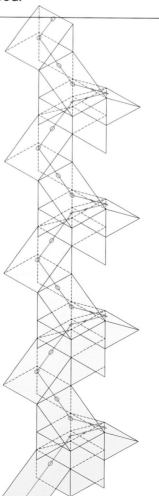
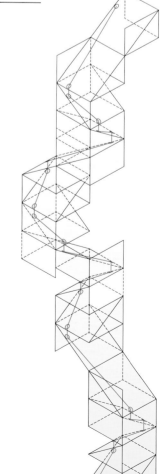

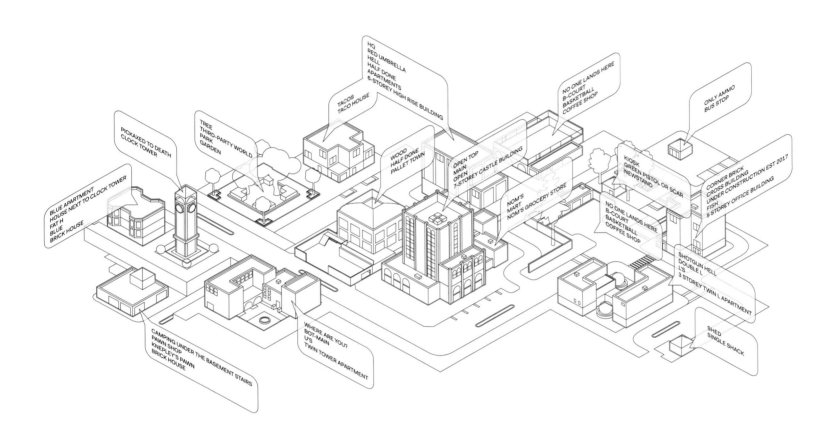

13

Buildings defined by their user-created callouts
in the previous named location of Tilted Towers.
Players attach names to buildings that relate to their
physical characteristics as a more efficient way of
communicating with one another during combat.

7.4   Community Semantics

With a mass online community and fast-paced gameplay, communication between team members is an essential tactic for strategizing against opponents. The game offers a set of formally named locations and POIs; however, due to the number of features within these locations, teams often build up their own vocabulary for identifying different buildings at a finer grain. Although the game provides a mechanism for placing markers on the map that are visible to teammates in real-time, verbal communication remains a vital tool for differentiating between buildings.

Teams often create unique callouts for buildings based on their appearance, shape, behaviour or likeness, making it easier for players to describe their location or intended move. In the case of Tilted Towers, a named POI in Chapter 1, this was one of the first areas to be introduced that was densely packed with rooms, chests, windows and high-rise buildings. As such, the area attracted many players, becoming a hotspot for fast-paced combat. Players invented ways to communicate their positions to one another, shooting from a 'fish'-shaped building to one with an 'open top'. Architectural features became definitive in their naming, characterizing them to form a visual identity [Fig. 13]. As locations appear and disappear across the chapters and seasons, the ever-expanding vocabulary and range of callouts within the game continues to evolve. We can see similar semantic connections in reality – in a city like London we can visit 'The Gherkin', 'The Shard', 'The Cheesegrater' or even 'The Walkie Talkie', buildings given popular names that represent their built form. But rather than representing an iconic status, the callouts provide players with a language to quickly identify themselves and others within an architectural space that is composed of more generic buildings.

In *Fortnite*, we can see that the design of the world, iterated and evolving over time, is one of the key mechanisms for retaining players and providing new and interesting experiences. As Jessica Reyes explains, 'rather than focusing on a single hero or a group of protagonists, Epic Games set out to make its island the main character',[6] acting as a dynamic and adaptive environment to enable several possible futures to take place. As *Fortnite* continues to develop and encapsulate different industries into its world, it has started to be discussed as a form of metaverse,[7] a persistent virtual world with its own economy and cross-cultural lore that can bring together rappers, movies, cartoons and sports cars into one environment. All these various layers of *Fortnite*'s world recalls Katherine Isbister's argument that games can become 'rich possibility spaces for emotionally meaningful social interaction'.[8] *Fortnite*'s transition from game to cultural phenomenon has ultimately mirrored the growth of the medium, with worlds now designed for perpetual change, to host diverse and contradictory stories.

☐ Callouts:

17 Buildings
62 Names

6   Jessica Reyes, 'The Entire Fortnite Timeline Explained', looper.com/340798/the-entire-fortnite-timeline-explained/.

7   The term 'metaverse', originally used in Neal Stephenson's 1992 novel *Snow Crash*, denotes a persistent online environment accessible from around the world. Figures such as Epic's CEO Tim Sweeney have been key in shaping contemporary discussions around how a metaverse may become our 'Web 3.0': Dean Takahashi, 'Why We Need an Open Metaverse', VentureBeat, venturebeat.com/2021/01/27/tim-sweeney-the-open-metaverse-requires-companies-to-have-enlightened-self-interest/.

8   Katherine Isbister, *How Games Move Us: Emotion by Design* (MIT Press: Cambridge, 2016), 53.

Sections

KATAMARI DAMACY

Details

Year	2004
Developer	Namco
Publisher	Namco

Platforms

PlayStation 2

Katamari Damacy's world appears to be a messy and illogical one, assembled from thousands of everyday objects spinning around a giant ball, yet beneath the chaos lies a complex, spatial choreography.

☐ Maps:

9 Stars
8 Constellations
1 Moon

8.1   Worlds within Worlds

From point-scoring to status or skins, games encourage us to consume items and experiences that allow us to advance within their structures. As Weir writes, this heightens 'the emotional impact of advancement.'[1] In *Katamari Damacy*, the player's progress is foregrounded in the centre of the screen, taking the form of a rapidly expanding ball as an amalgamation of objects collected from different parts of the world that the player has interacted with. The *Katamari* universe is otherworldly yet familiar and intertwined. Made up of different islands that form the basis of each 'continent' on 'Earth', it is only at the end of the game where the player is large enough to roll across the entire surface of the Earth that this familiar geography is presented to them [Fig. 1].

Working to restore the stars in the sky (which have been accidentally destroyed by the King of All Cosmos), the game jumps back and forth between being heavily rooted on Earth to looking back on it from outer space – described by Hall as 'an external "meta" world'.[2] From this view, the player enters a level by choosing either to 'Make a Star' or 'Make a Constellation'. These two modes ask players to find and capture objects in slightly different ways, providing alternative experiences of the same stage and creating a whimsical entry point to the game's levels as worlds within worlds [Fig. 2].

While on Earth, the game offers the player an insight into spatial environments at multiple scales, from a domestic house to a suburban town, and eventually the entire planet. The player's sense of this scale is initially set by the objects that surround them – being positioned under a car or next to a matchstick on a table gives an indication of how big they are relative to the rest of their environment. *Katamari Damacy* often uses the same surroundings presented differently in each stage, by changing their playable extent and the starting and finishing scale requirements for the player. Objects that acted as obstacles or barriers in previous levels later become consumable, unlocking new portions of the world for exploration. This can be seen most explicitly in the early stages of the game taking place at the scale of a house, where the player first experiences the world within the extent of a single tatami-lined living room. Spiralling up, down and beneath a *kotatsu*, and in and out of the recessed *tokonoma* spaces that line the main room, we are given an explicit insight into the ground-level particularities of a traditional Japanese house, where materials and threshold conditions are depicted with great accuracy [Fig. 3].[3] Within the architecture itself, the room is messy, inhabited by open books and snacks scattered among matchsticks and half-played dice games. Even within the confines of this initial room, glimpses through to the yard are offered through ripped holes in the *shoji* screen, reinforcing this 'lived in' narrative yet also hinting at a world beyond, even if it is not immediately accessible. In the next level, the *shoji* screens open on to an *engawa* in the backyard, and finally, the internal *fusuma* slide open to reveal the rest of the house. Here we scuttle across corridors through to other living spaces, eventually making our way on to the *genkan* and out of the house into the streets. By roaming through these spaces the player covers every square inch of this house, engaging with the distinctive local vernacular of Japanese domestic space.

1   Gregory Weir, 'Analysis: How Katamari's Scale Makes You High', gamedeveloper.com/design/analysis-how-i-katamari-i-s-scale-makes-you-high

2   L. E. Hall, *Katamari Damacy* (Los Angeles: Boss Fight Books, 2018), 2.

3   Key elements of a Japanese room can be defined as follows: *kotatsu*: a low table surrounded by a blanket; *tokonoma*: a recessed alcove in a room for display; *shoji*: a paper covered partition door; *engawa*: a wooden edge around a tatami floor; *fusuma*: sliding panel; *genkan*: entryway area for removing shoes.

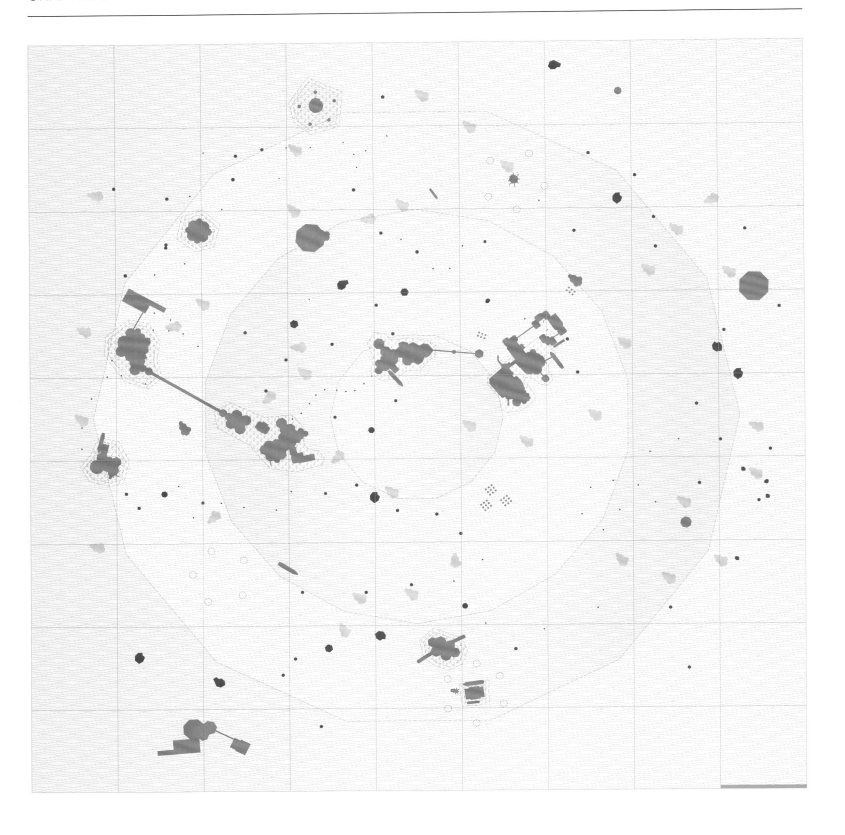

1

Mapping the final level in the game, where the player grows large enough to consume every object on the Earth's surface.

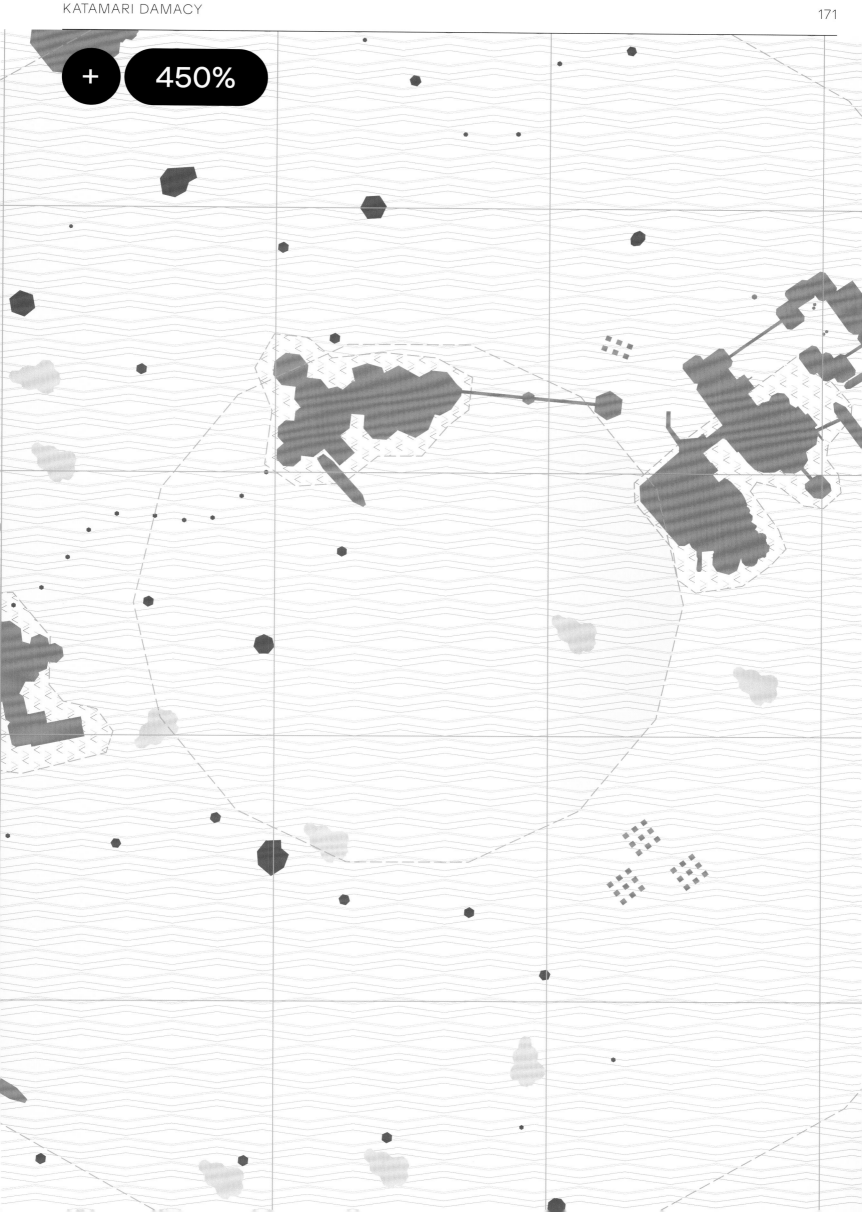

450%

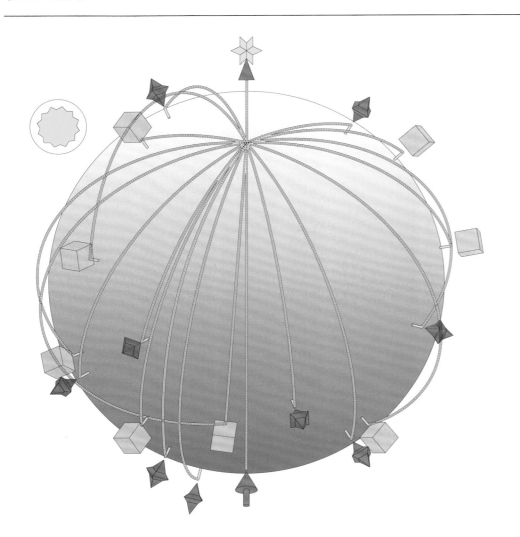

2

Constellation map locating the players' access points into each level on Earth.

3

Charting the expanding floor territories of different levels taking place within the same house.

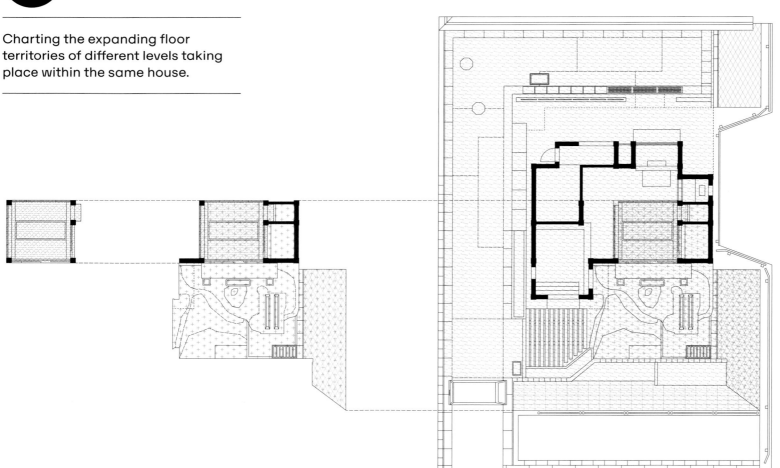

Object recognition and the changing agency of those objects also happens within levels as well as across them, binding the world together. Depending on the rate of growth, the player could be small enough to traverse the footings of a pylon at the beginning of the level and large enough to subsume it by the end. Different stages allow for various rates of growth, with some offering the player the opportunity to snowball rapidly, while others generate a more gradual journey where the katamari always stays below knee-height.

At a larger scale, certain environments will be transformed more dramatically, with the layout and typologies of buildings in the world adapted to the density of the level and the size of the katamari required of the player. While the urban elements change, the general landscape of the stage remains the same, such as an island next to a mountain and a deep valley. The easy reconfiguration of buildings and infrastructure within these landscapes also serves to remind us that these are also objects like any other, just bigger. As stages become bigger in scale, so do the buildings. Apartment blocks replace smaller family houses. Buildings are choreographed and carefully arranged to guide the route of the katamari through the expansive network of objects, carefully reacting to its transformative scale. The placement and configuration of buildings also serves to constrain the katamari, with courtyards surrounded by houses preventing a smaller ball from escaping and high-rise buildings around the edge of the valley preventing a larger katamari from straying too far [Fig. 4].

While this may appear chaotic and random at first glance, *Katamari Damacy*'s gameplay is tied to a progression that is often quite linear – requiring players to deduce an order from the chaos of objects surrounding them. To reach an optimum size within each level, objects need to be consumed in a particular order. If they are missed, the katamari will not be able to scale up to its full capacity and allow the player to explore each level in new ways. These objects are known by the community as 'bottlenecks', and the katamari must reach a minimum diameter before it can consume them [Fig. 5]. Players identify bottlenecks by first rolling organically, being repeatedly too small and bouncing off the same objects, informing the paths they take when they roll again. Rather than attempt to consume everything in sight, players must exert a level of control by consuming things in a certain order to allow the katamari to grow exponentially. Types and categories become secondary to their size, creating surreal juxtapositions between the appearance of objects and their meaning. We can see smaller objects like cherries, aubergines and canned mackerel fused together while a slightly larger katamari might contain candles, paint, buckets and pots. The resultant effect is, as Churchley describes, 'an aesthetic experience that is as mathematical as it is entertaining'.[4]

The same notion can be seen at an architectural scale in the game, when the player eventually grows large enough to 'Make the Moon'; in other words, it is capable of engulfing everything on the Earth's surface. The buildings themselves become bottlenecks, with a whole district needing to be consumed in a meticulous choreography of scale and time. Every building has a diameter for the katamari to reach before it can consume it, and any buildings spared from this will have been too big for the katamari when it was in that location, resulting in the player leaving them in place or returning to the location if they have time [Fig. 6]. When the katamari reaches this scale, swelling until it towers above the rooftops, we are reminded that every element in the game is something to be consumed. Kazemi explains this as an ontological relationship, stating, 'while at one level the house is a container for smaller objects you can pick up, at another level it becomes an object you can pick up in its own right'.[5] Earlier stages of the game were spent collecting objects under tables within houses, which felt sturdy and immobile, until the house became an object itself, uprooted within the wider environment of the world.

□ House:

1 Building
3 Levels

4   Ross Churchley, 'Exponential growth in Katamari Damacy', rosschurchley.com/blog/exponential-katamari/.
5   Darius Kazemi, 'The Prince of Objects: Katamari and Ontology', tinysubversions.com/2012/05/the-prince-of-objects-katamari-and-ontology/index.html.

Different urban configurations within the same landscape, planned to respond to the increasing scale of the player.

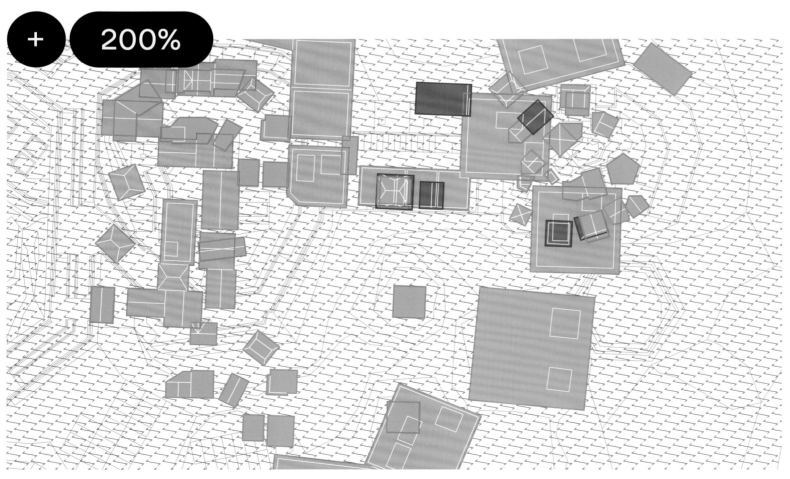

Highlighting various 'bottleneck'
objects, which must be consumed
at a particular point in the game
to allow the katamari to grow to
a certain size.

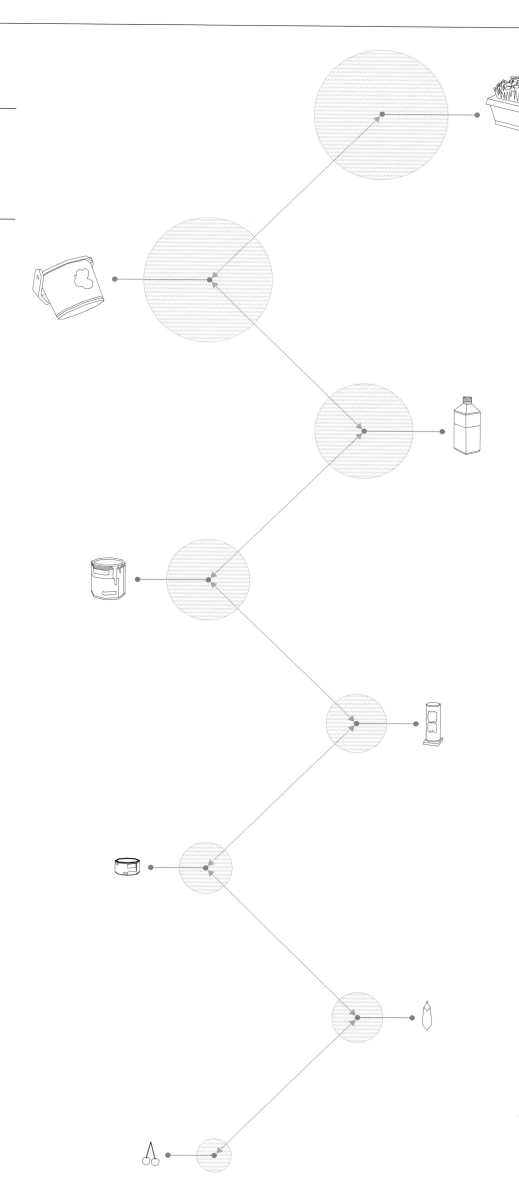

6

Buildings as bottlenecks, associated
with a particular diameter that the
katamari must reach before it can
uproot each architectural feature.

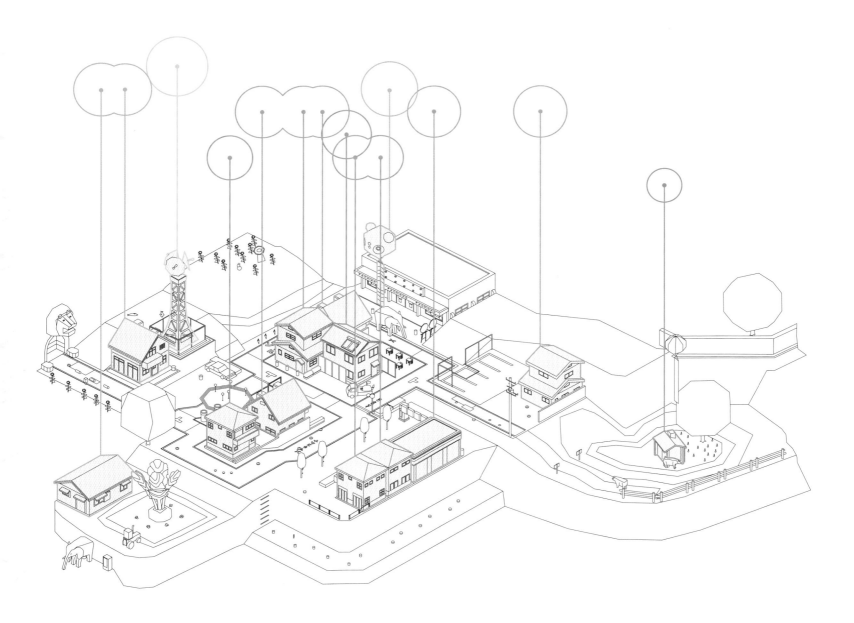

+ 350%

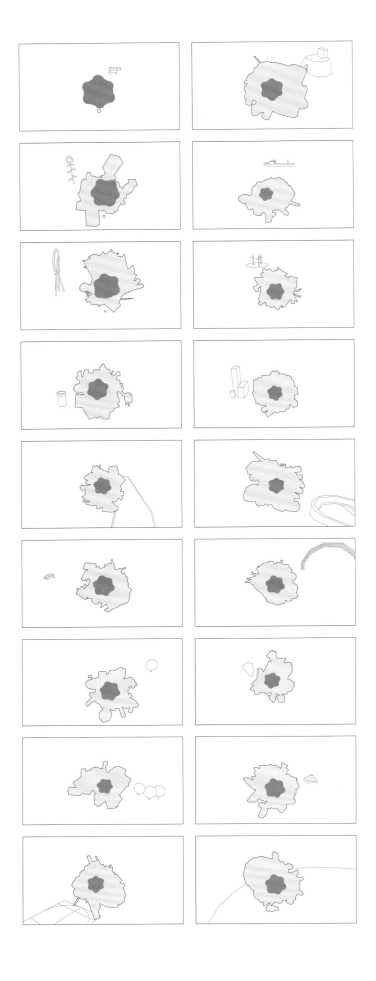

7

Analysing the relationship between the katamari and its surrounding environment as it gets bigger throughout the game.

8.2   Controlling the Clump

The player is represented by the Prince, the game's protagonist, who navigates the ball around the world. When starting a stage, the Prince is visible, playfully steering the katamari on its path. As the katamari accumulates more objects and increases in size, the presence of the Prince on the screen decreases, almost disappearing and becoming secondary to the katamari. The player's identity shifts from embodying the Prince to embodying the katamari. Each time the katamari reaches a target increment of growth, the camera expands up and out to adjust the player's view of the world to the shift in scale. The ratio between Prince, katamari, the objects that have been accumulated and the surrounding world changes, allowing the camera to adjust the player's perspective alongside the scale. While in the early stages of the level the katamari's scale is comparable to that of a sunflower, it later becomes larger than a mountain [Fig. 7]. Flattened on to the space of the screen, the relative proportions of the Prince, the katamari and the world show us how this vast agglomeration of objects ultimately dominates the environment.

The power of the katamari is also expressed through the game's control system. Players must operate both sticks of the controller to make the Prince push the katamari around, flipping them in opposite directions to make sharp turns – almost giving the control scheme the feeling of operating a piece of heavy machinery with caterpillar tracks. As we navigate around the world it is less that we are moving the Prince and rather that we are manhandling the katamari in the direction we want it to go. This turns what might be a relatively simple journey in spatial terms into a complex choreography of movements on the controller, and as with watching a skilled pilot manoeuvre a vehicle, the actions we see on screen from an accomplished player can hide the complex operations required to produce them [Fig. 8]. The controls also give the player the ability to disembody the katamari by zooming upwards into the sky and look downwards, producing a wider view of the area surrounding the katamari. This helps to locate the player within their surroundings, and allows them to survey the boundaries of each stage, identifying hazards and planning their future paths.

The katamari is at first characterized by its technicoloured skin, textured to contrast with its surroundings. As it becomes covered in objects, the presence of the naked, bumpy katamari fades, its new form defined by a thick crust of calculators, hamburgers and vending machines. Yet even at its largest diameter, we see glimpses of the katamari through gaps in the field of objects, growing alongside its outer dimensions rather than getting lost within it. By allowing the katamari to grow with the spatial scale of the game and always remaining present on screen, the player is reminded visually of where they started; that their gigantic ball of junk was and is still a katamari beneath it all [Fig. 9]. In its initial phases, the katamari's patterns of movement are closely defined by the manner of objects that stick to it. Its mobility and rhythm become altered by these objects as it turns, and it rotates higher off the ground if long and thin objects like baseball bats affix to the katamari at a perpendicular angle. Clusters of objects form like growths on its sticky skin, with the assurance that every time its developing and eventual geometry will be completely unique, adding to its character and charm [Fig. 10].

8

Encoding the manual methods of control the player can exercise over the katamari and its unique patterns of movement.

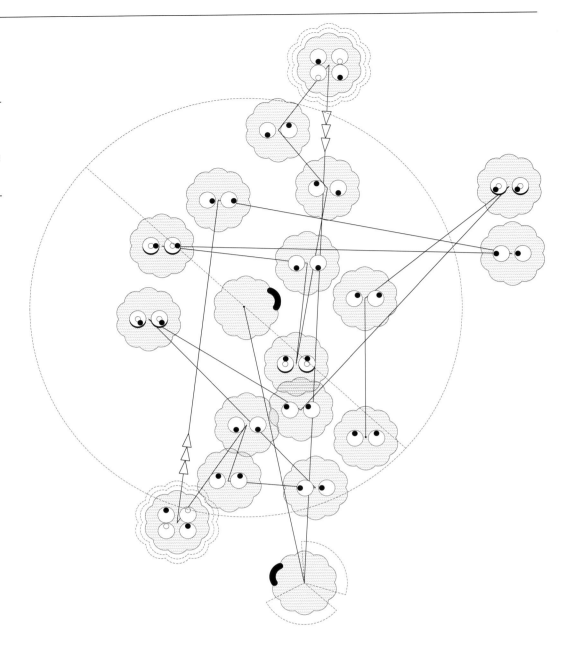

9

Katamari material studies.

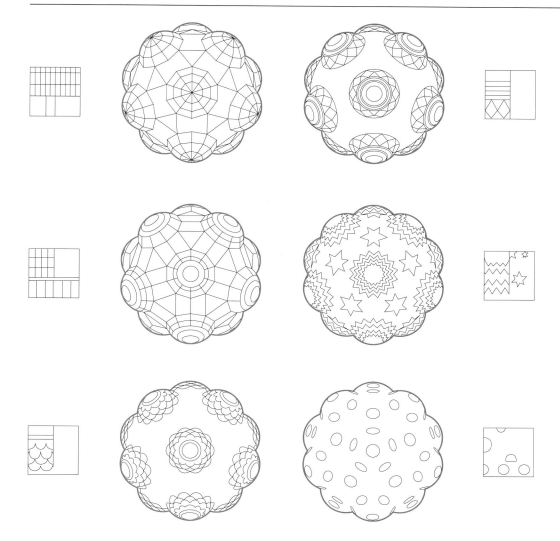

10

Understanding how the katamari's movement is impacted by the different types of objects it picks up, and their proportions.

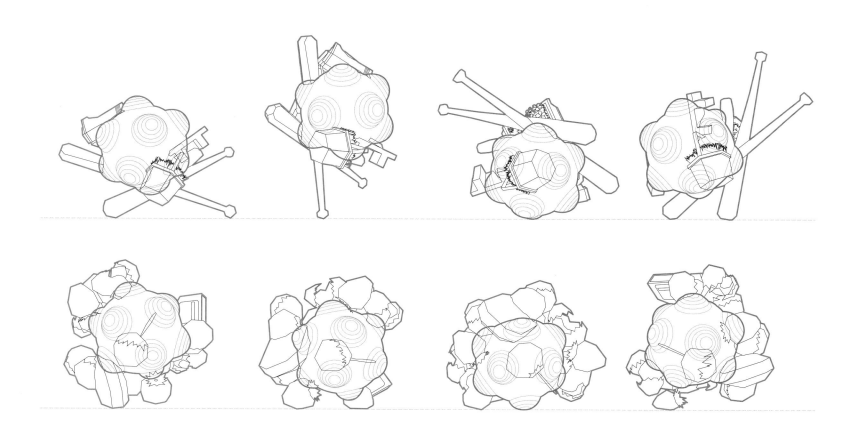

The entire path taken by a katamari
in one single level, and all the objects
it consumed, colour coded to relate
to each stage of growth.

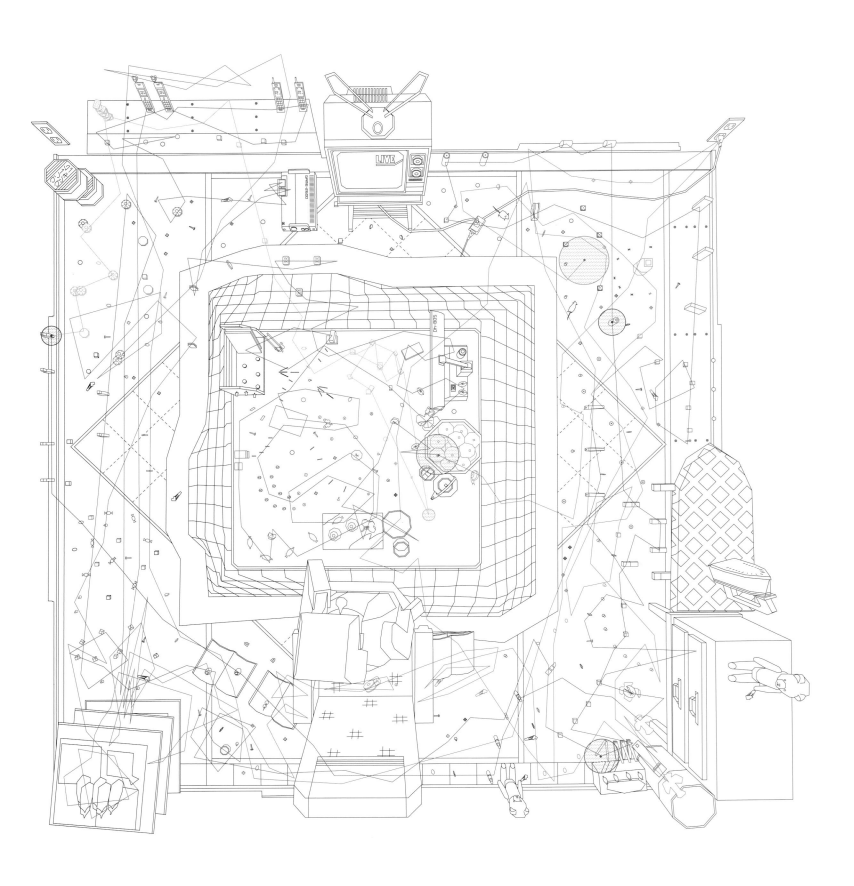

Physics seem present but imperfect, which encourages the player to go back and forth over their previous paths to pick up objects that were initially missed. By transcribing the entire path of one playthrough on a level located in the living room of a house, viewed from above, it is possible to see these routes as spirals and zigzags attempting to collect as many objects as possible. The katamari takes a non-traditional, non-linear path through the space, deeming every surface navigable, whether the sides of cushions, a timber door frame or a human leg. While the katamari can continue to roll relatively easily forwards, backwards, left and right, the player can also control it to charge, break and shift, adjusting its position more dramatically to respond to the dynamic terrain. By encoding each shift in scale as a different coloured line, the map becomes a reading of time, mobility and progression as various objects can be visually associated with each stage of the game and size of the katamari [Fig. 11]. At times, the katamari appears to defy physics, traversing upwards across vertical surfaces such as stairs, fences and walls if it gains enough traction. Although the process can be bulky, awkward and cumbersome, the feeling is eventually cathartic as the katamari negotiates these different geometries to proceed on its way.

While in some levels the katamari starts and remains relatively small over the course of play, in others, the difference in size between the katamari at the start of the level and at the end is more extreme. This relationship between size, scale and time varies across the game, to enable diverse experiences of space to take place, starting intimate and leisurely and becoming unforgiving and extreme.

In 'Make a Star 8', the katamari can grow by 120 times its starting size, if it achieves its target goal, from 10 cm (4 in.) to 12 m (39 ft 4½ in.). By mapping this growth

on to a plan of the level [Fig. 12], we can see how the katamari starts centrally within the space, occupying flat plazas and gaps between buildings, before moving into wider outskirts and territories of the map. The design of this level draws the player to the periphery of the space through the size of objects. We might consider this to be an inversion of typical urban principles, where bigger buildings tend to occupy the centre while the outlying areas decrease in scale. This is also linked to the contextual setting of a deep valley, visualized through a sectional drawing [Fig. 13]. Here the relationship between the game's geography and the scale of the katamari is inherently linked. The larger the katamari, the higher and wider distances it can move, gaining access to new 'off-road' portions of the map that are more rugged and extreme.

☐ Katamari Size:

10cm Start
12cm Target

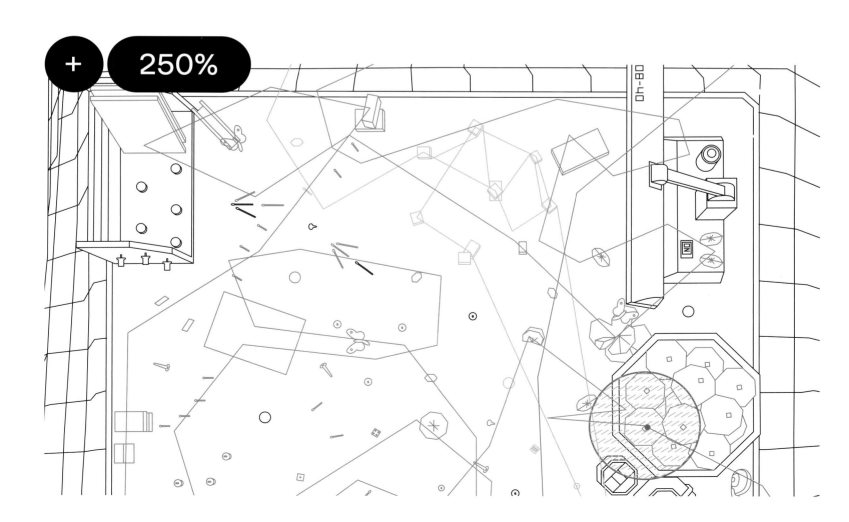

Plan showing the route taken by a katamari across a bigger landscape, showing its relationship and interaction with both urban and natural forms.

Section through a valley, revealing how the katamari can access higher and more extreme terrain as it gets bigger.

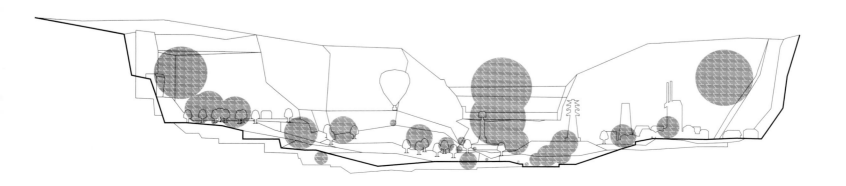

14

Matrix showing an assortment of objects in the game, ordered into the following categories: necessities, electronics, sport, fruit and vegetables, food, containers, garden, danger, cleaning, and decorative.

8.3　Lost and Found

As the game's developer Keita Takahashi describes, *Katamari Damacy* is a tale about mass consumption – filling the world with brightly coloured objects to roll up, and feeling empty when they're gone.[6] The objects were designed to resemble everyday things that a Japanese person would recognize instantly, such as a PET bottle, a vending machine or a yen coin. Rather than using actual products, items were made to look similar to real-world brands.[7] Through these decisions, objects have a degree of likeness without needing to be completely realistic, allowing them to speak about the act of consumerist branding itself, rather than any specific brand in isolation.

With the game's systems requiring so many objects in the world, they are designed to appear clunky and primitive, possessing less polygons than their real-life counterparts, with colours, textures and logos that look just about right. This aesthetic sets a tone for the game and the design of the world – playful, friendly and not too precious, validating the player's goal to consume everything in sight. While the impulsive reaction may be to attempt to collect everything indiscriminately, selective and meticulous rolling will ultimately lead the katamari to the most success. In this way we can imagine that the game is also reminding us that there are connections within our consumerist world of objects – we have drawers in our kitchens for objects of a similar size – and our real-world wardrobes, garages and classrooms are designed for specific objects in space. *Katamari Damacy* simply orders and arranges them in a different way. As McKenzie Wark argues, 'nothing is really qualitatively different…it's all just stuff', but at the same time the game provides 'a universal code that allows anything to be connected to anything else'.[8]

The game has a detailed and accessible inventory for the player to use at any point, a 'collection' of all the objects their katamari has acquired across different levels. Although inventory systems are common in games, we are often conditioned to collect rather than to think. By allowing players to sort objects in several different ways – organized by name, object type [Fig. 14], size and location, players can define what they feel is missing from their collection. This might be all the objects relating to danger, all the objects found on a baseball field, or all the objects which are 'somewhat small'. These different ways of categorizing the objects reframe their hierarchy depending on the player's inclination. This gives them autonomy over their actions, so they can go back over their tracks to revisit particular spaces or specific parts of the world to build up their collection. It also slows down the pace of the game, revealing objects that were picked up at speed, unintentionally or by chance, offering logic to the chaos that took place during the game. This mechanism can be likened to the transformation of a traditional database of objects through the incorporation of narrative – as media theorist Lev Manovich writes: 'We want new media narratives, and we want these narratives to be different from the narratives we saw or read before.'[9] While *Katamari Damacy* holds a finite number of items within its database, there are nearly limitless possibilities in the way players experience them and how these objects are perceived as a result.

As the game reaches its climax, *Katamari Damacy*'s world of objects grows to the scale of a planet, the 'continents' sticking to the ball as it rolls, tearing the Earth's surface off and leaving it as an expansive blue plane. Here we see the ultimate manifestation of the katamari logic, removing not only objects, but the ground itself from the ecumene, 'the relationship between humanity and the earth's surface'.[10] By subsuming everything into the logic of object-to-object connection, *Katamari Damacy* allows us to escape the planet and roll our human-made, synthetic world off into the future.

6   Keita Takahashi, 'Katamari was comment on consumerism', eurogamer.net/articles/katamari-was-comment-on-consumerism.
7   Keita Takahashi, 'How Katamari became one of the most eccentric games ever', gamesradar.com/uk/how-earnest-little-prince-rolled-eccentric-classic/.
8   McKenzie Wark, *Gamer Theory* (Cambridge, MA: Harvard University Press, 2007), 84.
9   Lev Manovich, 'Database as a Symbolic Form', manovich.net/index.php/projects/database-as-a-symbolic-form.
10   Augustin Berque, 'From "Mediance" to Places', PCA-Stream, pca-stream.com/en/articles/augustin-berque-from-mediance-to-places-98.

☐ Scale:

1,438 Objects
0.015m Ant
700m Tornado

Sections

MINECRAFT

Details

Year	2011
Developer	Mojang Studios
Publisher	Mojang Studios, Microsoft Studios, Sony Interactive Entertainment

Platforms

PlayStation: 4/3/Vita   Wii U

Xbox: One/360   iOS   Linux

Microsoft Windows   macOS

Android   Nintendo Switch/3DS

Kindle Fire   Oculus Rift

Minecraft is a game of almost limitless complexity, and many popular servers become worlds within worlds, possessing their own culture, lore and architectural styles.

☐ Maps:

1.38 × 1018 m³
60,000km Wide
383m High

9.1 A Survey of Servers

If there is one game that has transcended the industry and become what media theorist Lev Manovich calls 'cultural software'[1] – a computer program used for generating culture – then it is *Minecraft*. The game, which in its most basic form involves the mining and collection of raw materials and then the construction of structures with which to protect oneself, has such deep and complicated systems, and such a large player base using them, that defining 'the world' of the game is nearly impossible. One reason for this is that a basic *Minecraft* world is procedurally generated [Fig. 1]. A second is that there are innumerable different servers, maps and experiences available for players of the game. And thirdly, the game itself is being applied in non-game situations. *Minecraft* is used by architects and NGOs to help in the design of urban space, for example, with the organization Block by Block.[2] It has been used to hold music festivals with thousands of fans (Fire Festival, Coalchella[3]), as well as virtual graduation ceremonies during the Covid-19 pandemic.[4]

This creative platform has allowed certain types of server, hosting different forms of games within a game, to emerge – and some of these can be directly contradictory in their aims, despite sharing an underpinning structure. By examining these different servers in detail, we can see how *Minecraft* facilitates different world formations, social structures and game mechanics. These range from tightly controlled role-playing servers, where players engage with typical tropes of a fantasy landscape and build up their expertise, to anarchical free-for-alls, where deviant behaviour and hacks proliferate along with innovative experimentations in machine learning and AI. By seeing these servers as divergent outputs of the same system, it is possible to understand how each server satisfies the spatial and social impulses of the players drawn to them. In this way *Minecraft*, with its low accessibility barrier, but high ceiling for creative and skilful play and productivity, may be not only one of the best games, but the best piece of any software to understand the spatial imagination of millions of players who are not trained as architectural or spatial designers, but engage with this practice every single day.

1   Lev Manovich, *Software Takes Command* (London: Bloomsbury, 2013).
2   The Block by Block Foundation is a collaboration between UN Habitat, Mojang and Microsoft: blockbyblock.org.
3   The *Minecraft*-based team behind Coalchella (*Minecraft*.xxx) have produced several music festivals, most recently Lavapalooza, attracting international DJs.
4   Tom Phillips, 'University students graduate in official *Minecraft* ceremony', Eurogamer, eurogamer.net/articles/2020-05-18-university-students-graduate-in-official-*Minecraft*-ceremony.

1

Archetypal map showing several *Minecraft* worlds in their 'vanilla' format, created using a basic, unmodified version of the game. This is the building block on which all other servers are founded, yet they move far from these typical beginnings.

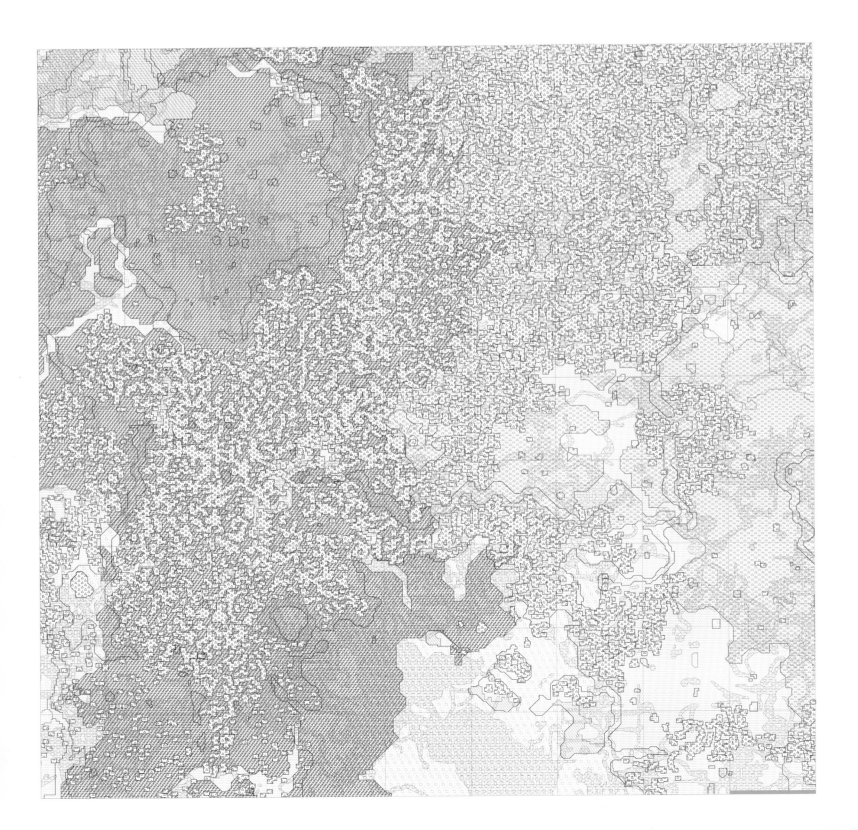

+ 400%

2

Map containing part of the central areas of 2b2t.
Giant walls spawn at the centre of the world, designed
to trap new players. Hanging above this is the giant
Masonic Eclipse and oWo, two symbols made by rival
groups, dominating the server from an aerial viewpoint.

9.2   2b2t, the 'Wild West' of the Internet

There is arguably no *Minecraft* server more notorious than 2b2t (2builders2tools), an unregulated free-for-all 'anarchy server' where the depths of *Minecraft*'s complexity and its social boundaries are tested. Such servers are operated with little or no moderation or rule structure, providing a free zone for players to build and destroy anything and anyone they wish. 2b2t has been running since 2010, and has been described in media features as 'the worst place in *Minecraft*'[5] and 'a place of beauty and terror'.[6]

The anarchical nature of 2b2t has produced a convoluted landscape that combines several principles key to the hierarchy of the world. The central spawn, a zone of 1,000 by 1,000 blocks, is bounded by a huge wall of obsidian blocks. The spawn has been the site of many different structures, built with the intention to disrupt and kill new players entering the server. As one moves further out into the world, the server is littered with private bases and stashes built by players, a vast number of which are in ruins due to being 'griefed' (destroyed) by other players. It is common for the coordinates of bases, or even projects under construction, to be leaked to other players, who then move in to ruin them. The cycle of construction and destruction is a key to the momentum of 2b2t's world. There are also many large, collaborative building projects within the world, produced by teams who often augment player labour with artificial intelligence bots.

As of late 2019, the centre of the 2b2t map has been dominated by a huge masonic symbol, named the Masonic Eclipse and constructed by a group known as the SpawnMasons. According to the 2b2t Wiki, this comprises over 28 million blocks of obsidian material, and dwarfs the large walls that surround the spawn [Fig. 2].[7] This giant structure is designed to exert dominance over the world, and to be seen from an aerial view. These impulses are mirrored in reality, where we need only look at the Palm development in Dubai to see real-world architecture 'presented in the media as an icon to be seen by orbiting satellites in space'.[8] Such is life in 2b2t that a second huge symbol, oWo, appeared sometime later, the product of a rival group who built the entire thing by hand with the aim of creating the largest human-built structure in the world.

Another example of collective building, this time a piece of usable infrastructure, is the Nether Highway System that runs out from the central spawn. As of mid-2021 this had reached the world border, the edge of the server that is 30,000 km (18,641 miles) from the centre of the world [Fig. 3]. Like the Masonic Eclipse, this has been achieved through the use of obsidian blocks placed by bot accounts using an AI system called Baritone, but it also leverages one of the unique properties of *Minecraft*'s dimension system. The Nether dimension is a dangerous one – full of fire, lava and hostile creatures, and accessible only via an obsidian portal – but it is also highly useful for creating such a large-scale transit system. The Nether maps on to the Overworld at a 1:8 scale, meaning every metre travelled in the Nether equates to 8 m (26¼ ft) in the Overworld [Fig. 4]. As such, the various groups constructing highways must 'only' complete 3,750 km (2330 miles)-worth of thoroughfare to provide total coverage in any of the cardinal directions.

The cycle of building and griefing on 2b2t has produced many visually striking spatial forms unique to the landscape of the server. We could see these as an architectural vernacular, a style common and local to 2b2t, produced through an emphasis on destructive building techniques. The spawn area of the server and its immediate surroundings are populated by giant mounds, towers, walls and triangular forms. These are produced by a technique called 'lavacasting', where players take advantage of *Minecraft*'s liquid flow simulation to pour and solidify vast tracts of lava blocks into cobblestone. This is a technique so ubiquitous on servers like 2b2t that it is used as a verb.

5   Andrew Paul, 'The Worst Place in Minecraft', Motherboard by Vice, vice.com/en/article/xywekq/the-worst-place-in-minecraft.
6   Roisin Kiberd, 'The Minecraft Server That Will Kill You 1,000 Times', *Newsweek*, newsweek.com/2016/09/23/minecraft-anarchy-server-2b2t-will-kill-you-498946.html.
7   2b2t Wiki, 'The Masonic Eclipse', 2b2t.miraheze.org/wiki/The_Masonic_Eclipse.
8   Marc Angélil and Cary Siress, 'Dubai Inc.', in Log 08, summer 2006.

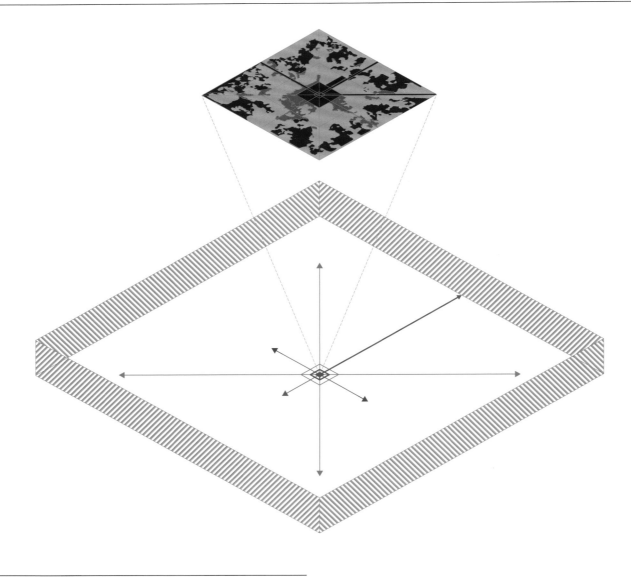

3

Diagram demonstrating the Nether Highway System in 2b2t, which has reached the very edge of the world in one direction and is undergoing construction in the others.

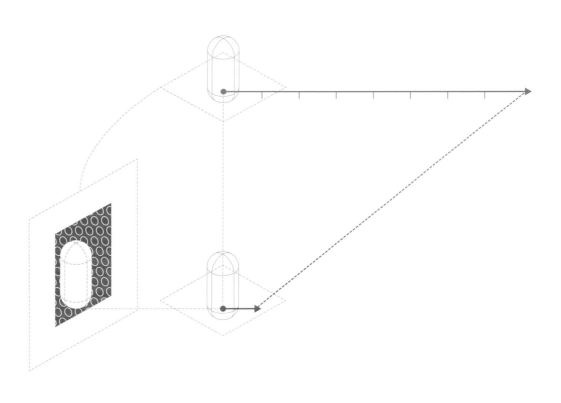

4

Distance in the Nether translates to eight times that in the Overworld, meaning that constructing highway systems there is highly efficient when spanning the world.

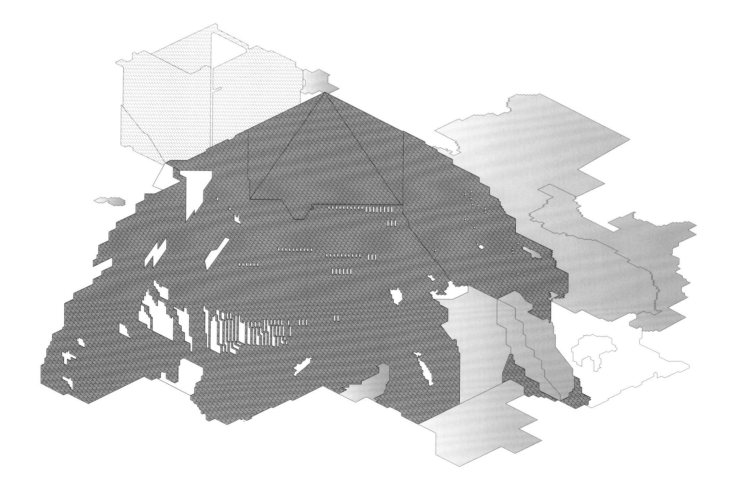

5

Two typologies of 'lavacast' architecture, steps and pyramids are emblematic of 2b2t's architecture of 'griefing'. These structures, made by pouring water on to flowing lava, allow players to quickly build on to and destroy other structures.

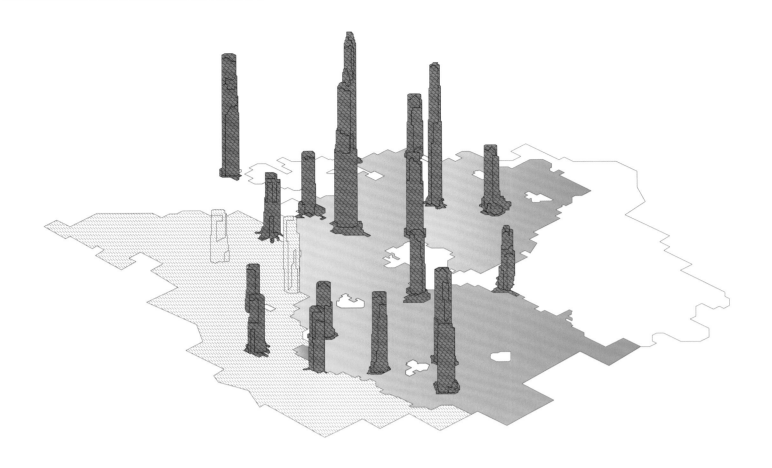

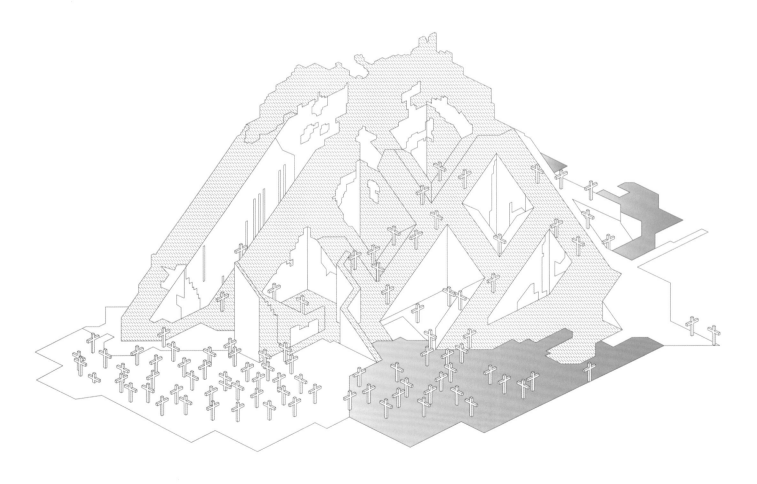

6

Lavacasting can also be applied in the design of huge
towers, and combinations of techniques produce
massive landscapes of solidified cobblestone blocks that
dominate the horizon.

Colossal triangular forms emerging from the ground within the 2b2t spawn are in fact giant staircases, laddering up block by block. Due to their scale, and the fact that they do not connect on to any other structure, the staircases have no use as access routes and instead become giant ruins, impositions on the landscape, making progress between them painfully slow for new players. By contrast, pyramid-type structures can simply envelop other buildings in a huge body of stone so large it appears well beyond the scale and scope of a typical *Minecraft* avatar. Unlike a traditional pyramid, which would have been stacked from the bottom up, this type of structure flows down from the top, entombing everything below in a giant cobblestone sarcophagus [Fig. 5]. Towers are relatively trivial to lavacast given that the technique relies on gravity, but the simplicity of the technique enables the quick creation of huge structures, producing vast clusters of mute and inexpressive skyscrapers. Many of these will actually be hollow structures, containing any number of storage or trap elements within. Combinations of these techniques, involving principles from stair and pyramid building, can produce more complex and expressive forms, where the flow of lava on to other types of blocks and the resultant distortions this produces can be seen in the striations of the structure [Fig. 6].

While these typologies are not unique to 2b2t and can be produced in a 'vanilla' *Minecraft* server, their ubiquity is due to the small amount of resources and time required to produce a large and significant building. Lavacasting works by the player building a simple formwork from stone or other blocks and then using a bucket to place lava at the top of the structure, allowing *Minecraft*'s fluid simulation to let it flow to the ground. In a staircase scenario, the lava will flow down the steps of the formwork and vertically over the side, producing a closed form [Fig. 7]. By placing another block above, and then pouring water on to this, the cold water chases the lava down to the ground, solidifying it as it goes. The same principle works for pyramids, where the player can use blocks to move themselves higher and higher into the air, to quickly generate a huge structure [Fig. 8]. By returning lava to their bucket again, players can game *Minecraft*'s resource system to build huge structures quickly and for little material cost.

While lavacasting is not the only building technique employed in 2b2t, it is the most emblematic of the tensions that allow the server to thrive in its own unique way. They are architectures of maximum disruption and minimum effort. Ultimately, they are monuments to griefing, and in an environment as uncontrolled as 2b2t, perhaps we can even consider them 'natural forms'.

☐ 2b2t:

11+ Years
14200gb+ Data
730,000+ Visitors

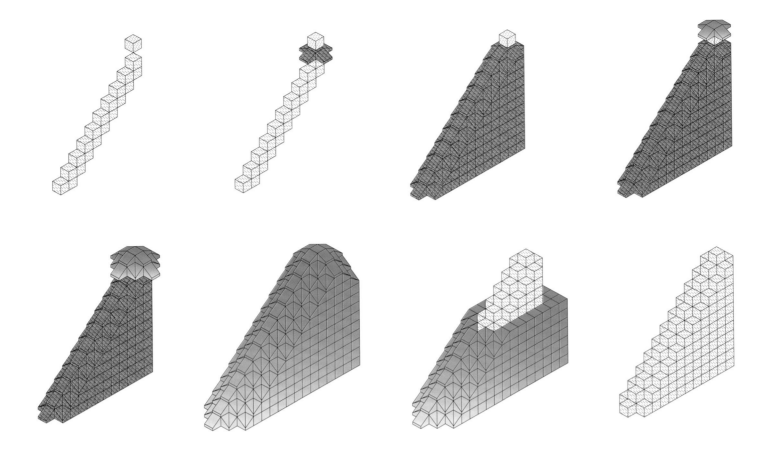

7

Diagram demonstrating the steps required to lavacast a staircase, by exploiting the flow and gravity systems of both lava and water. By pouring lava over a scaffold and chasing it with water to solidify it, large structures can be built very quickly with little material cost.

+ 300%

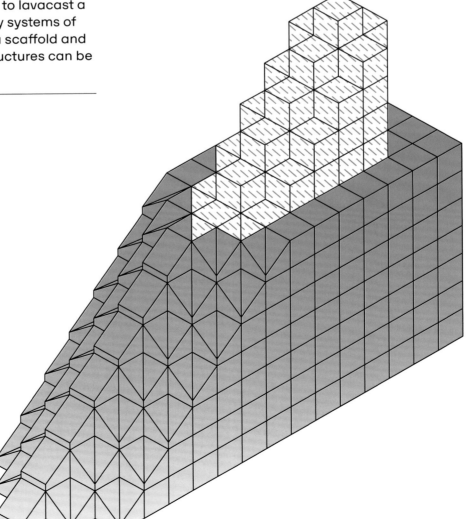

The procedure of applying lavacasting techniques in a pyramid configuration, allowing players to rapidly cover large expanses of the world using very few blocks.

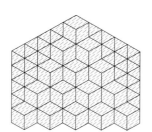
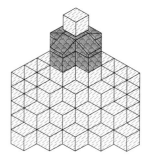
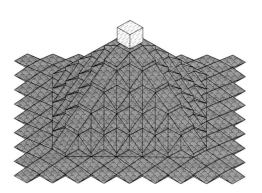
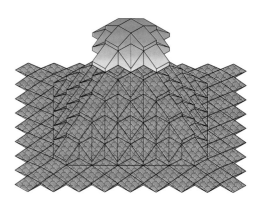
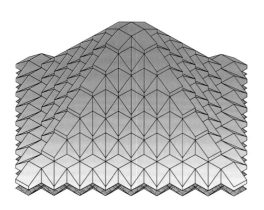
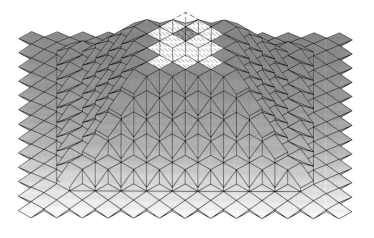
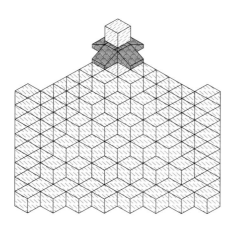
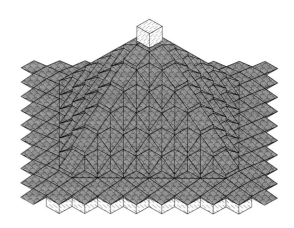

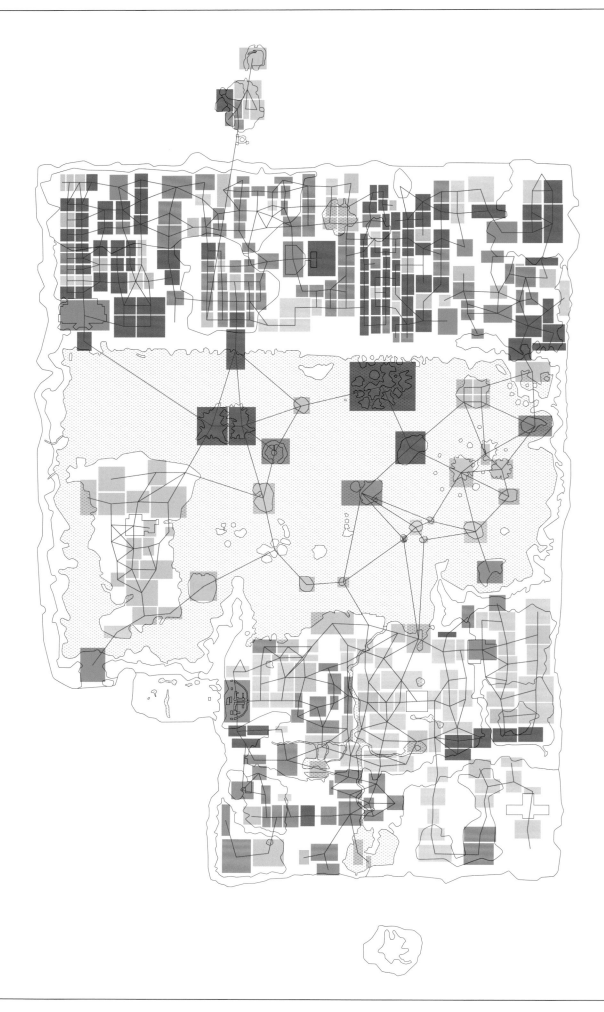

9

Map of the Wynncraft server, showing different areas broken down by resource type and quantity, alongside some of the main travel routes used by players on the server.

9.3 Wynncraft, the landscape of levels

In stark contrast to the uncontrollable anarchy of 2b2t, many other *Minecraft* servers provide worlds that have a much more structured experience. The popular server Wynncraft, for example, is a role-playing environment, taking the form one would expect of any typical role-playing game (RPG), down to the fantasy setting. This server provides a vast landscape for players to explore, building up their skills and abilities while also obtaining resources and equipment to trade and enhance abilities. Any new player entering Wynncraft will even be treated to a short narrative sequence that introduces them to some of the basic mechanics of the server, in a style very similar to other notable RPG games.

Wynncraft's map draws from more typical fantasy and RPG tropes, by dividing the world into different districts, each of which has a specific level, denoting the difficulty of enemies in relation to the skill of the player. At the centre of the world sits the Ocean, a giant expanse of sea populated by various islands. Unlike a sprawling anarchy server, the edges of Wynncraft are well defined by a series of snow-capped mountain ranges, meaning that players are contained within the surrounding landscape.

Despite these constraints, there are still community-made extensions and mods that are commonly used in Wynncraft. 'Wynntils', for example, adds a series of features into the game to help players navigate and organize their lives. It also provides data that finds its way into other mapping tools made by the community. Because so much time in Wynncraft will be spent gathering resources, there are websites designed to offer an easy breakdown of material locations for players, as well as detailing the drop rate of Emeralds (Wynncraft's currency), in any given zone of the map.[9] By transcribing such maps we can see that although Wynncraft has a highly articulated fictional environment, it can also be abstracted to stricter territorial divides defined by their numerical rate of resource production [Fig. 9].

As players start to obtain more resources and level up, they can also start to define their own small portion of the world. Housing islands enable players to create their own personal spaces, accessed through a hot-air balloon. This 81x81-block circular island form is suspended far above the world of Wynncraft, which allows every player the possibility of customization and to build their own unique property while keeping the bounded fiction of the world below separate and consistent [Fig. 10].

As in many RPGs, the world is divided into different areas with assigned levels, making it difficult for players to travel the world without first engaging with it to increase their abilities and strength. And as with other games of this type, this also encourages tactics such as 'grinding', repetitive actions made to quickly boost a character's statistics. As the community has identified through various guides,[10] there are many different grinding areas within Wynncraft that provide the player with the opportunity to earn experience at a high and consistent rate. These guides often provide precise in-game coordinates, and examples of the XP that can be achieved per kill. The Province of Wynn is a low-level area, where the Nivia Woods provide a consistent source of experience for new players in a place with a clearly defined boundary. As players progress through the game, they may choose a more difficult spot such as Castle Dullahan, which is also visited as part of a quest when the player is in the medium-to-high levels. At higher levels, players might grind near Lutho in the Silent Expanse, an area for powerful characters that is notable for the Eyeball Forest, a dangerous and morbid place where the eyes of lost souls became part of the woodland [Fig. 11].

As the prevalence of these spots shows, because the RPG mechanism privileges a numerical definition of player expertise and power, rather than the total free-for-all of 2b2t, where power is asserted through a complex set of social relationships, the world of Wynncraft structures this for the player. This creates a secondary landscape on top of the narrative space, one that is tightly defined by the player's experience and power. True freedom in Wynncraft is to be so powerful that these distinctions no longer matter.

9   Wynncraft 1.20 map by bolyai based on a map from the 'Wyntills' utility, kristofbolyai.github.io/Territory-map/.

10 Post by user ItzAzura entitled 'List Of Grinding Spots Level 1–106' on the Official Wynncraft Forums, 9 September 2019, forums.wynncraft.com/threads/list-of-grinding-spots-level-1-106.255238/.

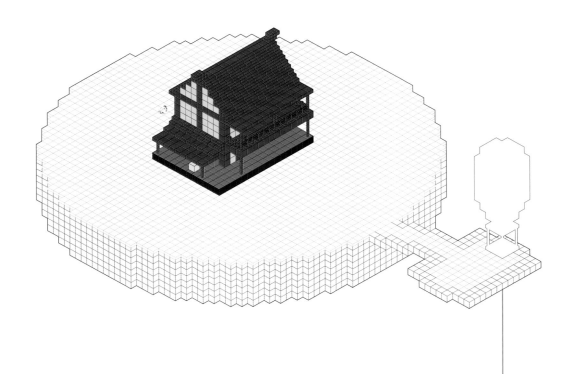

10

Configuration of Wynncraft's housing islands, accessed by a hot-air balloon. Here players can build their own individual houses without affecting the world below.

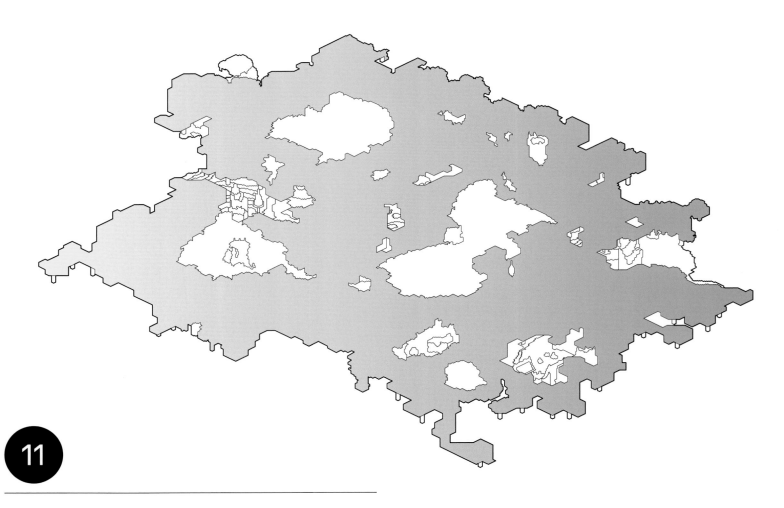

11

Popular grinding spots in Wynncraft such as these provide areas for different levels of players to rapidly grow their abilities and resources, making them well-travelled destinations in the world.

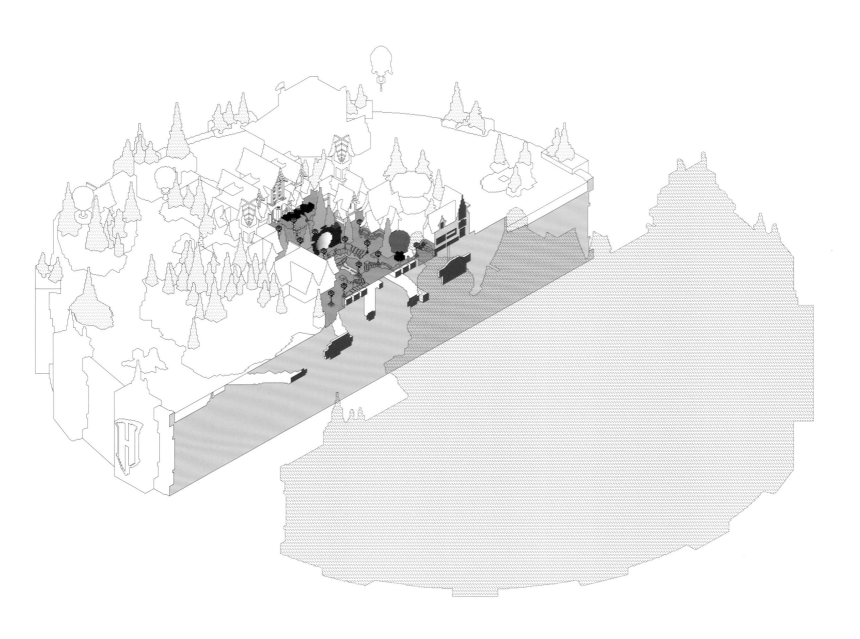

12

Sectional isometric through Hypixel's lobby space as the centre of the server's world, connecting out into all the other lobbies and games that that server provides. This space is designed to provide amenities, news and shopping opportunities to keep players engaged with the world.

9.4 Hypixel, a Labyrinth of Lobbies

Hypixel is, by most measures available, the most popular and well-travelled *Minecraft* server on the internet today.[11] The server is something of a hybrid, providing a series of games-within-games and a sequence of worlds and hub levels to facilitate this. The spatial design of Hypixel provides an environment that includes many popular types of game, meaning that one server can satisfy the needs of players who might enjoy many different forms of experience. To accommodate all the varied types of games it offers, Hypixel relies on a system of 'lobby' spaces that direct people from a main hub into different parts of the server. Ironically, lobby is an architectural term that has been adopted by game designers to signify an area of the game where players are held while waiting to enter a match. Typically, lobbies might take place in the game's menu, yet in Hypixel we see the lobby reattached to its original meaning as a place at the entrance of a space where people can spawn and gather before proceeding further into the world.

The main lobby of Hypixel is one of the most emblematic spaces of the game, and it is often altered during special events. It provides facilities along with a bank of fast-travel points that open out on to another series of lobbies, which in turn can provide access into further different spaces [Fig. 12]. From here, players can choose multiple game types, being sent into further lobbies from which they will be placed into arenas.

Each of these sub-lobbies has a different design but retains common features. To the left as the player faces forward will always be the Leader Board, while to the right is the Guide, giving information about that specific game type. Each lobby provides amenities such as the Mystery Vault (for randomized prizes) and vendors for the purchase of in-game currency. The most striking feature of each lobby is the huge Hypixel logo that frames the space – this branding is repeated in every lobby. This reminds us that we are in a carefully curated, proprietary server where we are never too far away from a vendor promising microtransactions. In the Housing Lobby, we can even find HYKIA – a version of the ubiquitous Swedish home store, where we can purchase custom furnishings for our home. These strategies are reminiscent of the architectural tactics employed in Las Vegas. By packaging many game types together under one umbrella and using thematic branding and spatial design to keep the player interested, Hypixel mirrors real-world casinos that want to provide total 'integrated resorts' which we never need to leave for other experiences.

The design of casino space has been called the 'ergonomic labyrinth'[12] – a place that is hard to escape but provides pleasure while trapping us. By recording all the connections that spread out from Hypixel's central lobby, into all the various sub-lobbies, arenas and housing areas, we can see a complex labyrinth of spaces that keeps the player stimulated within the Hypixel ecosystem by always providing a new and interesting diversion [Fig. 13]. Although these connections change, during the 2021 Summer Event the Main Lobby provided twenty-two portals – eighteen of which connect to other lobbies, and four of which connect directly to games that Hypixel wishes to highlight. In total this provides around eighty different options for players, accommodating many thousands of people playing Bed Wars (a game about destroying and defending beds) while fifty people opt to play Hypixel's version of football.

By far the most popular mode on Hypixel is the persistent game SkyBlock, a derivation of a popular survival game type in *Minecraft* where players inhabit floating islands. Hypixel's version of this is a world-within-a-world, with its own economy, towns and biomes for the players to explore [Fig. 14]. Similar to other RPG-based servers, SkyBlock allows players to build expertise in seven different skills, and gradually unlock different parts of the map. Here, as in Wynncraft, player levels start to define areas that can and cannot be visited. This persistent world will store player progress and save alterations to their house, yet should the mood for something different (like playing *Minecraft*'s version of Quake) take us, the main Hypixel lobby is just a '/hub' command away. There is no need to leave.

11 A search for 'Top Minecraft Servers in August 2021' returns Hypixel as the most occupied server, with over ten times the users of the next most popular server: topminecraftservers.org/sort/players.
12 Natasha Dow Schüll, *Addiction by Design: Machine Gambling in Las Vegas* (Princeton NJ: Princeton University Press, 2014), 54.

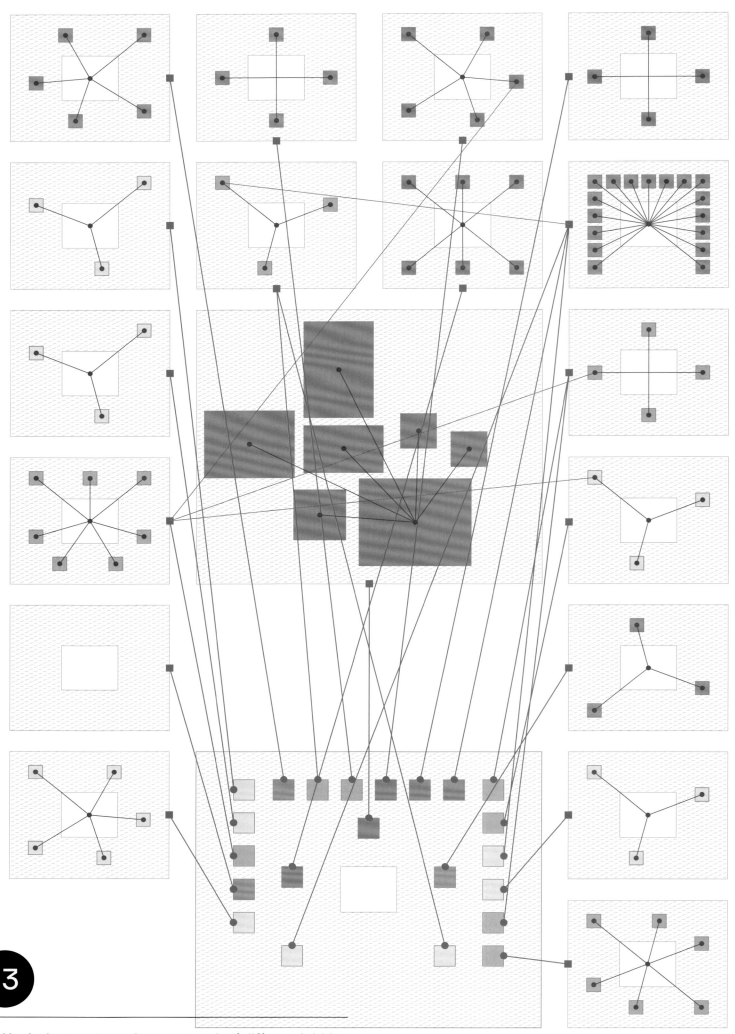

The Hypixel server has a large network of different lobbies
providing a wealth of different game types. This mapping
demonstrates all the lobby connections within the game,
colour coded by their popularity.

☐ Hypixel:

21m+ Visitors
140,000+ Players
80+ Modes

The world of SkyBlock is a game-within-a-game on Hypixel, providing a fantasy setting and RPG-style mechanics. Players can build a life within this world, unlocking and travelling to different islands, while easily connecting back to all the server's other game arenas.

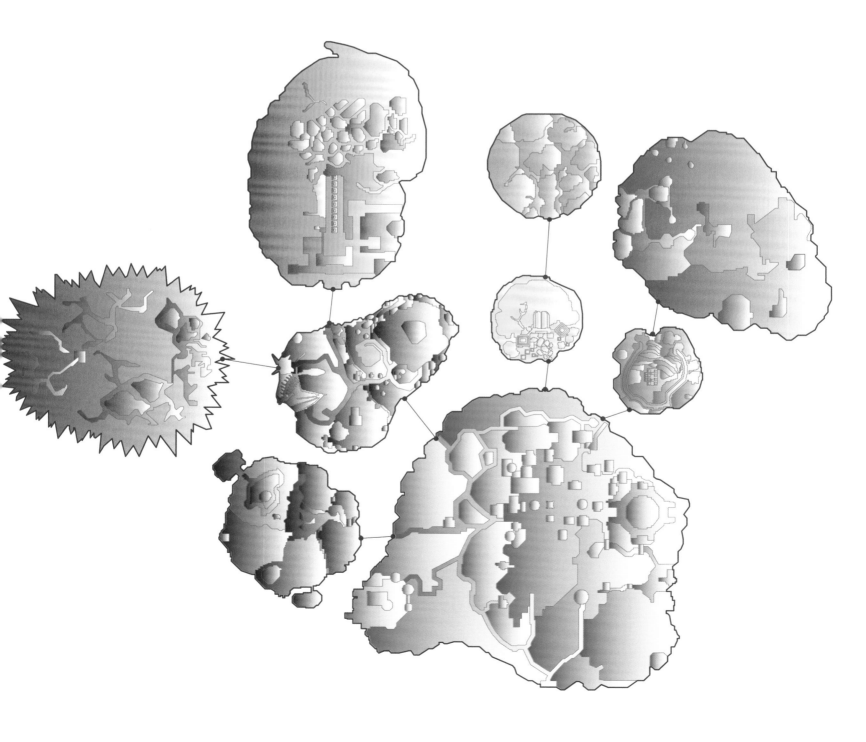

○ VIDEOGAME ATLAS

Sections

NO MAN'S SKY

Details

Year	2016
Developer	Hello Games
Publisher	Hello Games

Platforms

PlayStation: 4/5

Xbox One   Xbox Series X&S

Microsoft Windows

Nowhere is the spirit of exploration more present than in the universe of *No Man's Sky,* which combines procedural generation, the aesthetics of 1970s science-fiction and symbolic social systems together.

☐ Maps:

255 Galaxies
18.4 × 10^{18} Planets

10.1 Planetary Procedures

Recent years have seen a reinvigoration of the 'space race', led by a new generation of space industry figures that have their sights set on Mars. Space has been drawn back to the fore in public discussion through both novel scientific missions and publicity stunts. But the dream of prospecting new worlds beyond our own is of course not a new one, and has persisted as a key theme for videogames for as long as they have existed. The romantic notion of high-technology space pioneers is one that continues to captivate, and this relationship forms the basis of the success of Hello Games' *No Man's Sky*, with its emphasis on exploring scenic planets in a stylishly retro spacecraft.

No Man's Sky is built on a vast procedural system that generates a universe of 255 galaxies through an algorithm, broken down into regions, star systems and planets for the player to discover. In their starships, players can jump between star systems, exploring the planets contained within, scanning and documenting flora and fauna, and taking advantage of their natural resources for trading or the crafting of equipment. Once on planets, players can log their discovery to the game's servers and establish a home base, enabling more advanced exploration and resource-finding activities to take place. Planetary locations can also be shared by means of a set of visual 'glyphs' that allow other players to visit in their own games. While the size of the game's universe is beyond human comprehension, Hello Games' own Galactic Atlas serves as a visual mapping of planetary discoveries made by players within the first galaxy, Euclid. This information helps us to understand the form of the game's interplanetary structure, albeit at a tiny scale compared to the entire universe [Fig. 1].

The visual style of *No Man's Sky* and its universe is highly reminiscent of 1970s science-fiction art, with the developers citing influences that evoke a 'feeling of the frontier, that feeling of adventure'.[1] This included Ralph McQuarrie's visionary work for *Star Wars* and Chris Foss, the British artist noted for his 'intricately detailed, sharply delineated starships, majestic planetary backgrounds, and airbrushed spacescapes'.[2] Such a setting draws

the game close to a historical period in which space travel and exploration captured the imagination of both the public and designers. Following the Moon Landing of 1969 and NASA's 'Blue Marble' photograph of 1972, otherworldly imagery proliferated in the popular imagination, not least through NASA's own visual explorations of life in outer space presented in its 1977 publication *Space Settlements: A Design Study*,[3] involving artists such as Don Davis and Rick Guidice. As such, *No Man's Sky* is seemingly nostalgic for a point in history where the possibilities of otherworldly exploration were arguably more exciting and visually striking than they might be today.

Hello Games' hosting of the Galactic Atlas emphasizes one of the important social mechanics of *No Man's Sky*, which is the ability to communicate and share locations with others across the universe. Given the nature of the procedural generation used in the game, without such interfaces players might never encounter one another. This has allowed forms of community to flourish within the game, with a series of alliances and groups that have come to constitute 'Civilized Space' – regions with defined and collaborative populations of players. Vast maps of all these civilizations have been documented by the game's community.[4] By using this information to visualize the path through galaxies as a linear journey (which is the way the game typically requires players to navigate), we can see that there is a heavy weighting towards Euclid, the first galaxy of the game and the one that has become by far the most socialized space [Fig. 2]. The second most populated galaxy is Eissentam, a 'lush' galaxy type that produces the most visually interesting and hospitable planets. As we can see from this mapping, there are vast parts of the universe that remain untouched by Civilized Space to this day, perhaps demonstrating the labour of jumping between galaxies and the desire for socialization.

1   Grant Duncan, 'The Art Direction of No Man's Sky', GDC 2015, youtube.com/watch?v=v4Q_chMbcAE.

2   Steve Holland, *Sci-Fi Art: A Graphic History* (Lewes: Ilex, 2009), 60.

3   National Aeronautics and Space Administration, *Space Settlements: A Design Study* (Washington, DC: US Government Printing Office, 1977).

4   No Man's Sky Fandom, 'Civilized Space Maps', nomanssky.fandom.com/wiki/Civilized_Space_Maps.

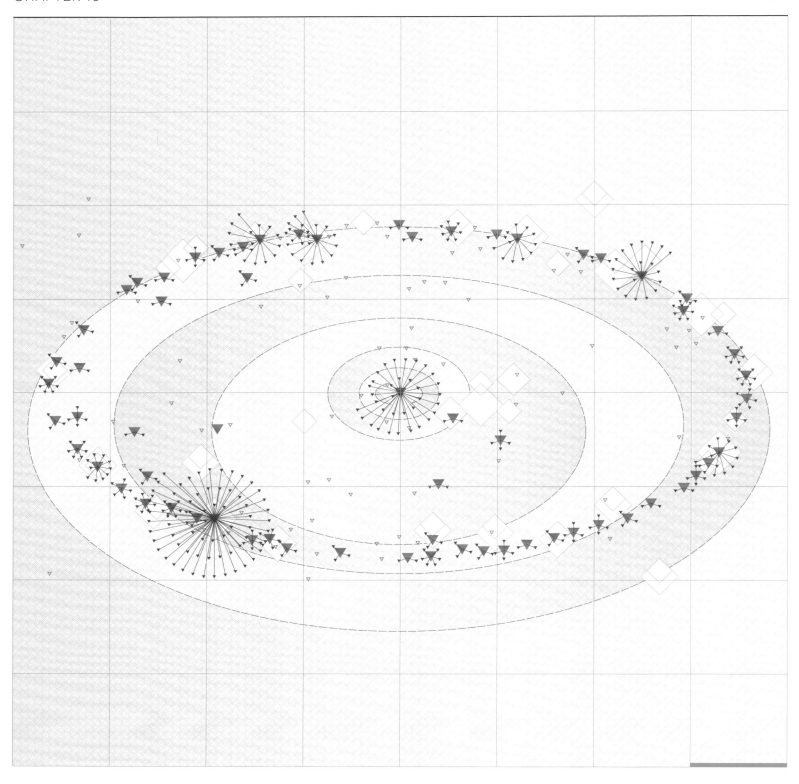

1

A map of the Euclid Galaxy, showing star systems
and planets logged by the community on the
Galactic Atlas.

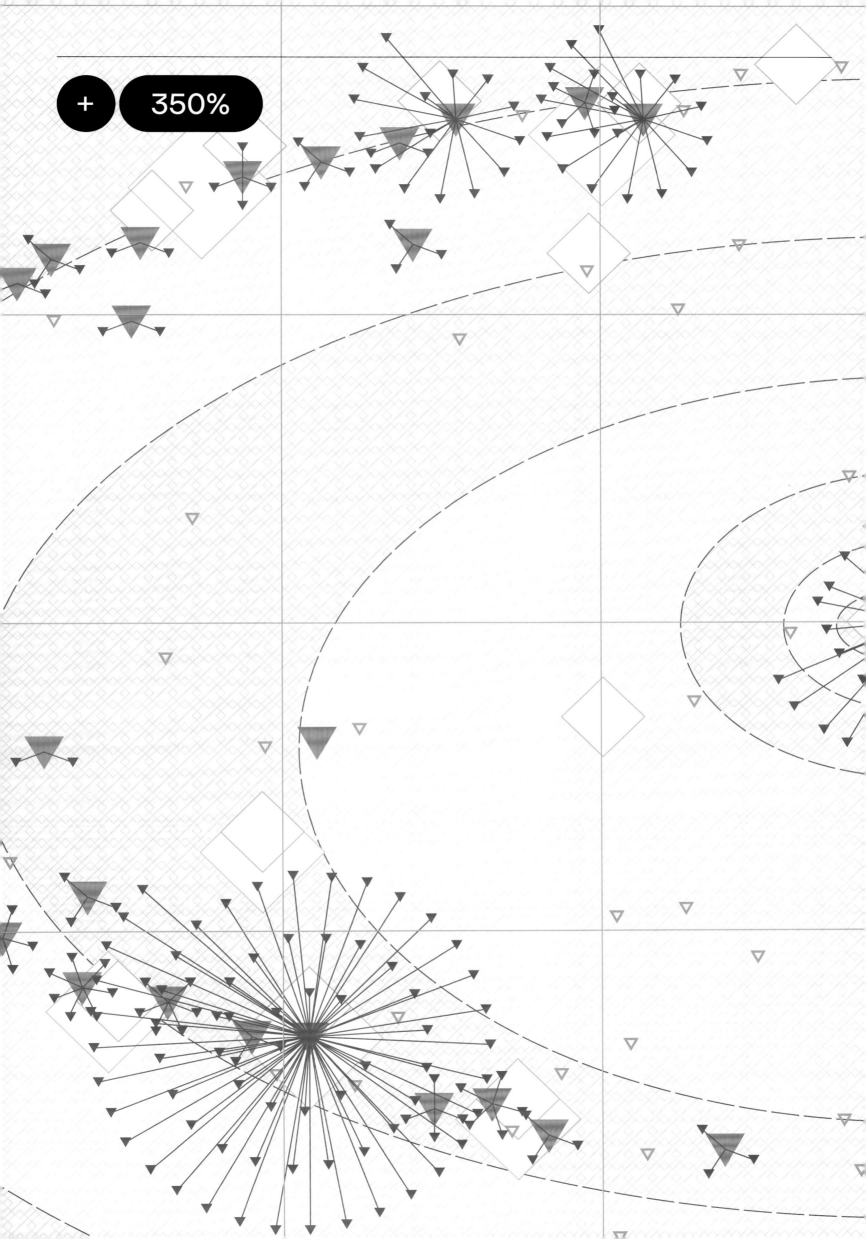

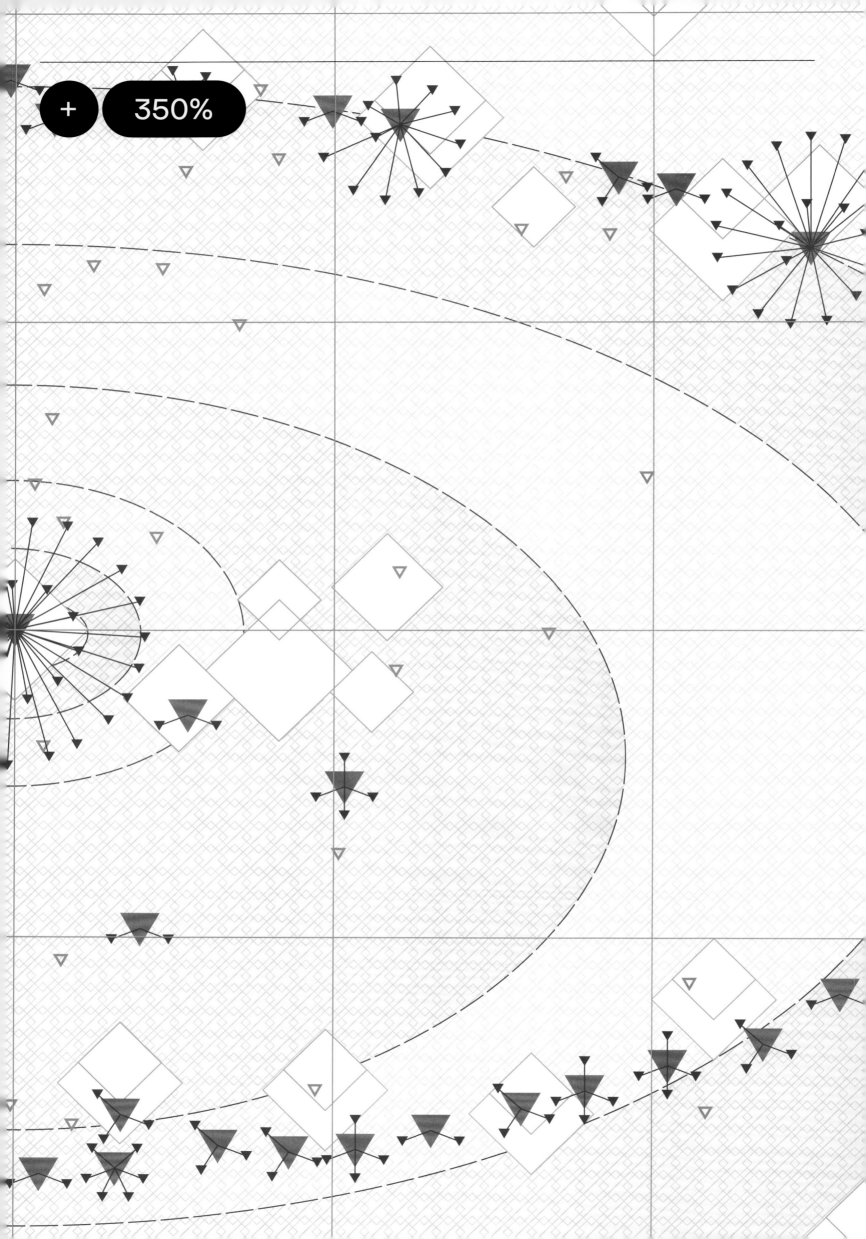

+ 350%

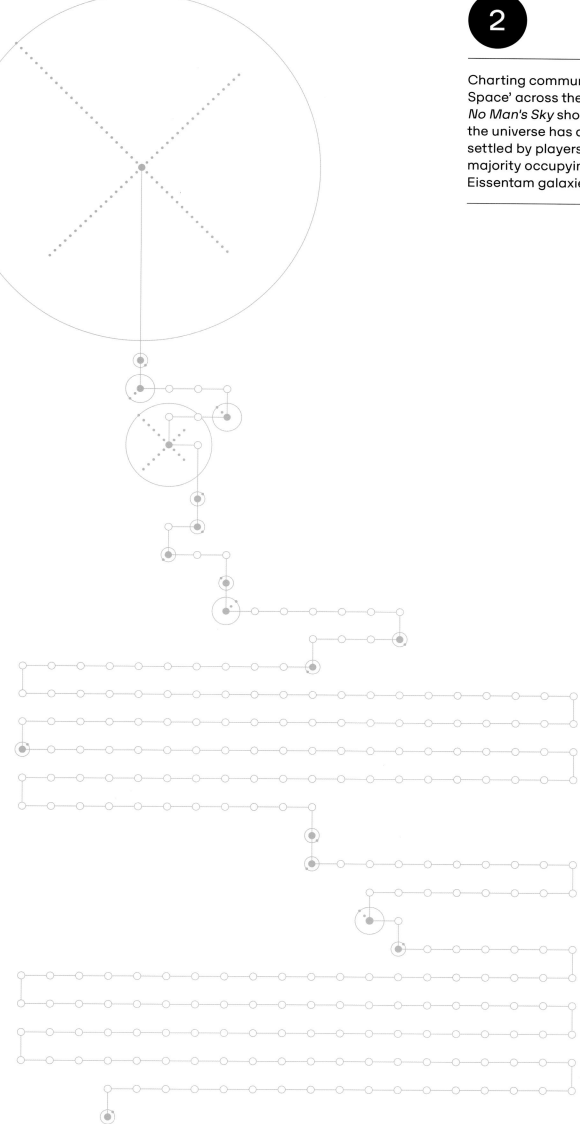

Charting communities in 'Civilized Space' across the 255 galaxies of *No Man's Sky* shows how little of the universe has actually been settled by players, with the vast majority occupying the Euclid and Eissentam galaxies.

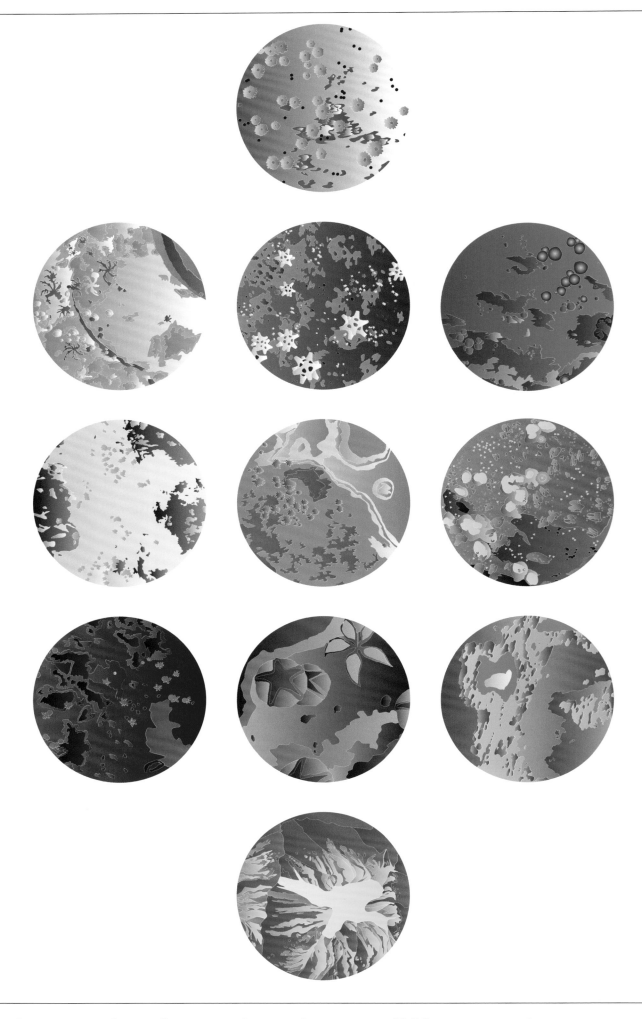

Visual samples from the eleven different planetary biomes used in procedural generation. Every planet encountered in the game will be some derivation of these overarching logics.

10.2   Material Economies

While galaxy types define the regions, star systems, and planets within them, when the player touches their starship down, they will meet a procedurally generated world based on one of eleven different biomes. Biome types define elements such as the weather and environment, ecosystems and landscape formations. By sampling a series of different planets based on each of these biomes, we can get a visual sense of the environments they produce, from Earth-like 'lush' planets to 'dead' planets that are similar to our own Moon [Fig. 3]. Much like real-world discussions between scientists concerning the number and scale of biomes existing on Earth,[5] in *No Man's Sky* biomes have historically been flexible, undergoing a series of revisions as the game is updated. There have been fundamental reworkings of how planets are generated during the game's post-launch development, resulting in a series of 'galaxy resets' that have seen entire planets change. Archaeological scholars such as Andrew Reinhard have studied such resets, identifying how 'a large group of human players was displaced by a digital climate change event'.[6]

Star systems are broken down into four overriding types, each of which contain planets with a different primary resource. Within these, each planet has a unique composition defined by its biome, and they possess various combinations of natural minerals. While these resources differ from planet to planet, their function as part of the crafting and economy within the game remains consistent, meaning that planets in different star systems are tied together into a network of landscape exploitation [Fig. 4]. This organizational structure combined with that of the biome means that some planets may have a very high concentration of a specific and valuable resource, attracting players towards them and turning whole planets into networked industrial zones for mining and extraction.

Once a player lands on a planet, they will undoubtedly examine its physical attributes while also calculating its resources through a process of scanning using their Multi-Tool's visor. Here the landscape becomes quantified in terms of elements that are of use. This might be deposits of materials, hazardous flora and animals or caches of information. Ships and vehicles can also be outfitted with scanners to help with finding further points of interest. While the mechanics of scanning assist in discovery, once a planet has been thoroughly logged, the landscape becomes understood predominantly as a set of resources to be exploited by the player [Fig. 5]. Players will continue to use their scanners and visors to navigate between resources marked on the landscape, making their movements highly strategic.

Players are rewarded for the identification and indexing of plants, minerals and animals – providing them with a motivation for discovery beyond the utility of the materials they harvest. By examining matter from one star system within the game, we can see that it forms a network of resources that closely tie to the logic of the game's systems. In the game's 'Normal' mode, players will invariably encounter easy sources of materials such as Carbon, Sodium, Oxygen and Ferrite Dust that are key to the harvesting, life-support and building technologies they carry. While there is variance in species across planets, there is a backbone of materials that runs across the natural landscape, allowing the player to stay moving and productive. In this context, all planets become 'habitable' [Fig. 6]. In contrast, the game's 'Survival' and 'Permadeath' difficulty modes increase the scarcity of resources, making survival less trivial. As these essential elements will still be available in some quantities, continued exploration from planet to planet is always viable.

5   One Earth, 'Bioregions 2020', oneearth.org/
    bioregions-2020/.

6   Andrew Reinhard, 'Archeology of Abandoned Human
    Settlements in No Man's Sky: A New Approach to
    Recording and Preserving User-Generated Content
    in Digital Games', in *Games and Culture*, vol. 16, no. 7
    (New York: SAGE, 2021), 857.

Mapping a small sample of thirty-six star systems visited in the game demonstrates how they are connected by common resources, with some defined by the star system type and others varying from planet to planet.

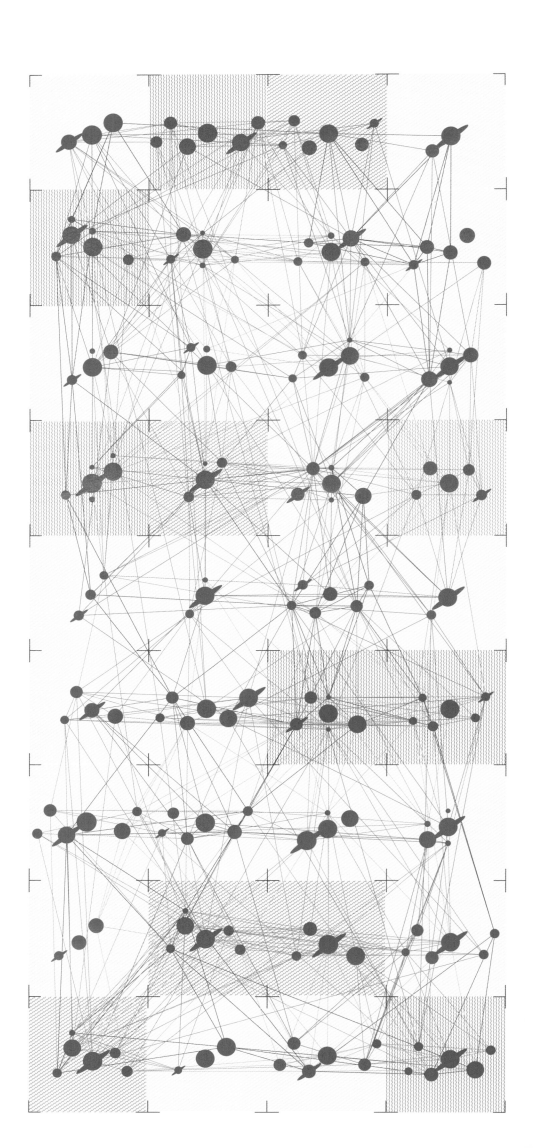

Seen through the player's analysis visor, planets become encoded as landscapes of material utility, with deposits of resources or points of interest highlighted to enable a more efficient exploitation of the natural environment.

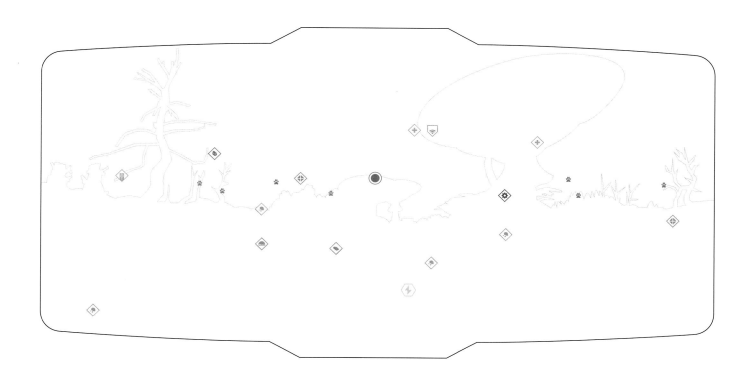

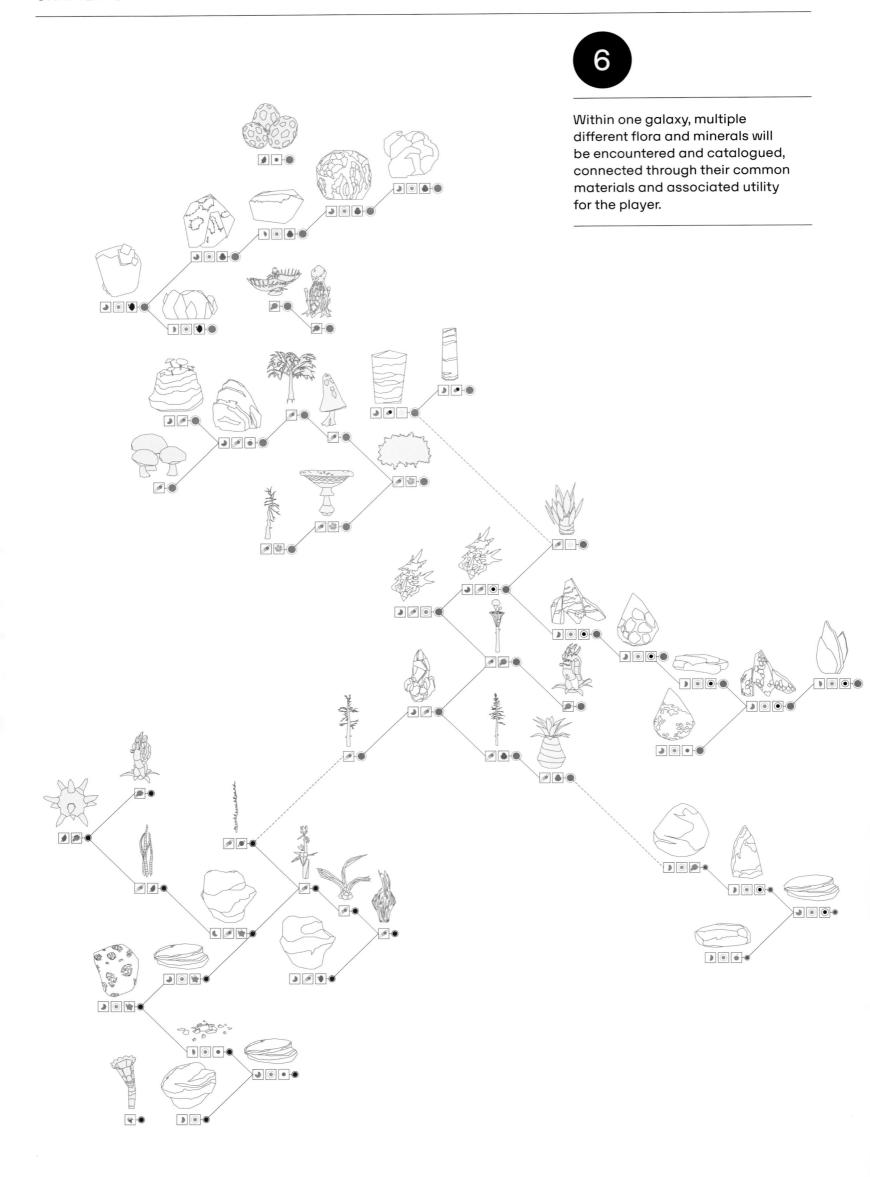

6

Within one galaxy, multiple different flora and minerals will be encountered and catalogued, connected through their common materials and associated utility for the player.

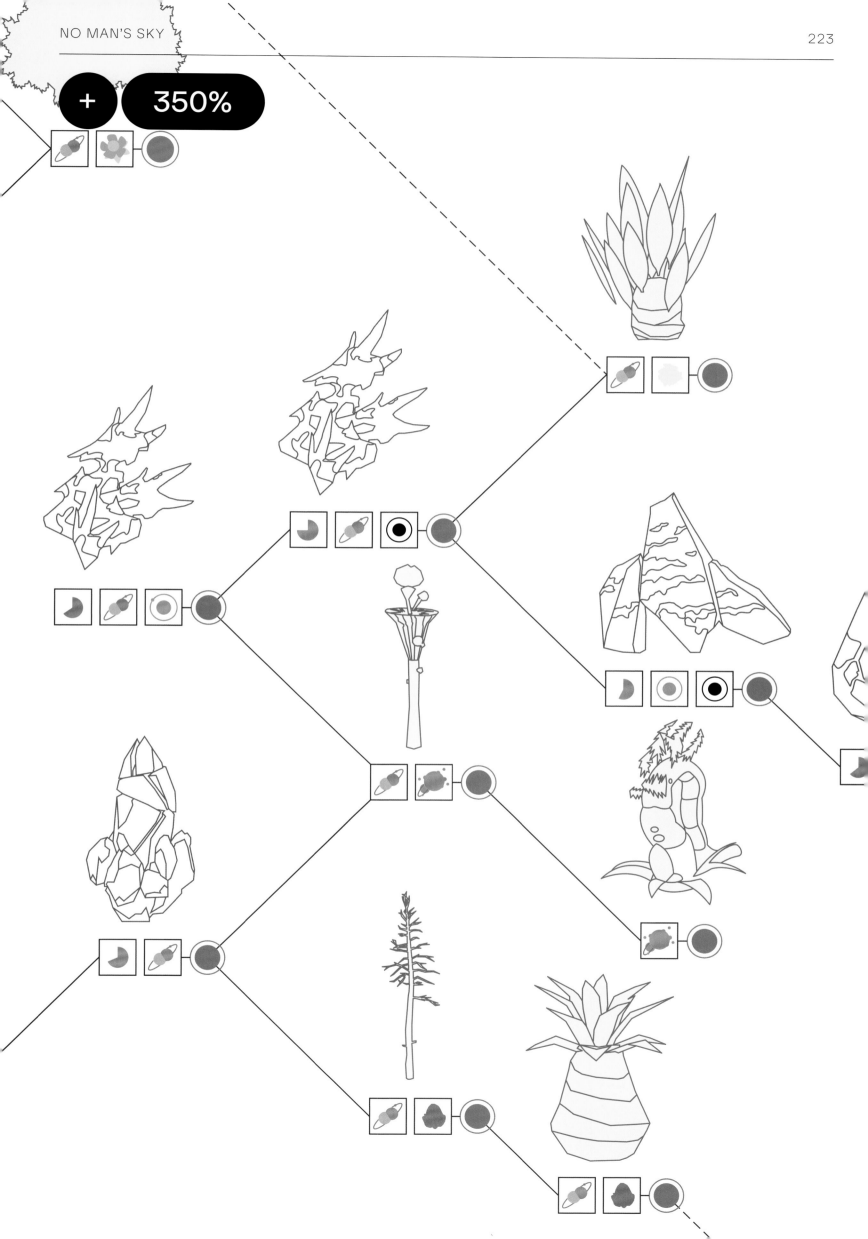

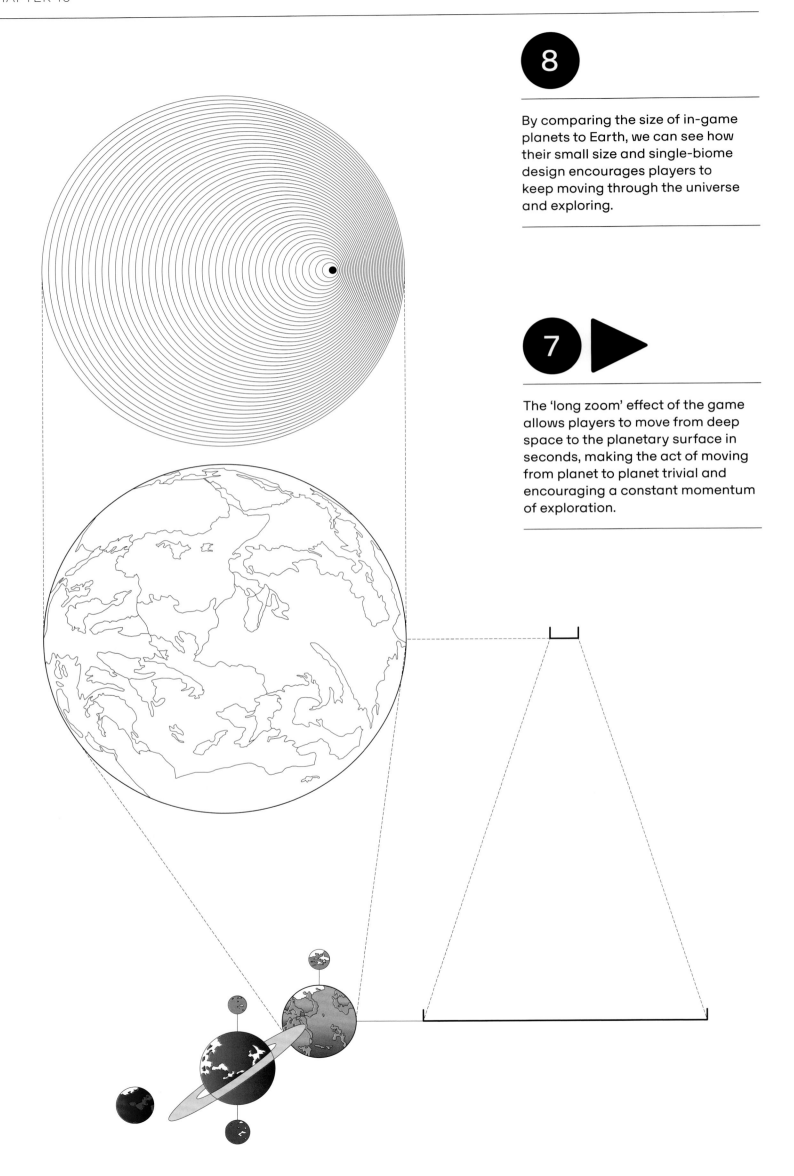

8

By comparing the size of in-game planets to Earth, we can see how their small size and single-biome design encourages players to keep moving through the universe and exploring.

7 ▶

The 'long zoom' effect of the game allows players to move from deep space to the planetary surface in seconds, making the act of moving from planet to planet trivial and encouraging a constant momentum of exploration.

10.3   Long Zoom Landscapes

One of *No Man's Sky*'s striking features is the ability to travel all the way from deep space to a planet's surface in one smooth movement. Players can scan a remote planet in the distance and have their boots on the floor ready to explore within a matter of seconds, before jetting back off into the universe again. The ease with which starships escape and enter planetary atmospheres incites players to keep discovering what is produced by the game's algorithm. This is facilitated by systems that use 'Uber Noise'[7] to generate planets as vast spheres enveloped by a 128-m (419-ft-11⅜-in.)-thick crust of voxel-based terrain that can be manipulated and mined by the player. According to the developers, voxels are 1 m (3 ft 3⅜ in.) in size and broken into 36-m (118 ft 1⅜ in) cubic regions, allowing for the voxels to be polygonized into a more naturalistic-looking terrain [Fig. 7].[8] Various 'level-of-detail' systems allow for the vast worlds to be streamed around the movement of the player. In its entirety, this process evokes the idea of the 'long zoom',[9] Steven Johnson's way of describing our modern reliance on satellite imagery that can take us from a view of our back garden to a planetary scale in seconds, and the aesthetic condition of being able to visualize our world in vastly different orders of magnitude. Through the generation of new planets and the ability to seamlessly jump between them, long-distance scale can be trivialized. This suggests that the game attempts, as Alenda Chang argues, 'to make the complexity of infinite worlds accessible'.[10]

While the full extents of *No Man's Sky*'s universe are vast and unknowable, players have come to understand that the scale of planets can be calculated through methods such as the placing of beacons at poles to record distance, or simply circumnavigating the planet on foot. As in-game units are not explicitly dimensioned to reality there are questions regarding the accuracy of such methods; however, 1u appears to map to 1 m (3 ft 3⅜ in.), given that looking straight down with our in-game scanner records the floor at 1.6–1.7 m (5 ft 3 in– 5 ft 6⅞ in.) below our eyeline (and that building elements use a 5u grid that maps to 5m (16 ft 4⅞ in) rather well). In a post entitled '2 Years of Math and Discoveries in 1 Post', Reddit user 'Ittriumn' details planetary calculations using

beacons that place the average scale of a *No Man's Sky* planet at roughly 1/49 that of Earth.[11] Through a visual comparison using an in-game star system we can see the orders of magnitude in difference that this represents [Fig. 8]. The scale of these planets reinforces their single-biome logic and provides a greater number of smaller expanses to drive the player perpetually onward. Rather than a vast and varied planet, players move between many smaller, discrete planetary environments.

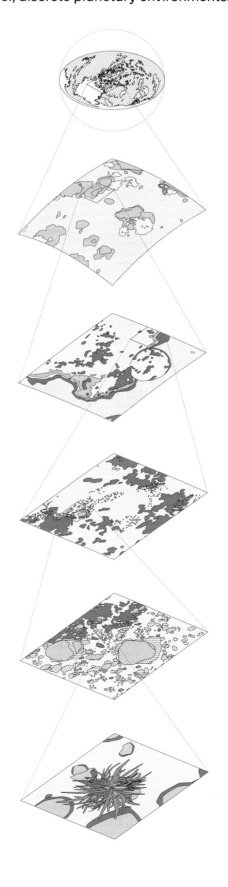

7   Sean Murray, 'Building Worlds in No Man's Sky Using Math(s)', GDC 2017, youtube.com/watch?v=C9RyEiEzMiU.
8   Inness McKendrick, 'Continuous World Generation in No Man's Sky', GDC 2017, youtube.com/watch?v=sCRzxEEcO2Y.
9   Steven Johnson, 'The Long Zoom', *The New York Times*, nytimes.com/2006/10/08/magazine/08games.html.
10 Alenda Chang, *Playing Nature* (Minneapolis & London: University of Minnesota Press, 2019), 100.
11 Reddit user Ittriumn, '2 Years of Math and Discoveries in 1 Post', reddit.com/r/NoMansSkyTheGame/comments/8a5326/2_years_of_math_and_discoveries_in_1_post_ittriumn/.

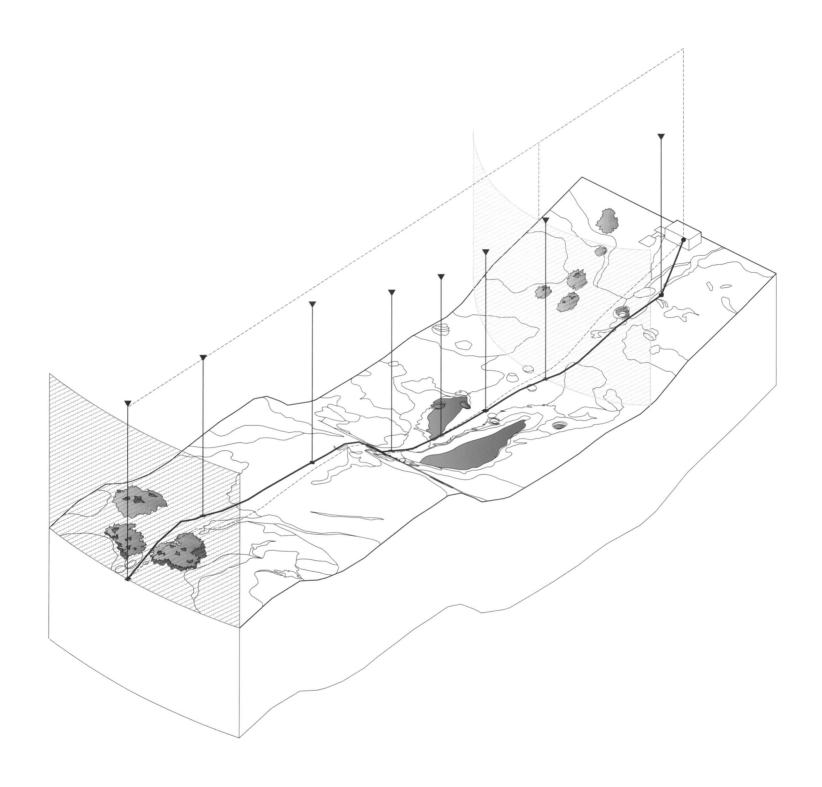

9

Isometric diagram showing how players can extend the borders of their planetary bases by placing single small objects at the periphery of the existing boundary, growing the edges step by step.

10.4 Extraterrestrial Architecture

Once players discover a planet, they can begin inhabiting it by engaging with the game's sprawling building system. This provides over 600 different unlockable blueprints to construct, power and decorate their bases. In reality, contemporary concepts for extra-terrestrial building have focused on techniques such as moon-dust deposition and 3D printing;[12] however, *No Man's Sky* utilizes a component-based system that is again reminiscent of 1970s innovations in space architecture. Fred Scharmen describes how NASA's 1975 settlement guide 'recommends using prefabricated standardized panels and frames',[13] and the game's components evoke this – even referring to a 'Universal Building Standards 2.3b' for compatibility. These bases are notionally limited to a 300u radius around the Base Computer system at their centre, establishing a set of restrictions that govern where players can build. As with many games that facilitate player creativity, the community has sought to subvert some of these limits. Numerous online guides have demonstrated[14] how the initial restrictions of a base can be extended to around 1000u through 'pushing' the extents of land by placing singular objects. Applying such techniques by placing single floor-plate elements at the base's edge, we can see how players can capture more territory step by step, bringing it under their direct control [Fig. 9]. These techniques effectively allow the player to colonize more of the planet through the placement of seemingly disconnected objects that confer ownership through mere presence.

Despite the open field of space given to us, *No Man's Sky* does provide other 'fixed' points to orientate ourselves towards. The most notable of these might be the space stations we encounter, with their uniform interior spaces and a consistent set of amenities. Further to this is the Space Anomaly, a giant Death Star-like space station and social hub that players can summon to their position. By activating the 'quick menu' in space, the Space Anomaly is projected directly to the player's targeting reticule, warping into view as a giant ball with an access point at its centre. As players enter, we find the interior of the structure is a long, rectangular hall with various types of buttresses, pipes and circuits disappearing into the distance. By comparing the size of the entrance on the station's surface to the space within, it becomes hard to reconcile the inside and outside of the space station, perhaps emphasizing its anomalous existence [Fig. 10]. Such an interplay between inside and out is common in such forms, with Scharmen arguing that 'the ineffable object' such as the Death Star (or in this case the Anomaly) 'must break down into accessible structure. The thing must become a world'.[15]

This manifests in the interior of the Anomaly, which functions as a permanent and shared space for players, an extra-terrestrial lobby, where we can see others land, trade and warp to featured bases built by other players. By surveying the interior of the Anomaly through screenshots, we can build an indicative floorplan of its facilities, demonstrating how it works as a series of hubs providing different facilities for players to refine their equipment and abilities [Fig. 11]. With its language of neon strip lighting and smoothed 'greebles', the interior of the Anomaly is somewhat different to the generic, functional space stations we would normally encounter – marking this shared space as something outside everyday space life.

12 Foster + Partners, 'Lunar Habitation', fosterandpartners. com/projects/lunar-habitation/.

13 Fred Scharmen, *Space Settlements* (New York: Columbia Books on Architecture and the City, 2019), 298.

14 Spoon, 'How to Extend the Limits of your Base – No Man's Sky Guide – Frontiers Gameplay', youtube.com/ watch?v=OVhvSO2TrYA.

15 Fred Scharmen, *Space Settlements* (New York: Columbia Books on Architecture and the City, 2019), 307.

10

Drawing exploring the relationship between the monumental Space Anomaly and the player, who can summon the station at will before exploring its large interior, which serves as a social space.

11

Plan of the Space Anomaly interior derived from screenshots, showing how the station functions as a social space and also provides many amenities, allowing the player to significantly enhance their capabilities in every aspect of the game.

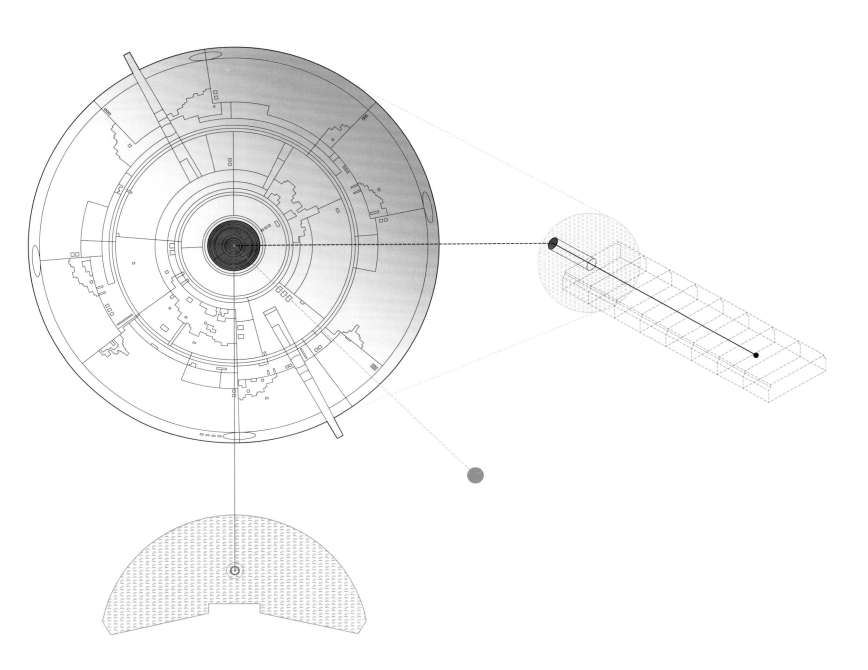

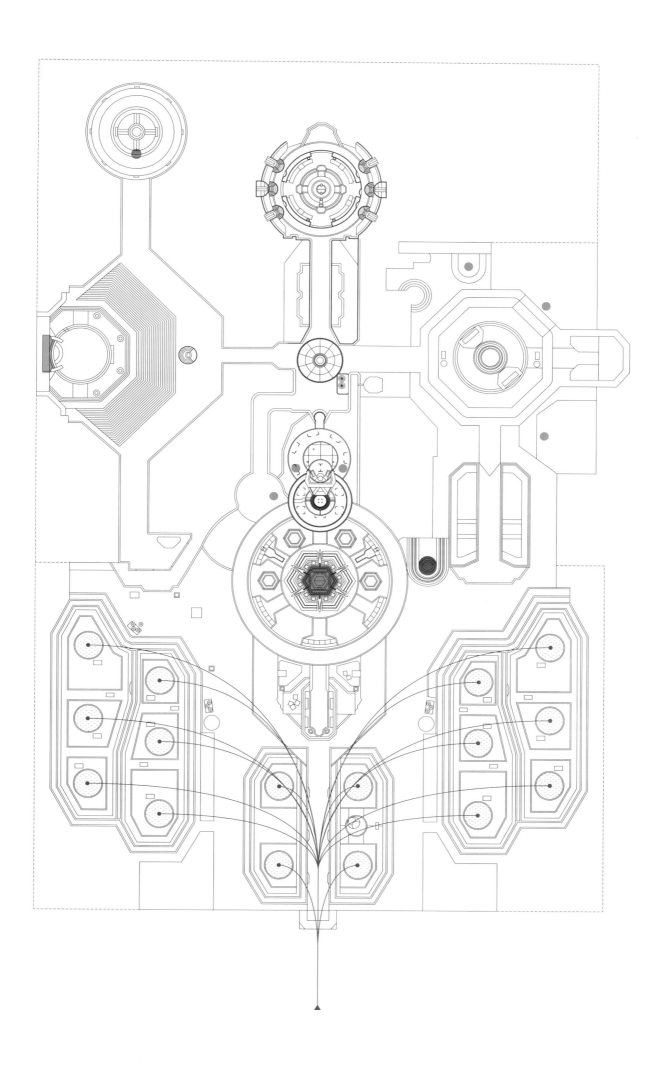

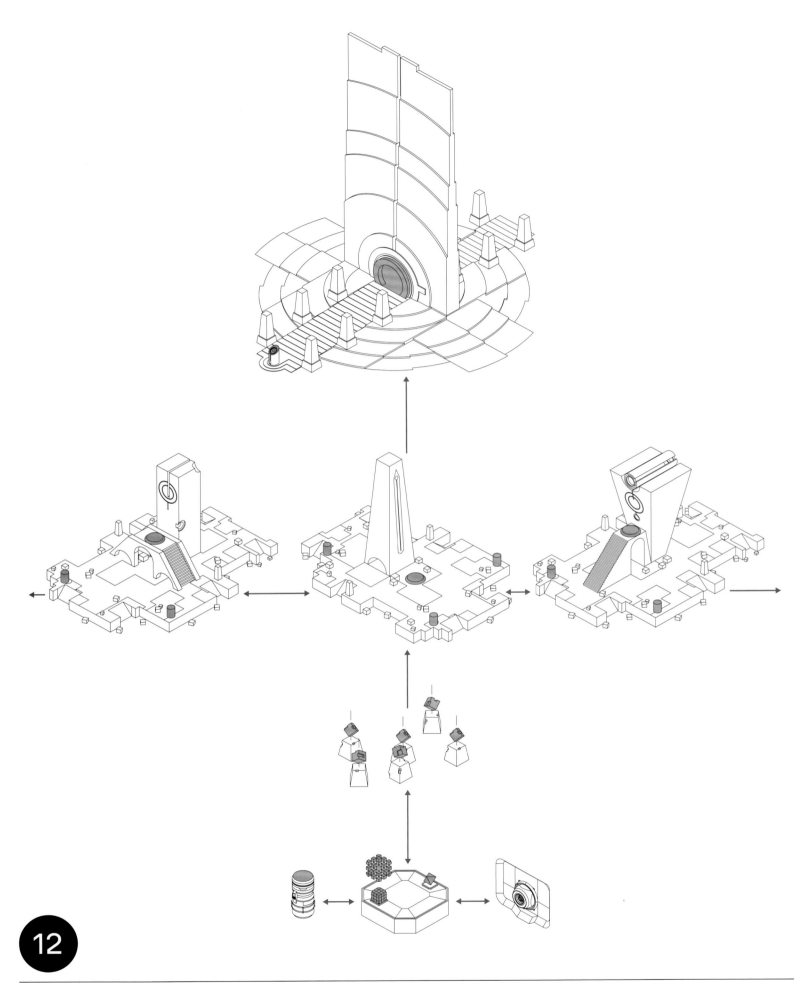

12

Network diagram demonstrating the processes typically required to locate a Portal and enable the game's quick-travel system. Players will seek out alien structures that provide clues to Portal locations.

10.5   Shared Space

The sharing of planets, facilities and experiences in *No Man's Sky* is largely predicated on glyphs as a system of communication. When players take screenshots in-game, glyph codes are displayed in the bottom left, allowing others to find the depicted location. Glyphs are the encoded inputs used in Portals, which forms the game's fast-travel system, allowing players to visit new worlds without physically journeying to them. Gaining access to Portals is not a trivial activity and requires much exploration. While each planet possesses a Portal, its location is not marked, making random encounters unlikely. Instead, players typically scan planetary surfaces for Salvaged Data and trade this on space stations for cartographic maps of alien structures. These lead to Monoliths that, following a riddle, can provide the position of a Portal. As such, simply locating the infrastructure for fast travel requires a significant amount of resource gathering and exploration [Fig. 12]. It also celebrates a typical and beloved trope of science-fiction that *The Encyclopedia of Science Fiction* terms a 'macrostructure' or 'big dumb object', involving 'the discovery, usually by humans, of vast enigmatic constructions […] built by a mysterious, now-disappeared race of Alien intellectual giants'.[16]

Upon finding a Portal, players must also learn sixteen glyphs to be able to 'dial' a known destination. While these glyphs can be obtained through the main storyline, there are many guides and walkthroughs for obtaining them quicker, by visiting 'grave sites' of Travellers – strange characters met on space stations. For example, the site 'Xaines World'[17] provides a list of planets near space stations containing Travellers, 'dialable' with a minimal glyph 'vocabulary'. Following these instructions, new forms of social space cluster around these sites, not unlike a form of pilgrimage. It is common to find Communications Stations gathered around the Portal, with motivational messages from other players. It becomes clear that within the vast universe, these are well-travelled paths. Many 'grave sites' also have infrastructure built around them, from vast 'support centres' providing vehicles and resources, through to more simple structures that are built around the graves themselves as a form of mausoleum [Fig. 13].

While facilities might be helpful, the simpler and more monumental structures can feel contemplative; moments of respite in a large and unforgiving universe.

The messages indicated by floating Communications Stations also demonstrate how *No Man's Sky* attempts to offer us certain social and indexical anchor points within the universe. These have been a key part of virtual archaeologists such as Reinhard's research, providing traces of human activity in worlds since lost.[18] While navigating on a planet's surface we can encounter messages in the landscape in their actual locations, but these messages also persist at a planetary scale should we leave and jet into space. Here the game maintains a certain density of visual information – consistently highlighting social points, significant bases and so on [Fig. 14]. This allows for points of interest to be maintained across vast distances, giving a strong impression of 'life' on planets, drawing players towards them.

16 'Macrostructures', *The Encyclopedia of Science Fiction*, sf-encyclopedia.com/entry/macrostructures.

17 xainesworld.com/no-mans-sky-portal-glyphs-fast-travelers-graves/

18 Andrew Reinhard, 'Archeology of Abandoned Human Settlements in No Man's Sky: A New Approach to Recording and Preserving User-Generated Content in Digital Games', in *Games and Culture*, vol. 16, no. 7 (New York: SAGE, 2021), 868.

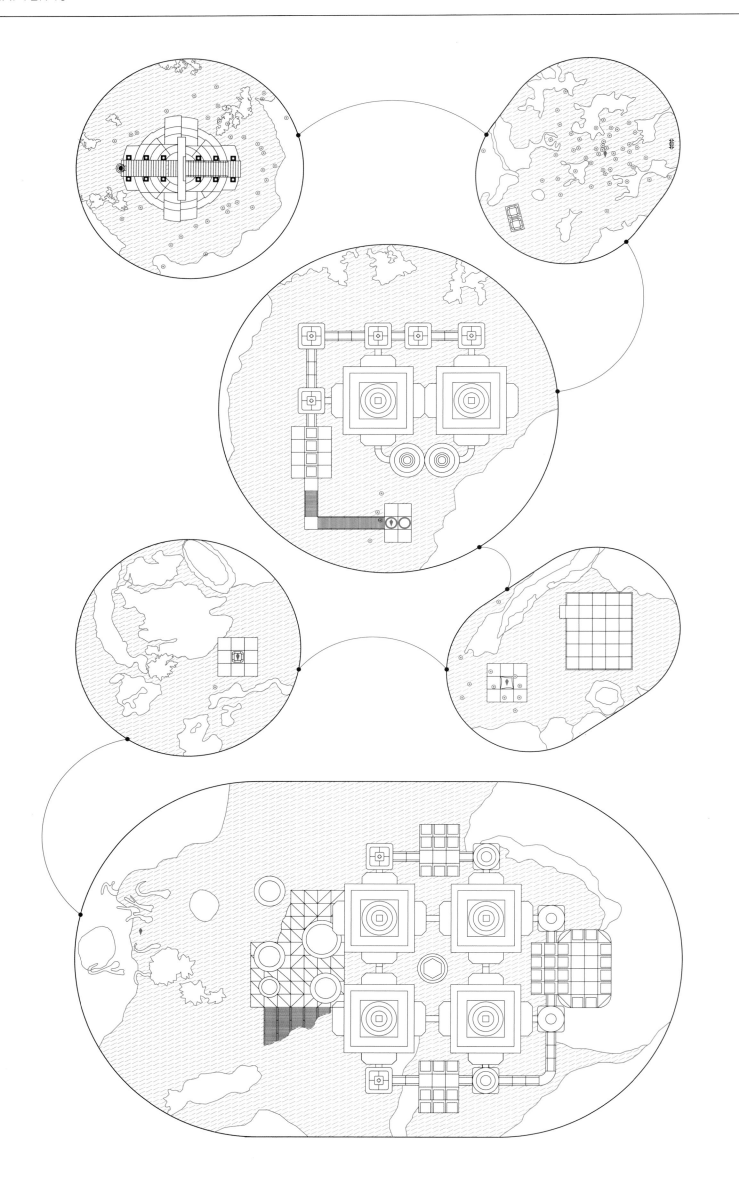

Examples of 'pilgrimage' sites formed around Portals and Traveller Graves by players hunting Portal Glyphs. Here we can see both 'support centres' providing amenities and symbolic structures designed as mausoleums for the grave sites.

14

Diagram showing the relative scales of communication notifications on the planetary surface and in deep space. This allows players to identify social spaces on planets at vast distances.

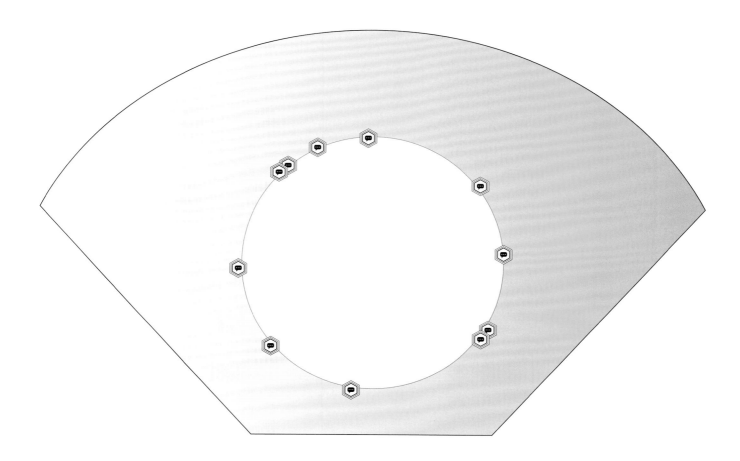

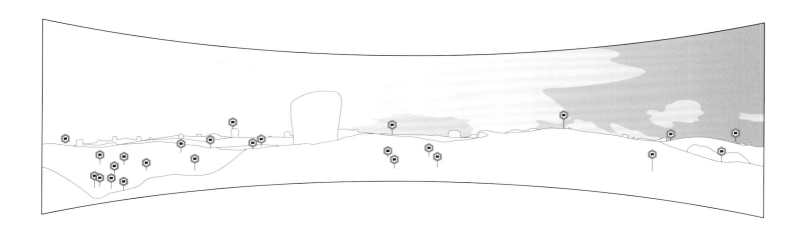

15

Popular types of environments as shared on internet communities, including Earth-like planets, ship farming stations, Activated Indium farms and curious 'megabuilds'. Through Portal glyph codes and planetary positions, other players can visit as galactic tourists.

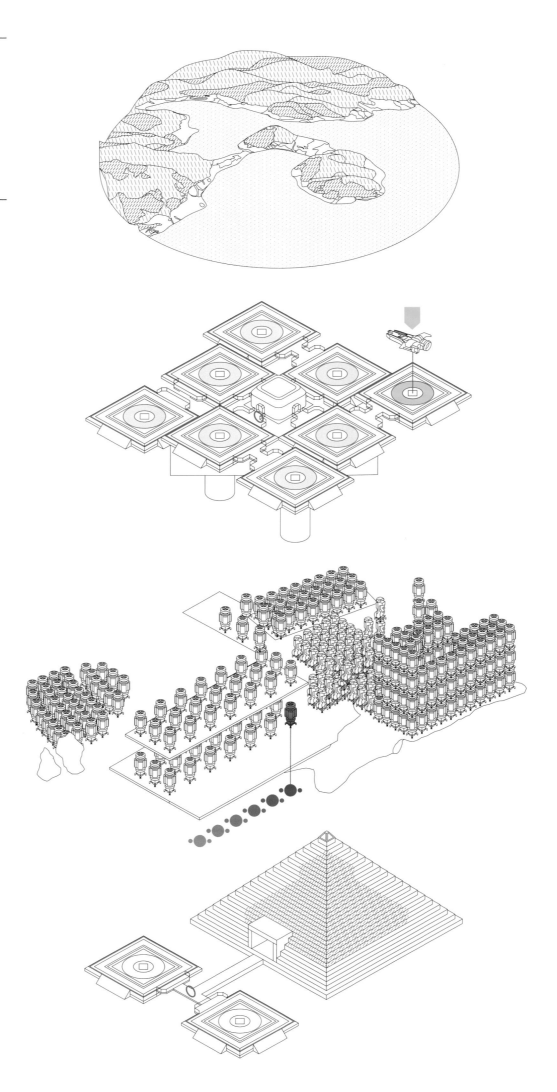

Once players gain the ability to fully program destinations to the Portal, another layer of *No Man's Sky*'s social space unlocks – the free communication of addresses connecting various parts of the game's community and economy. By looking at the top-ranked post on the 'NMSCoordinateExchange' Reddit (with over 164,000 subscribers), we can discern the types of places people tend to share and visit through the Portal navigation system. One of the most popular post themes is beautiful planets, particularly those with Earth-like features (including one resembling the Windows XP desktop background). Other well-shared locations include planets in star systems that spawn rare starships or freighters. These systems often contain user-made 'ship farms' – structures containing many landing pads to attract rare ships for purchase. One system boasts more than forty bases just dedicated to farming a rare black fighter ship. Certain planets are extremely rich in expensive minerals such as Activated Indium, supporting players in the construction of huge facilities for extracting and sharing these resources, and players often compete to have the largest capacity processing facilities [Fig. 15]. While these huge structures can make the game run slowly due to their complexity, they can also provide hundreds of millions of units from a quick visit. Additionally, posts containing 'megabuilds' and unusual base architecture remain popular, such as a giant pyramid built by Reddit user Freeherder that contains a maze within its sarcophagus.

In each of these cases, players are searching for stability in a near-infinite universe: a place that looks like home, somewhere to locate a specific ship, or a place to marvel at the idiosyncratic design ideas of another explorer. The development of *No Man's Sky* from a simpler exploration game to a fully formed community has, for some, moved it away from its emphasis on frontierism. But the impact of this is that players no longer encounter only a universe formed through procedural complexity, but one that is inhabited by people creating emergence through the societies and structures they build, nestled on small rocks deep in space, waiting for the next reboot to come.

☐ Portals:

1 per Planet
16 Glyphs
281Tn Combos

Sections

PERSONA 5

Details

Year	2016
Developer	Atlus
	P Studio
Publisher	Atlus

Platforms

PlayStation: 3/4/5

By connecting the minutiae of daily life in Tokyo to the fantastical world of the Metaverse, *Persona 5* takes its compact streets, minimarts and vending machines, reinventing them as amenities for the otherworldly.

☐ Map:

25 Neighbourhoods
6 Explorable Districts
10 Transit Lines

11.1 The Fantastical Everyday

Many games transport us to strange imaginary worlds where, as players, we gain new and unexpected capabilities. Yet these worlds may also be accessed through the spaces of our everyday. We play games sitting in living rooms, at a desk or on a subway train. In the world of *Persona 5*, a Japanese role-playing game (JRPG), this relationship forms the very core of the game and its world. The player is a high-school student known as Joker, and *Persona 5* revolves around a team of teenagers named the Phantom Thieves who attempt to repair Japanese society by changing the hearts of criminals involved in a governmental conspiracy. To do this they travel, by means of a phone app, to Palaces, buildings that represent the subconscious 'distortion' of a person's corrupted thoughts. Palaces are one part of a giant Metaverse, a parallel world created from the collective unconscious of all people. Yet even the use of the app, described by *Persona 5*'s director, Katsura Hashino, as potentially 'too mundane' for a game[1] serves to reinforce the relationship between normality and the fantastical, often sick, spaces created by the mind.

These journeys into cognition are offset against the day-to-day life of a high-school student, with players able to study for exams, date, play baseball at batting cages or visit the cinema. These activities take place across a highly compressed yet recognizable version of Tokyo, traversed by means of a subway map [Fig. 1]. Many of the locations within *Persona 5* are recreations of real places such as Shibuya's station square or Akihabara's back streets. As players explore the city, they mingle with passers-by, chattering Tokyoites represented as simplified figures without full faces that are visually distinguishable from the main characters. As the game's art director Masayoshi Sutou explains, this visual approach enables *Persona 5* to represent the bustle of Tokyo and the anonymity this can provide, while also maintaining the 'picaresque'[2] narrative centred around Joker and the Phantom Thieves.

By creating an interface between everyday, often mundane spaces and heroic adventures in the Metaverse, *Persona 5* encourages us to look closely at the relationships and places we inhabit in our daily lives, while at the same time considering how far the human mind and its depths can take us from this.

1   Personacentral.com, 'Persona 5 Director Katsura Hashino Interview About Development Process and Themes', translation of original Japanese 4gamer.net interview, personacentral.com/persona-5-director-hashino-development-interview/.

2   Ibid.

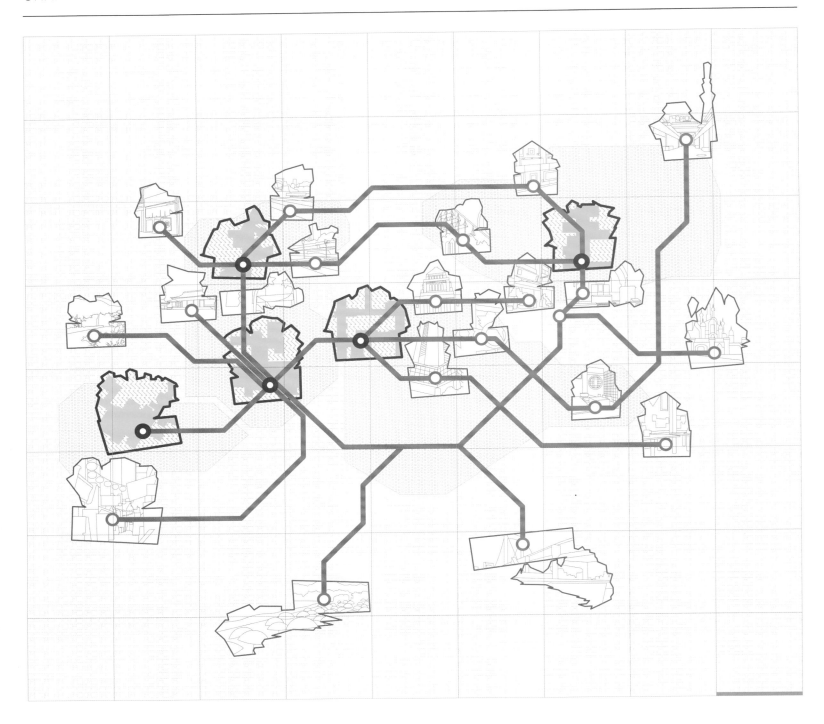

1

This version of *Persona 5*'s subway map, demonstrates the distinction between the areas of the game that are fully explorable by players and other areas that are experienced only through social activities and 'flat' depictions.

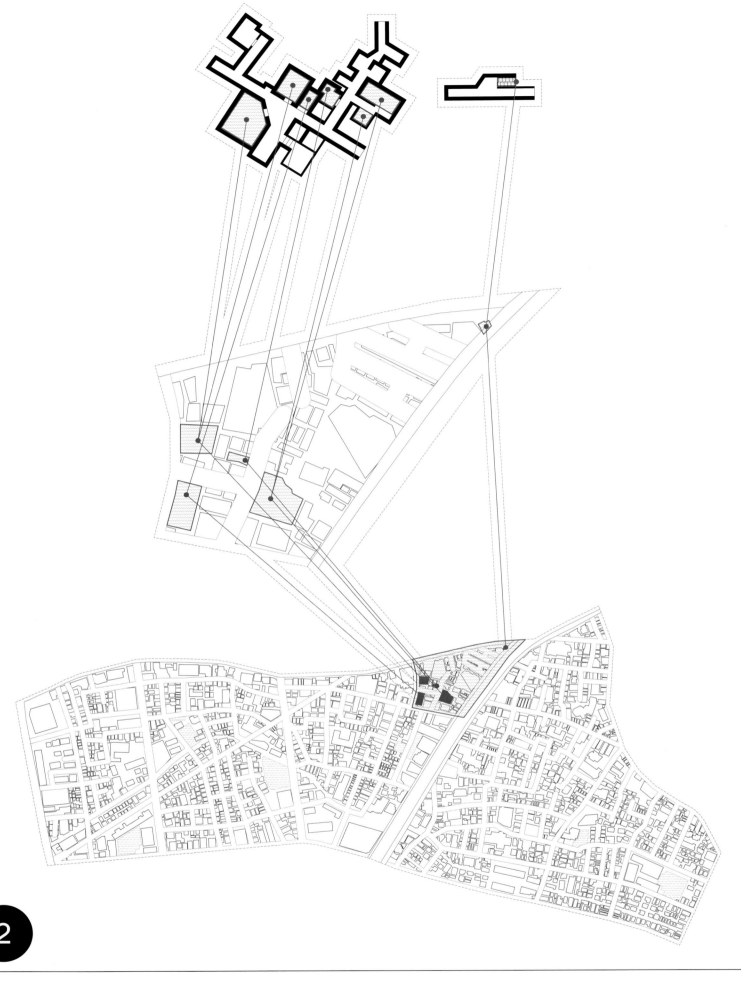

2

Comparative mapping of Yongen-Jaya's spaces to the real-world Sangenjaya, indicating how the close clustering of buildings in reality carries through into the space-planning of the game.

11.2   Yongen/Sangen

The main area of the game, where Joker lives, is Yongen-Jaya – a play on the name Sangenjaya, which is a real area in the Setagaya district of Tokyo. As the home neighbourhood, this area provides certain amenities and activities that can fill the time between school and journeys to the Metaverse. As many blog posts and photographic articles have detailed,[3] there is a very close relationship between the in-game neighbourhood and its real counterpart. While the streets have been somewhat compressed, by comparing their real position to that in the game, the real area does indeed have a similar level of density [Fig. 2]. Many local buildings are closely recreated and form part of the game mechanics, providing opportunities to buy equipment or increase Joker's social stats. Sangenjaya has also become a pilgrimage site for fans of the game, who retrace Joker's steps as they seek out these in-game locations.

By examining these buildings through architectural elevation drawings, we can see how closely Yongen-Jaya's architecture references reality while also understanding points of emphasis that demonstrate their function within the game. The local minimart, a yellow-fronted shop called Niku no Hanamasa, becomes the purple Super Muramasa in the game. The scale of the building's façade is compressed horizontally, with the relative proportion of the front door increased, presumably enhancing its visibility to the player [Fig. 3]. The store has no explorable interior – entering only produces a menu of food items to purchase. Traditional minimart confections such as squid snacks or nuts can be bought to heal allies in the Metaverse. Back in Sangenjaya, Niku no Hanamasa is flanked to the left by a small stairway hiding between the produce boxes and an electricity post, leading to the Sangenjaya Batting Center. The same centre appears in the game, where Joker can practise baseball to increase his proficiency, but it is relocated to the right of the façade, making it more visible and bringing it closer to the centre of the map. This move retains the ambiance of the area

while foregrounding the batting centre as a place for 'self-improvement'.

Likewise, the local cinema (which had been demolished by the time of the game's release in September 2016) retains some of the key features of the original building, such as the thin second-floor windows and the large sign on the street-facing corner of the building, while colourful characters have been removed from the façade and the clutter of promotional signs and schedule information boards dispensed with. In this way, the game retains a clear sense of the architectural identity of the local area, while also focusing the player's attention on the entrance, where various genres of films can be watched at different times of year, producing different social stat boosts [Fig. 4].

☐ Real Buildings:

1 Minimart
1 Bathhouse
1 Batting Center
1 Cinema

3   Alexandra Thompson, 'Exploring the Beauty of Japan through Persona 5', ARCGIS.com, storymaps.arcgis. com/stories/a15bc74a9efe42e483e1806c40d8275e.

Elevational studies of the minimart
in Yongen-Jaya, establishing how
its real-world counterpart is altered
and scaled to bring attention
to architectural elements more
pertinent to players. Here we can
also see the everyday items that
define the shop's role in the game.

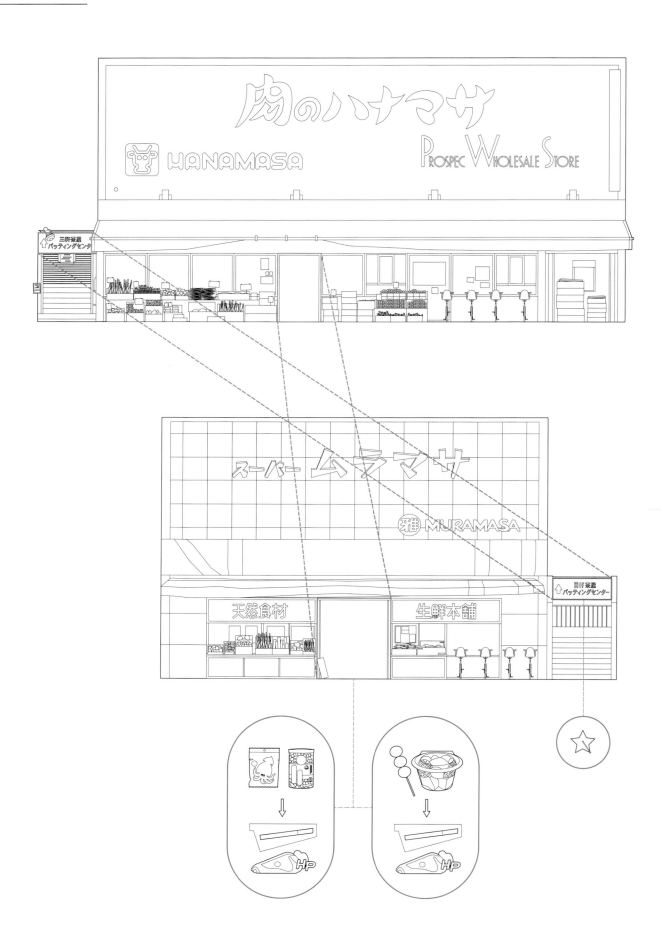

By comparing the in-game and
real-world movie theatres we can
see subtle changes that make
the entrance to the building more
visible – and how the films that Joker
watches in the cinema contribute to
'personal growth'.

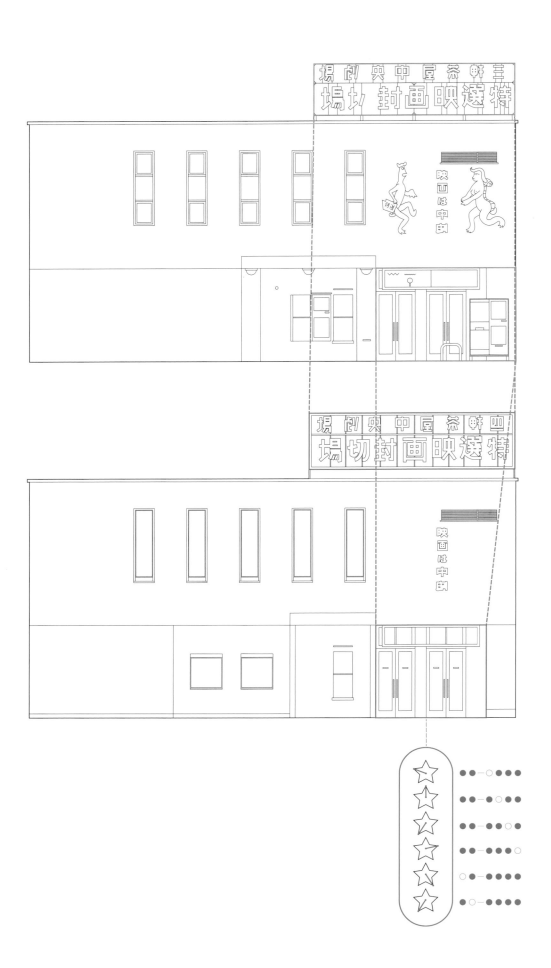

A tiny bathhouse and launderette are also faithfully recreated from their Sangenjaya counterparts, representing key spots for bathing to increase stats, or to clean dirty clothing found in the Metaverse to produce potentially rare armour for a cheap price. By comparing the space connecting these two facilities to its real-world counterpart, we can see some more minor architectural changes, such as moving the sign for the bathhouse and reducing the size of the vending machine covering it, presumably to enhance its legibility for players while still retaining the intimate scale that personifies these local landmarks in Sangenjaya [Fig. 5]. The tiny spaces full of details that we encounter are highly emblematic of Tokyo's urban form, which Hidenobu argues is because 'to find comfort in a compactly unified space is a peculiarity of the Japanese' and 'residents spare no effort in preserving their common environment'.[4]

Each of these spaces is deeply connected to *Persona 5*'s economy of everyday objects and activities producing supernatural effects in the Metaverse. This emphasis on the minutiae of daily life and the spaces in which it takes place is reminiscent of the pioneering work by Japanese architect and sociologist Wajiro Kon, whose drawing studies of Japanese domestic space during the industrialization of Tokyo were compiled into a field of research he termed 'modernology'.[5] Kon's work visually demonstrated the field of objects that combine to form domestic space – and likewise, the buildings of Yongen-Jaya, from the minimart to the electronics shop, all provide Joker with the ability to purchase and collect objects that appear on the face of things to be banal, everyday items, but that deeply enhance the abilities of the Phantom Thieves within the Metaverse.

The close relationship between real-world objects and the spaces where we buy them reinforces the sense of 'Tokyo-ness'. As photographer Kyoichi Tsuzuki has argued, 'when you live in Tokyo, your home is the entire city', to the point where 'you don't even need a refrigerator because there are convenient stores and vending machines on every street corner'.[6] Similarly, the Tokyo we experience as Joker provides everything we need to thrive in the game, from machines selling healing energy drinks, to trinkets we can buy for a crush or arcades to play games with others for personal growth.

4   Jinnai Hidenobu, *Tokyo: A Spatial Anthropology* (Berkeley, LA, London: The University of California Press, 1995), 126.
5   Wajiro Kon, *Wajiro Kon – Restrospective* (Kyoto: Seingensha Art Publishing, 2011).
6   Hou Hanru, 'Our Home is the Entire City – Notes on Japanese House Design', in *The Japanese House: Architecture and Life After 1945* (Venice: Marsilio Editori, 2016), 9.

5

Elevations of Yongen-Jaya's laundromat and bath house show how even subtle changes to the scale and placement of architectural elements can change their in-game visibility to players.

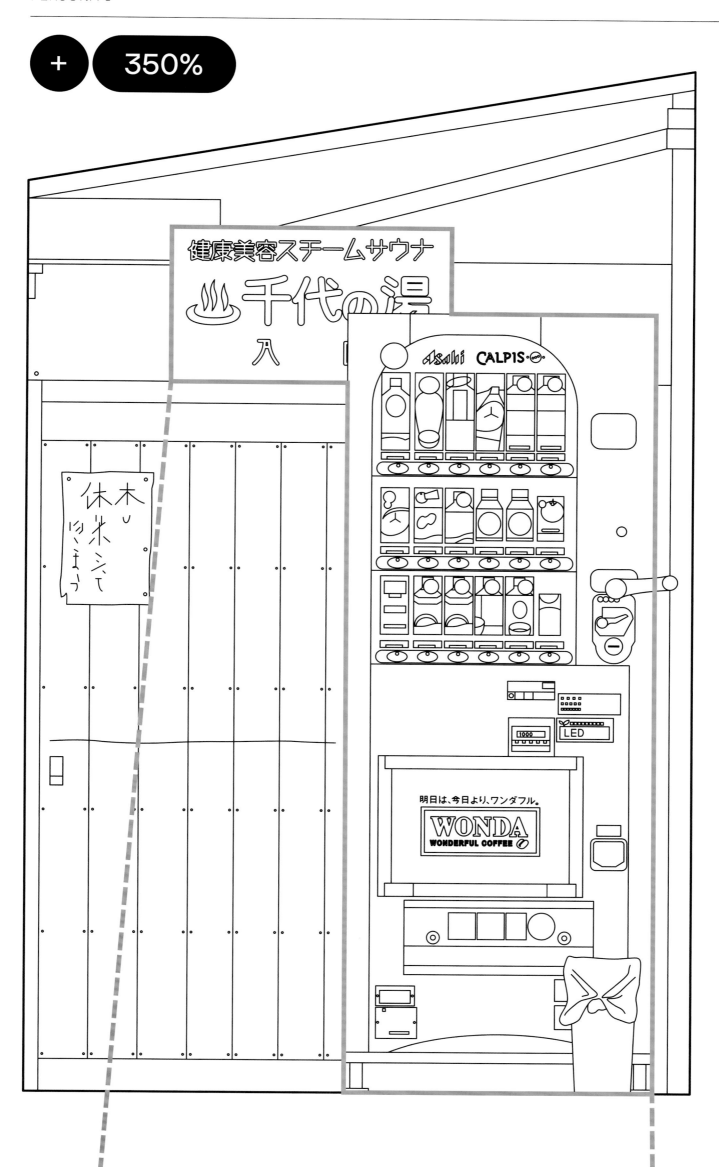

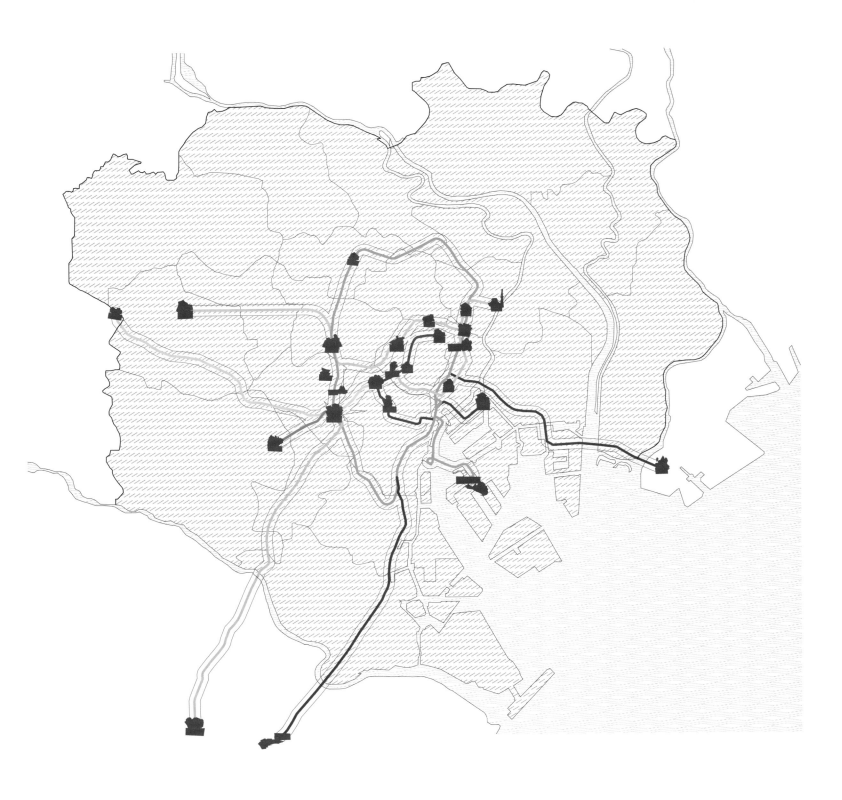

6

By overlaying the subway map locations on to the real
Tokyo, we gain a clearer understanding of all the areas
Joker and his friends travel to within the game.

11.3   Take your Time

In *Persona 5*, the way time is treated serves to reinforce how the whole city becomes a home for Joker. Days are split into chunks, with players needing to decide which activities they want to perform to pass the time. These can include going on dates, watching a film, working at a ramen shop, bathing or studying at a diner. While these activities cause time to pass, moving around Tokyo in the game does not. *Persona 5*'s map presents the city as a subway network, but it tends not to map accurately to real-world geography. By overlaying all the places Joker can visit on to the real extents of Tokyo, we begin to understand the reality of the journeys the game allows us to take. Although subway maps typically 'straighten out' the real routes of train lines, in *Persona 5*, the game works even harder to compress and distort these fragmented locations into one cohesive system [Fig. 6].

While travelling does not cause time to pass as such, many of the twenty-five locations in *Persona 5* are 'hangout spots', places where we can meet friends or love interests for activities that do use a chunk of the day. In contrast, the game provides several areas for Joker to explore at will, containing shops and other facilities. There are five of these hub areas: Yongen-Jaya, Shibuya, Shinjuku, Akihabara and the Shujin Academy in Aoyama. These districts provide over thirty shops for buying equipment, books and other trinkets, as well as places to meet and develop relationships with confidants who allow Joker to develop powerful abilities in the Metaverse. Travelling between and within these hubs does not cause time to pass until an activity is selected, meaning that the fifty-minute real-life journey between Yongen-Jaya and Akihabara can be made an infinite number of times, while practising Joker's baseball swing causes a whole evening to go by. Tokyo's public transportation system is efficient, but *Persona 5*'s is more so.

☐ Timeline:

9 Months
260 Days
344 Activity Slots

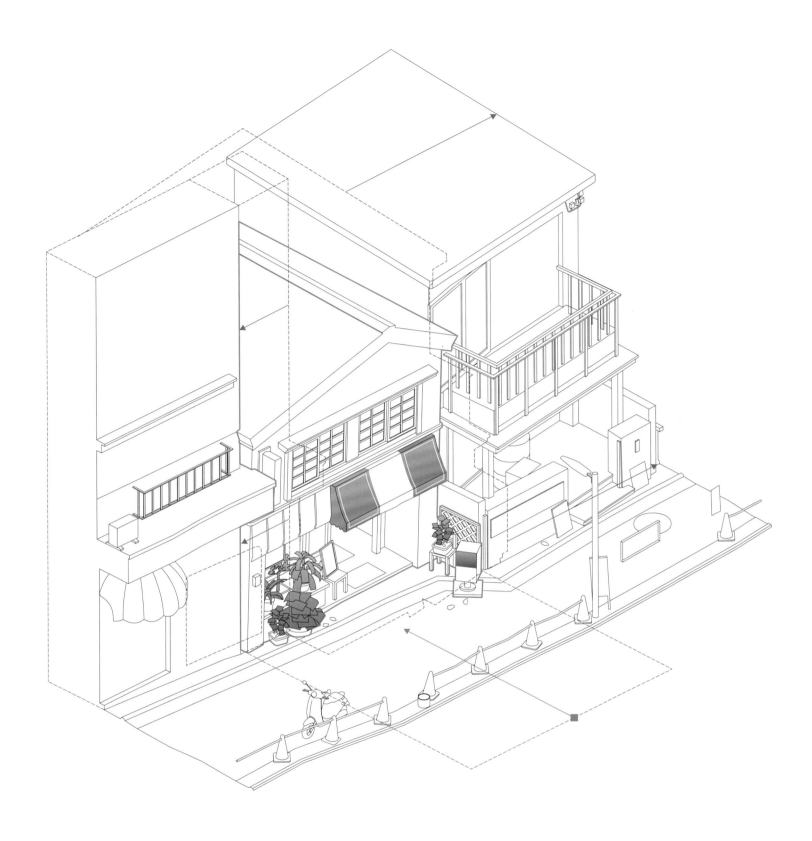

7

Isometric study showing how the developers have peeled apart two buildings in real-world Sangenjaya to accommodate the new two-storey building that contains Leblanc, the café that serves as Joker's home.

11.4 Coffee and Curry

While many of the buildings in Yongen-Jaya are faithful reproductions – with a twist – the main space that Joker inhabits during the game is an entirely fictional insertion. Café Leblanc, the coffee and curry house run by Sojiro Sakura, is a two-storey building, with Joker living on the first floor above the café, in a space that also serves as a hideout for the Phantom Thieves during the game. As with other buildings in the area, fans of the game quickly identified the street on which Leblanc is sited, near a Sangenjaya bar called Good-day Good-day (Good-bye Good-bye in the game). In reality, Good-day Good-day is flanked by two more bars, all sharing the same rounded-corner door fronts as part of the same building. In Yongen-Jaya, the most northerly of these bars, named A.Garden, has been replaced, and the two flanking buildings pulled apart to accommodate the insertion of an entirely new two-storey building that is around 7 m (22 ft 11⅝ in.) wide and only contains Leblanc [Fig. 7]. While this is still a small building, it is considerably larger than A.Garden's bar interior, suggesting that aside from the need to create a building to support the story, the existing spaces were too small, despite the game accurately depicting the street widths of Sangenjaya, typically less than 5m (16 ft 4⅞ in.) wide.

Slotting buildings into narrow gaps and combining the function of spaces are architectural approaches highly characteristic of Tokyo. Architects Yoshiharu Tsukamoto and Momoyo Kaijima from the studio Atelier Bow-Wow produced two influential books, *Pet Architecture Guide Book*[7] and *Made in Tokyo*, detailing these unique types of buildings, such as tiny houses surrounded by vending machines.[8] By levering the adjacent buildings apart to insert Lebanc, the designers may be imposing a fictional structure into the neighbourhood, but the effect of this is highly contextual and indicative of Tokyo's prevailing approach to fitting together a city.

As the story progresses, ventures into the Metaverse, whether Palaces or Mementos, are typically started from a Hideout. The Phantom Thieves' Hideouts change throughout the course of the game, but they too tend towards spaces of the everyday, where you might stop to check your phone or take a break from daily life: the roof of a school, a bridge at Shibuya station or Joker's bedroom. Hideouts provide a connection point for players to begin incursions, but they are rarely seen (apart from the spaces in Leblanc) from anything other than a static camera angle. By reconstructing some of these Hideout spaces from the game, it is clear *Persona 5* frames significant views through these static cameras rather than the freer viewpoint used in exploration sequences, while retaining the same visual language across both types of space [Fig. 8].

Transitions between static and moving cameras are used across many spaces. Fixed cameras are often used at the ends of streets, denoting where we might leave an area, or at contextual action points, such as a series of jumps we might make within a Palace. The interior of Leblanc is also a good example of this. During normal daytime hours the space is seen through a series of static, rotating cameras that follow the player's movement, but when the player calls a Hideout meeting at the same location, the game transitions to a camera with an entirely fixed viewpoint, allowing for the game to fade into the loading transition to the Metaverse [Fig. 9].

7   Tokyo Institute of Technology, Tsukamoto Architectural Laboratory & Atelier Bow-Wow, *Pet Architecture Guide Book* (World Photo Press, 2002).

8   Momoyo Kajima, Junzo Kuroda & Yoshiharu Tsukamoto, *Made in Tokyo* (Tokyo: Kajima Institute Publishing, 2001).

8

By recreating *Persona 5*'s hideouts as 3D spaces we can see how these mundane spaces, seen only through fixed cameras, use normality to contrast with the weird Metaverse spaces they link to.

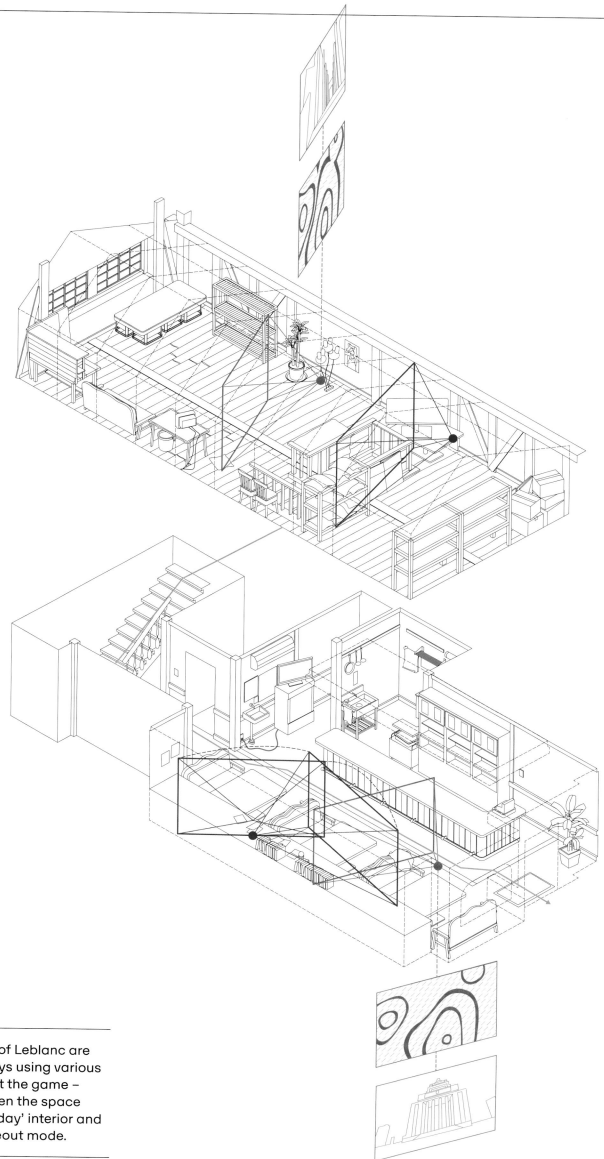

9

The interior spaces of Leblanc are seen in different ways using various cameras throughout the game – transitioning between the space viewed as an 'everyday' interior and the space in its Hideout mode.

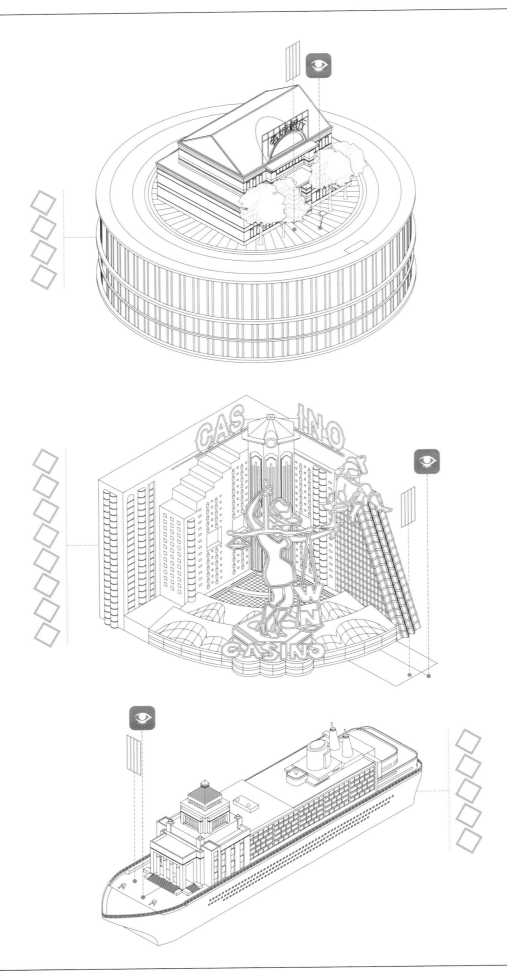

10

Recreations of Palace exteriors, showing the symbolic architecture they employ to represent the cognition of the people who constructed them. While each Palace is different, they share common elements such as Safe Rooms.

11.5 Palaces

For much of *Persona 5*'s storyline, our attention is focused on Palaces, elaborate structures built in the Metaverse that represent physical manifestations of the Seven Deadly Sins. Exploring the depths of a particularly distorted mind, these spaces are highly symbolic in both the visual and spatial form of the architecture, and in the design of puzzles and dungeons found within the structures. Players will encounter Palaces in various forms including a castle, a space station and a tomb within a giant pyramid, each of which has distinct shadow forms guarding them and labyrinthine puzzles that protect the treasure within. The fact that Palaces represent cognition as an architectural structure is actually quite appropriate, for as architectural critic Deyan Sudjic argues, this has always happened. 'Architecture feeds the egos of the susceptible,' he writes; 'they grow more and more dependent on it' to the point where 'it has become an attempt to construct a particular view of the world'.[9]

All Palaces share some similarities, such as a clear point of entrance from the real world, a connection point to the Velvet Room (where Personas can be managed), and a sequence of Safe Rooms that provide respite for the player and allow them to save. The interiors of most Palaces tend towards 'dungeon'-like designs, a series of connected spaces that can sometimes be hard to understand in relation to the exterior form of the building. By reconstructing the exterior form of three of these Palaces from their limited depiction in the game's cutscenes, we can start to comprehend their overall architectural approach more clearly in a way that is not always possible while exploring the interiors of the structure. At the same time, we can see how the symbolism of the spaces is recursive; certain gestures and motifs present at the larger scale are also found within the logic and aesthetic of the levels contained within [Fig. 10].

As an example, from the exterior we see Sae Nijima's Palace (the sixth one infiltrated by the Phantom Thieves) as a giant casino, emblematic of a 'rigged' legal system Sae participates in. The casino's form appears to be a mixture of various influences from Las Vegas, including the sloping block from the MGM Grand, and the iconic neon sign 'Sassy Sally', a cowgirl figure who adorned a Vegas strip club for some forty years. Within the Palace we find halls and halls of slot machines, creeping through staff corridors and attempting to win a huge jackpot by hacking a giant one-armed bandit. While the scale of these spaces is not necessarily so different to reality, the final battle of the Palace takes place on a giant scaled-up roulette wheel, where the symbolism of the rigged game of chance becomes more overt and more clearly spatial [Fig. 11]. Here the back and forth of the battle is combined with moments where the giant wheel becomes a key protagonist in the fight.

☐ Metaverse:

8 Palaces
8 Treasures
66 Mementos

9   Deyan Sudjic, *The Edifice Complex: How the rich and powerful – and their architects – shape the world* (London: Penguin, 2005), 12.

11

Plan of boss battle arena in Sae Nijima's Palace, transcribing how the rotating landscape of the roulette wheel becomes a spatial protagonist in the battle, requiring Joker to send one of his party away from the battle to deal with it.

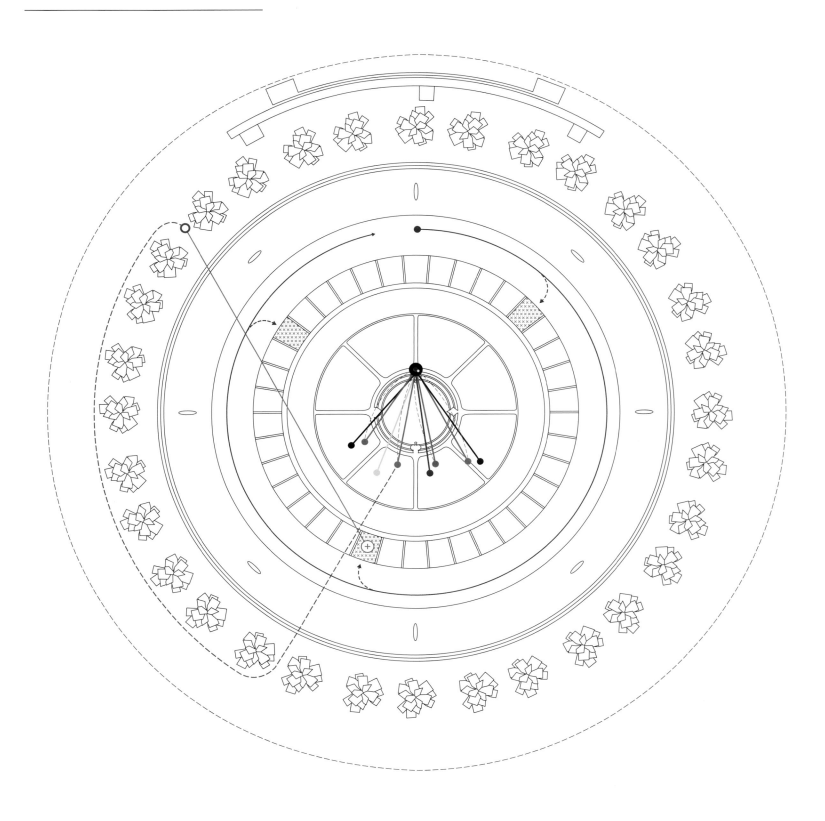

By mapping out the interior spaces of Masayoshi Shido's Palace, symbolism can be layered to produce new forms. Shido's perception of himself as captain of the ship produces an interior space that heavily references cruise liners in its visual form, with the midsection of the Palace seeing Phantom Thieves sneaking through countless corridors lined with cabin doors. Yet as floorplans, these spaces create a much more mazelike circulation than the linear layout of a real-life cruise ship.[10] The labyrinthine plan instead appears to be a spatial representation of Shido's perception of the player as a mouse, and in this Palace there are several puzzles that involve the player being transformed into a rodent by the power of carefully placed golden statues of Shido himself [Fig. 12]. Having managed to navigate this imposition, and several boss fights, players will eventually find themselves inside Shido's version of the National Diet chamber, with the stage magnified in size many times and covered in a giant Daruma, a Japanese doll charm said to confer good luck in perseverance.[11]

Here we witness the most overt signs of the relationship between the schoolkid Phantom Thieves and the powerful adults who control society. Yet seen through the spaces of the game, we can also conclude that it is the power of everyday Tokyo and its urban form that allows Joker and his friends to prevail. While the story presents Tokyo as a city full of uncaring and unengaged people, who might barely notice society's descent into ruin, it is through the fine grain of normal life that players can create a character with enough power to overcome this. By allowing players to re-enact intimate moments of daily life – such as taking ramen orders, working out, watching a film or snatching a moment to read a book on the train – each of these combine to have a much more significant impact in the Metaverse and conquer the sickening spaces created by warped ego.

While Shido's Palace is styled as a cruise ship, we find a complex network of mazes within the internal spaces. Here both the visual theme of the space and its plan layout work together to emphasize how the villain sees other people as mere rodents.

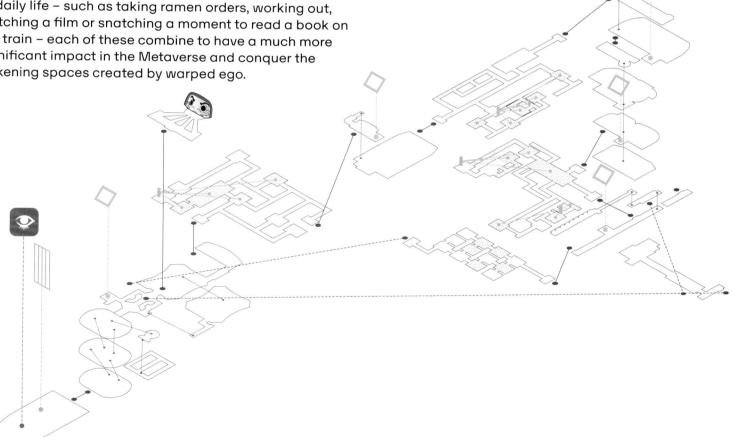

10 Royal Caribbean Explorer of the Seas, royalcaribbean. com/cruise-ships/explorer-of-the-seas/deck-plans/2061/07.

11 Live Japan, 'Japanese Daruma Dolls: The true story behind the insanely cute souvenirs!', livejapan.com/en/article-a0002401/.

○ VIDEOGAME ATLAS

Sections

STARDEW VALLEY

Details

Year	2016
Developer	Eric Barone
	Sickhead Games
	ConcernedApe
Publisher	ConcernedApe

Platforms

Microsoft Windows macOS

Linux iOS Android

PlayStation: 4/Vita

Nintendo Switch Xbox One

In *Stardew Valley* we encounter a landscape to be nurtured, square by square. With its gentle lessons in labour, the world demonstrates the value of time – and the impact of bypassing it with automated production.

☐ Map:

1 Nation
11 Points of Interest
40 Occupants

12.1   Lie of the Land

Throughout modern history, the homestead fantasy has perpetuated a desire for a self-sufficient lifestyle. While such independence is a necessity for many cultures, the idea of placing oneself in the wilderness and cultivating the land into a productive home has become an idealized form of identity in many other parts of the world. From growing vegetables, to raising livestock and the production of goods, the act of nurturing wilderness into a territory of our own has long been a desire of humankind. This impulse is represented very clearly by *Stardew Valley*, the popular farming simulation/role-playing game (RPG) hybrid published in 2016. The game's complex and comforting agrarian world was painstakingly built by one person – developer Eric Barone – over six years. *Stardew Valley* is inspired by the 1990s game *Harvest Moon*,[1] meaning it plays not only on our fantasies of a homesteading lifestyle, but also on the nostalgic aesthetics of videogame worlds we may have experienced as before. In a contemporary context, online movements such as 'cottagecore' have idealized rural life by aestheticizing this 'frontier spirit', tying it closely to the popularity of the game [Fig. 1].[2]

Stardew Valley allows the player to assume the role of a farmer after acquiring a plot of land from their elderly grandfather. The player quits their day job in the city, relocating to a rural region to begin their new life. They are given a choice of seven Farm Maps at the start of the game, each with its own individual layout and features driven by an overarching theme. Each farm offers various opportunities and constraints, comprising different distributions of water, grassland, farmland and foliage. Rather than just providing visual differences, the maps closely control the experiences that will follow for the player and help to guide their decision making. The chosen map influences not only the shape and layout of the farm, but also the specific skills the player can gain. While a 'Riverland Farm' encourages fishing, a 'Wilderness Farm' pushes players to learn combat and protect themselves from monsters that emerge at night, promoting different actions and styles of play as a result. Each farm also has a different in-game trajectory, meaning that some locations allow for rapid early development but are harder to cultivate later.

The interior of the player's farmhouse is furnished distinctively to complement the farm's theme. Both inside and outside the house, essential amenities remain common and consistent, such as the location of a bed, the provision of a greenhouse and a Shipping Bin to provide the player with an essential infrastructure for progressing through the game. Other decorative accessories are more diverse, in both their appearance and location. By overlaying the starting interiors, we can see how the different designs also give clues as to the exterior context, with the multiplayer 'Four Corners Farm' containing a larger communal dining table, and 'Beach Farm' reflecting the warm climate through its lack of a fireplace, common to all other farms [Fig. 2].

The *Stardew Valley* world is located in the fictional, bucolic setting of Ferngill Republic. The mainland is comprised of the player's own farm, and a surrounding valley containing a Town, Beach, Calico Desert, Cindersap Forest and Mountain. Subterranean spaces including an expansive network of Mines and a sewer can also be unlocked to give the player access to extended types of terrain and their associated resources. The wider archipelago, connected by Gem Sea, contains several islands including the exotic Ginger Island, made accessible after the player repairs a boat.

Initially, the player traverses between these lands on foot, limited by their character's base speed of running at five tiles per second, which can be increased through consumables such as espresso coffee and magic candy. With the primary outdoor territories totalling approximately 55,000 tiles, the player navigates from area to area through connecting entrances located at various points on each map's perimeter. As they progress through the game, fixing minecarts and bridges, and obtaining warp totems and Obelisks (permanent teleporters) for fast travel, navigating across the wider map becomes less cumbersome. This allows the player to customize their journey into a personalized infrastructure, shaping their own unique experience of the Ferngill Republic and turning it into a network of nodes that enable the player to move more rapidly from place to place, and ultimately become more productive in a shorter space of time [Fig. 3].

1   Tom Marks, 'Interview: What's next for *Stardew Valley*', PC Gamer, pcgamer.com/uk/stardew-valley-interview/.
2   Juniper Lewis, '*Stardew Valley*, Cottagecore, and the Politics of Fashion', *Gamers with Glasses*, gamerswithglasses.com/features/stardew-valley-cottagecore.

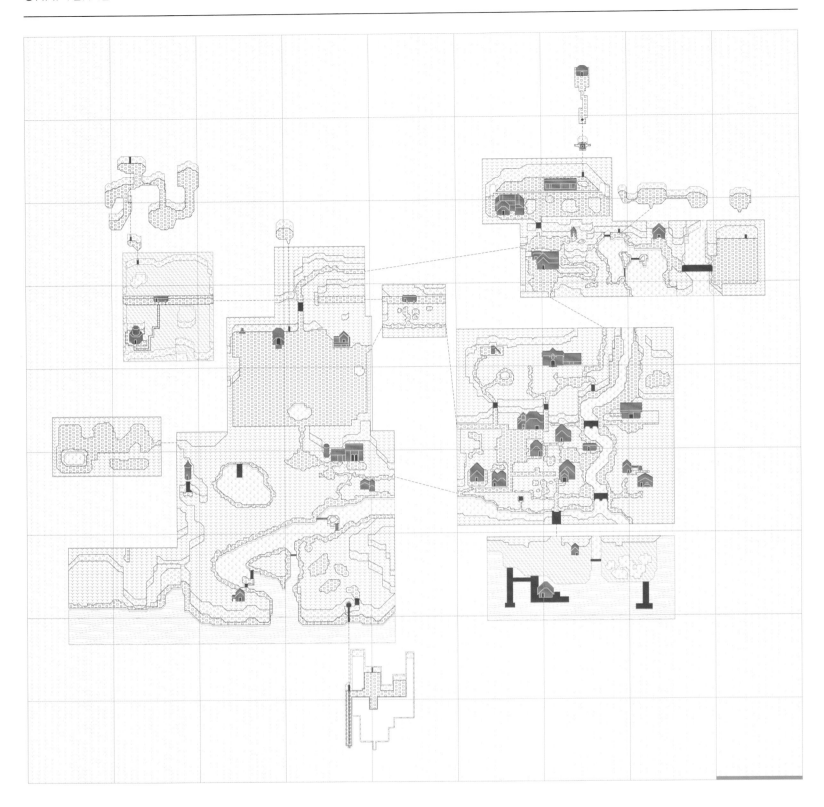

Map of *Stardew Valley*'s primary external territories, comprised of the player's own farm, and a surrounding valley containing a Town, a Beach, a Desert, a Forest and a Mountain.

+

350%

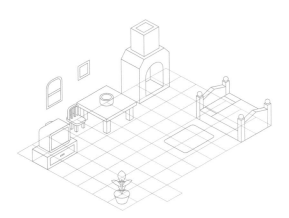

Interior layouts of the player's
Farmhouse, the design of which
is influenced by the farm's theme.
Many houses share common
furniture, but hint at the different
environments outside.

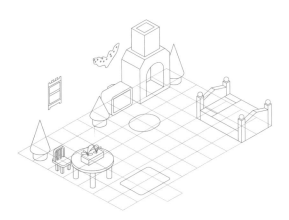

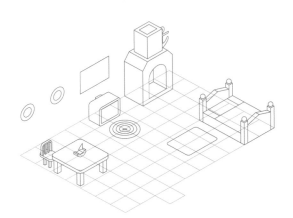

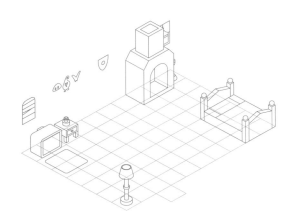

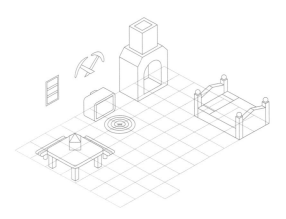

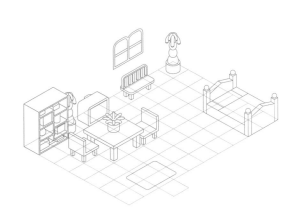

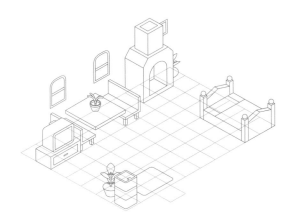

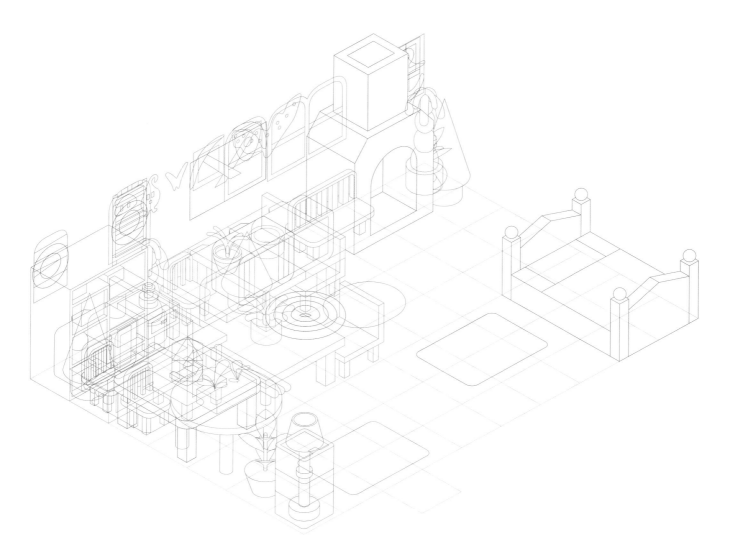

A mapping of a player's personalized infrastructure for warping and fast travelling across Ferngill Republic, allowing them to skip the game's strict time limits.

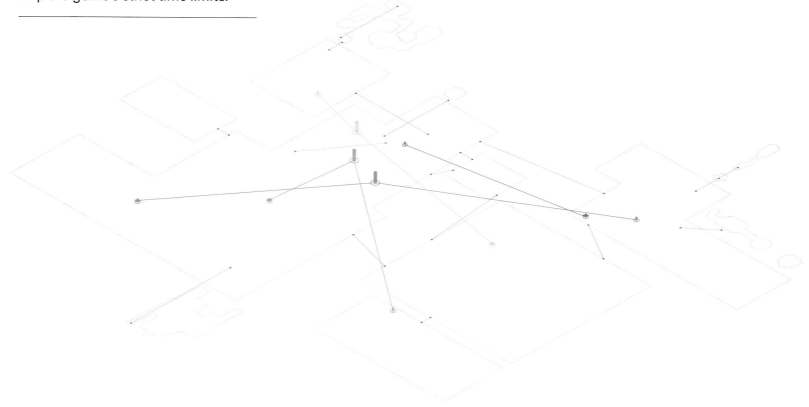

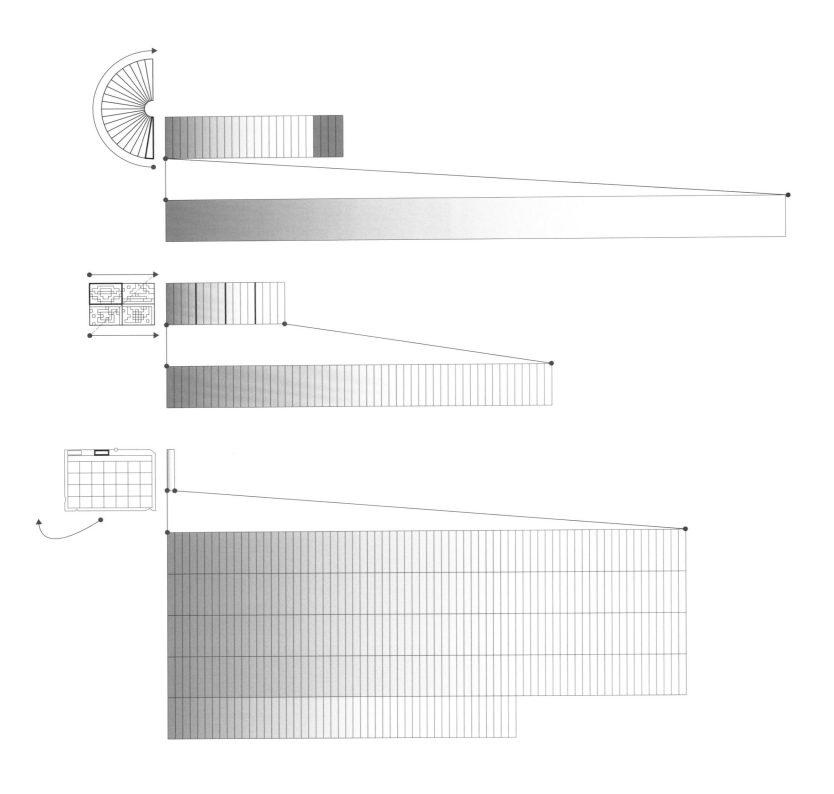

4

The passing of time in *Stardew Valley* operates
on a timescale of 1/327 of reality. This diagram
demonstrates that days are compressed to twenty
hours, and years become sixteen weeks long, split
rigidly into four seasons.

12.2   Intensified Agrarianism

The game's handling of time intensifies the motivation to unlock fast travel, as ten minutes of game time pass in seven real-time seconds. With a maximum playable day of twenty in-game hours, the player needs to return to their home by 2 a.m. every night. Failure to do so results in the player passing out and incurring financial penalties, which are revealed when they wake at 6 a.m. the next day. This suggests that although the player may seem to have endless objectives to fulfil, the act of rest (for four hours at least) is still essential to the game, restoring the player's energy and health and placing a critical importance on the Farmhouse and the bed it contains. Each year's four seasons lasts for only twenty-eight days, producing a 'year' that is only sixteen weeks long. As we can see, this further compresses the passing of time at multiple levels of scale, with one in-game year mapping to approximately twenty-seven real-world hours, operating on a timescale of 1/327 of reality [Fig. 4].

Stardew Valley's grid system encourages an intensely meticulous, itemized approach to setting out and orchestrating growth on the player's farm and the territories beyond it. This overriding spatial logic of the game informs the placement, density and configuration of objects. The grid is integral to the game's ability to maintain order, precision and control. Regulated by this grid, players develop their farm in innumerable ways without breaking the underlying systems of object placement and resource collection. The game is viewed from a frontal 'oblique' perspective, unnatural to the human eye. This way of viewing space has a long history and was commonly used in architectural design to communicate both elevation and depth for detailed space-planning.[3] As such, *Stardew Valley*'s viewpoint is ideal for viewing the farm in an orderly, unobstructed manner that extends the player's control over the landscape. Moreover, community tools such as the Stardew Planner allow for players to test and iterate various versions of their farm outside the game, effectively creating drawings of the yet-to-be-built.

Some objects crafted or obtained by the player have the ability to affect the territory around them when positioned, ranging from one neighbouring grid square to larger, more expansive diameters [Fig. 5]. These

consist of different strengths of sprinklers for watering crops; Bee Houses for making honey; scarecrows for protecting crops; bombs for clearing objects; and Junimo Huts for harvesting. These objects of influence work independently yet can interact with one another when arranged in different configurations by the player. Whether striving for efficiency, or prioritizing a distinctive radial or linear aesthetic, the combinations of sprinklers, scarecrows and crops are a much-discussed topic in Stardew's community. Finding the optimal relationship between different objects and the grid has led to endless pattern formations for players to utilize and adapt within their own farms [Fig. 6]. This becomes highly reminiscent of emerging real-world technologies for agricultural growing systems, including 'pixel cropping' – a technique where crops are planted in matrices of small squares, with the hope of developing beneficial relationships between different units.[4]

These methods also extend to the arrangement of machines on the farm. By advancing their skills and constructing Artisan Equipment, the player can generate Artisan Goods, which are produced or processed in a series of machines. Bee Houses produce different types of honey, which can be farmed on a large scale and sold for different values, depending on which type of flower the bees are placed next to. This production method leads to another array of unique spatial configurations, with masses of Bee Houses positioned ornately around differently flowers, serviced by sprinklers, within the protective range of scarecrows. Such designs demonstrate the carefully controlled balance and interplay between natural and human-made elements on the farm [Fig. 7].

3   Massimo Scolari, *Oblique Drawing* (Cambridge, MA & London: MIT Press, 2012).

4   'Pixel cropping', Wageningen University & Research, wur.nl/en/project/Pixel-cropping.htm.

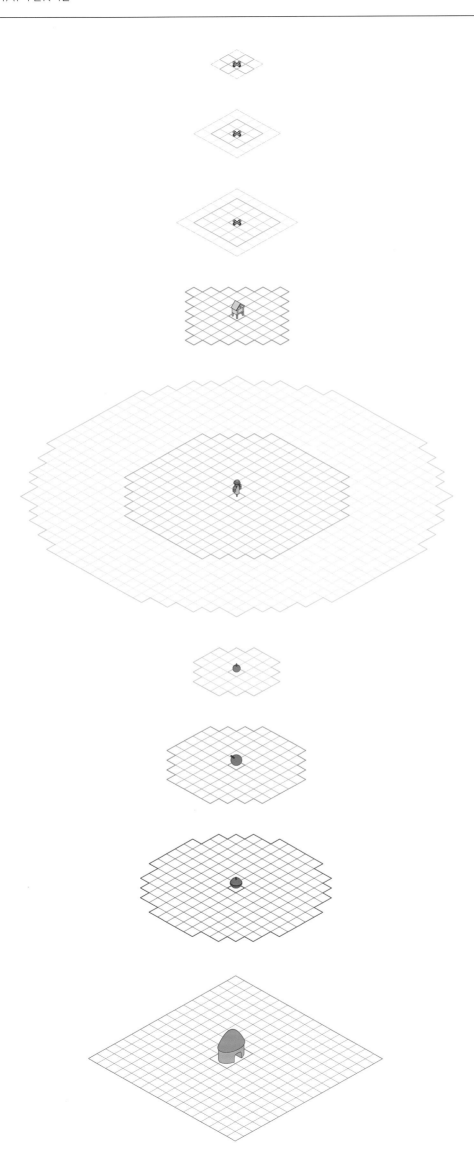

Objects of influence that the player can place in their farm, demonstrating the range of effect on their surrounding territories.

A map of community-made patterns generated by various crop, scarecrow and sprinkler arrangements. Some prioritize efficiency, while others prize aesthetic harmony.

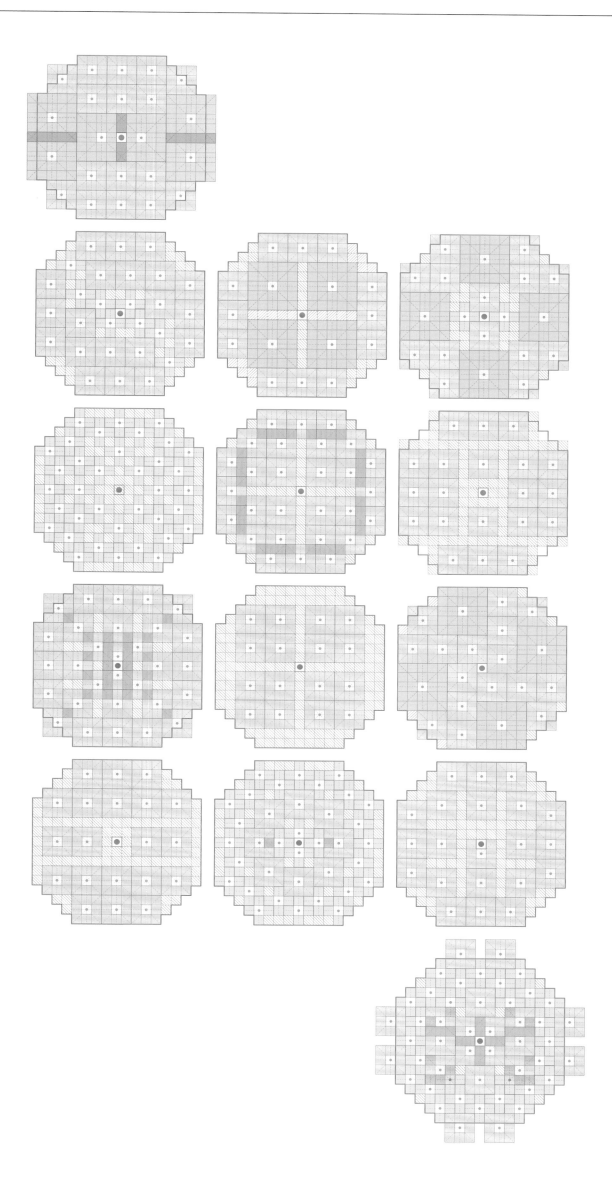

The design of Bee House formations, assembled to produce honey from flowers, demonstrates the balance and interplay between natural and human-made elements on the farm.

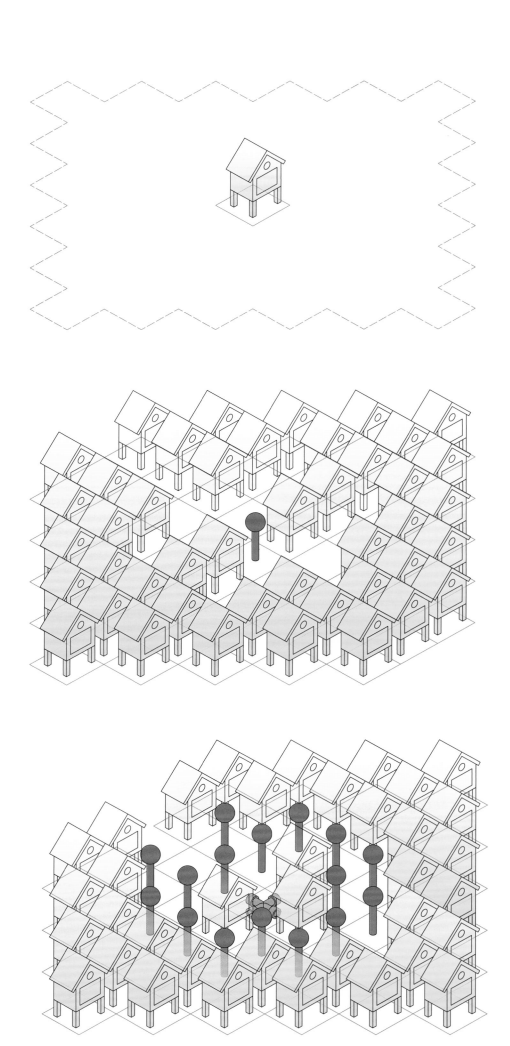

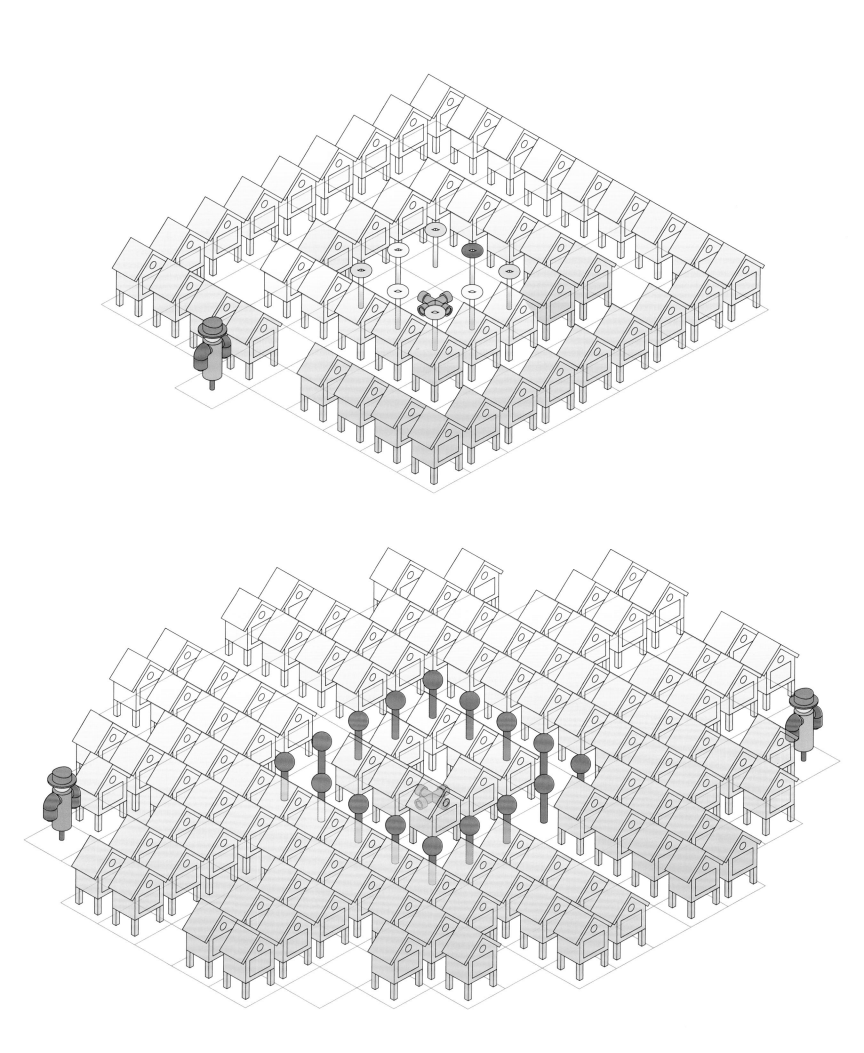

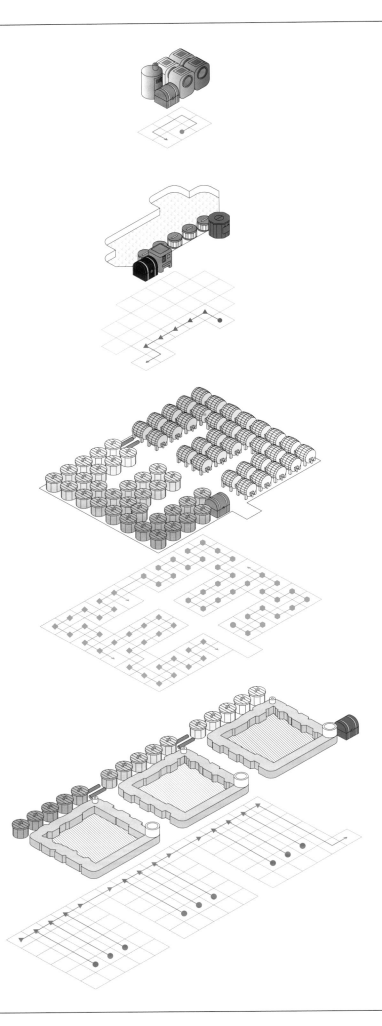

8

Diagram showing several types of automated machine created through modding, each of which processes resources across a chain link of individual components.

12.3 Automated Agriculture

While it is possible to progress and turn a decent profit over time in the base game, one of the most widely used mods for *Stardew Valley* is Pathoschild's 'Automate', which allows multiple machines to be connected via a chest, using it to either insert raw items for processing or to extract refined materials.[5] The mod has been downloaded over 1.4 million times, and players have created endless forms of machine by positioning different combinations of equipment in various landscapes and interiors. These machines vary from simple processing units to mechanisms that draw fish and animals from a series of connected ponds, processing them over time to create Aged Roe [Fig. 8]. Whole floors of sheds can be filled with units such as jars and kegs, allowing for the mass processing of produce into Artisan Goods such as Jams or Juices.[6] Each piece of equipment will process the goods in parallel, enabling large quantities to be generated within the typical in-game cycles that can sometimes be days in length.

Through mods such as 'Automate', *Stardew Valley*'s world is taken to its logical (efficient) extent: a set of highly automated agricultural systems requiring little to no human intervention. This of course also mirrors developments in real-world agriculture, where jobs and machines that once required human labour and interaction are likely to be given over to self-operating systems. Research projects such as 'Hands Free Farm' have been utilizing autonomous drone systems to work land,[7] while large manufacturers of farming machinery such as John Deere are developing a suite of autonomous and semi-autonomous tools for the modern farm.[8] The logic of the modded automated systems in *Stardew Valley* is somewhat simpler, generally derived from the proximity of one unit to another. Yet the drive towards systems that generate refined produce and resources with minimal human input, enabled by the mod, is one that we can see developing within the technological industries that serve agriculture.

The decision to automate is also central to the game's two alternate endings, centred around the fate of Pelican Town's Community Center. Initially appearing as a derelict building, the player can either choose to restore the Community Center or purchase a JojaMart membership, which replaces the Community Center with a commercial Joja Warehouse. If the Community Center is repaired, the player gains access to Junimo Huts that can be placed on farmland to assist the player in the harvesting of fully grown crops. These structures are inhabited by forest spirits called Junimos, which emerge in groups of three every morning to pick individual crops that surround the hut in a range of 17x17 grid tiles. Through mapping their movements, we can see that three Junimos travel synchronously on an individual path, darting around the hut range in linear patterns to pick the crops, intersecting one another, occasionally stopping to rest [Fig. 9]. The player can then retrieve the harvested crops from a bag located outside the hut. As an end-game feature, the Junimo Huts represent a specialist type of automation offered in the game, which rewards the player for choosing to improve the town in favour of the community. It demonstrates how even mythical creatures can be tamed to collaborate with humans.

5   'Automate' mod by user Pathoschild, Nexus Mods, nexusmods.com/stardewvalley/mods/1063.
6   Structures demonstrated by user BiiPolar Potato: 'AUTOMATE – A Stardew Valley mod guide with real playthrough examples', youtube.com/watch?v=ytX6DKYlge0&t=287s.
7   Nicola Twilley, 'A Field Farmed Only by Drones' in *The New Yorker*, newyorker.com/tech/annals-of-technology/a-field-farmed-only-by-drones.
8   John Deere, 'Future of Farming', deere.co.uk/en/agriculture/future-of-farming/.

9

Magical harvesting sequences
structured around the range of
a Junimo Hut, demonstrating how
the Junimo pick and gather crops
on the player's behalf.

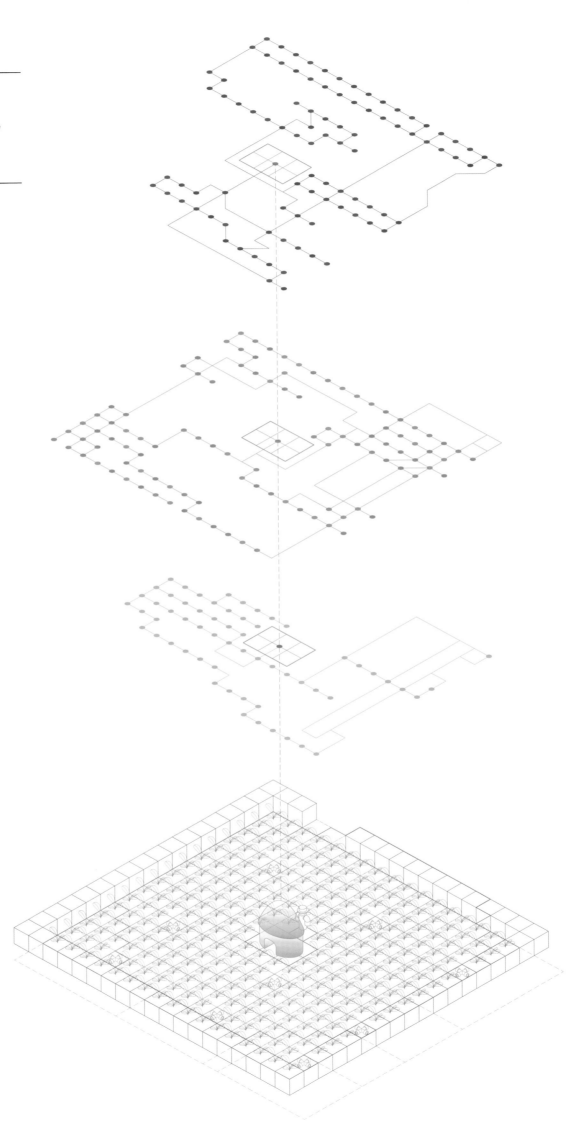

+ 350%

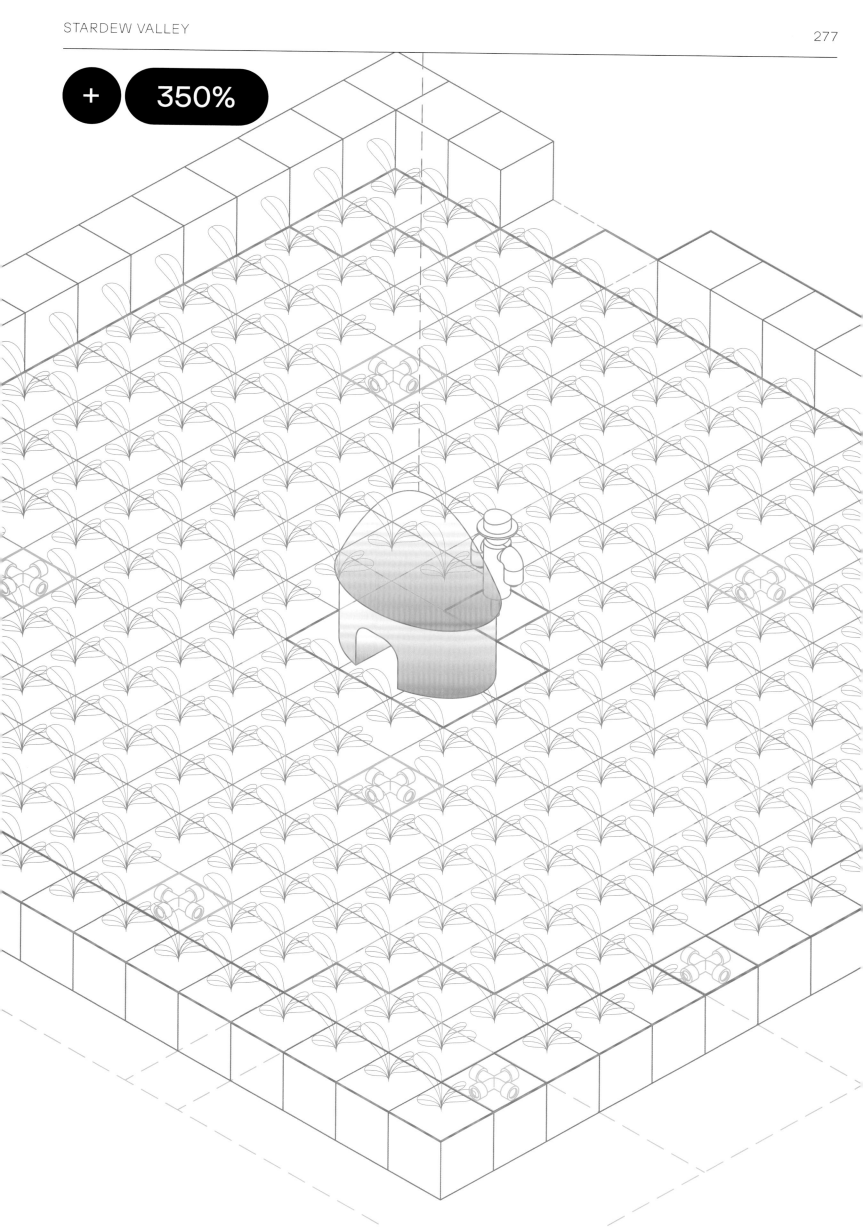

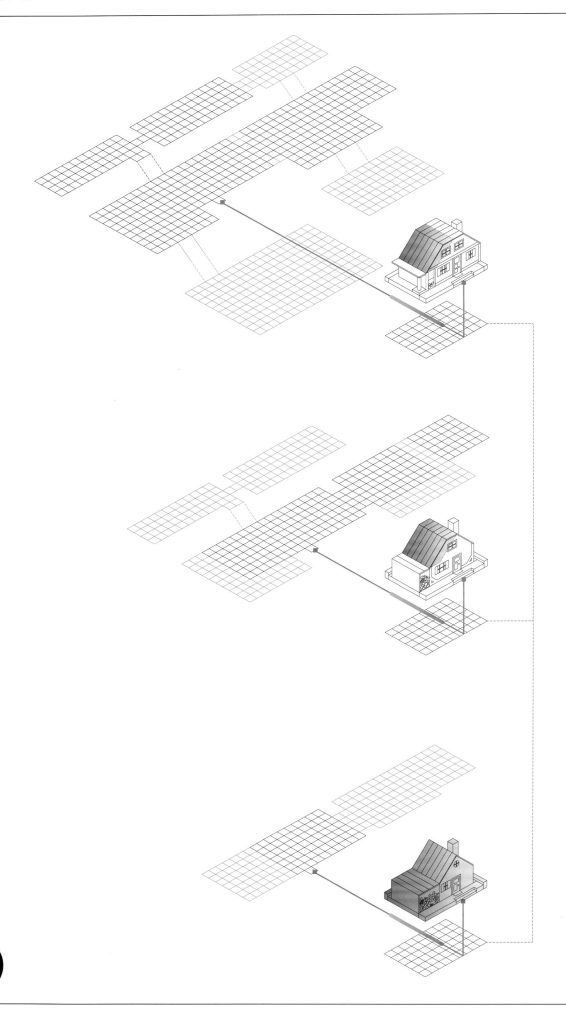

Comparison between the external presence of the Farmhouse and its interior volume, communicated through subtle tweaks to the exterior of the Farmhouse as it becomes upgraded.

12.4   The Homestead

The Farmhouse is the player's primary residence in the game, located in the northeast corner of their farm. Characteristic of its typology, it deploys a simple yet distinctive style on the exterior, comprising a timber structure and red slate roof tiles. Its external footprint occupies a 6x9 rectangle that does not expand as the player upgrades their farmhouse, limiting the impact on its surroundings. Yet as the player improves or renovates, the number of internal rooms and their size increases, becoming ever more disproportionate to the appearance of the house from the outside. While some indications are given of the parallels between inside and out, such as extra windows, and an elongated volume, the size of the internal spaces is compressed into a scaled representation of the house when viewed externally. Throughout history the architectural façade has been a component of experimentation for the expression of functions, size, materiality and structure. Proportions and openings typically become critical indicators of the space within, often designed to exaggerate or conceal levels and proportions. The Farmhouse's disjunction can be seen as an example of facadism, highlighting 'a divorce between interior and exterior'.[9] In *Stardew Valley*, the disconnect between the external area of the farm and the internal volume of the house demonstrates two parallel systems in play, allowing the house to act as a symbolic representation of the spatial possibilities inside [Fig. 10].

As the player progresses their farm, they will place additional buildings to accommodate animals, process resources or store items. Some of these can be upgraded in size, which subsequently unlocks new animals that are introduced to the farm. In a similar fashion to the Farmhouse, the upgrades to the external appearance are aesthetic rather than volumetric, even as the interior space increases. Once they reach their optimum size, the player is offered the ability to customize their appearance, by altering the colour of the façade, structural details and roof. Unlike the homesteader building their own simple yet unique home from the ground up, as we can see from the façades in *Stardew Valley*, the ability to personalize one's architecture is only possible once the buildings become more developed and highly articulated.

Elevational study showing the upgrade and customization possibilities for Farm buildings, characterized by their Homestead typology. Greater levels of customization are unlocked at higher building levels.

9   Jonathan Richards, *Facadism* (London: Routledge, 1994), 2.

A survey of the unique floor layouts of the Mines, demonstrating the random generation of entry points into the floor below. These floor typologies repeat as the player descends further.

12.5   Resources and Relationships

The player learns the limits of in-game life cycles and how they are defined by forces such as real-life seasons. The collection of materials and resources from nature is a key facet to the economy of *Stardew Valley*. Yet unlike reality, timber can be obtained without true forestation, and new mineral deposits appear every day. Another example of this condition is the perpetually lit campfires that can be toggled with the click of a mouse and survive heavy rain. Alenda Chang discusses these 'technological conveniences'[10] as contradictions to real-world natural resources such as fresh water and fertile soil, and their often-contested status. In contrast, *Stardew Valley*'s synthetic ecology is simplified and favourable towards the player, allowing super-natural conditions to take place.

While presenting a friendly face, the game also asks us to treat the natural landscape as a set of materials to be freely extracted, and this is particularly evident in the Mines. The player uses their tools to strike rocks which contain a variety of common and rare materials. Each level contains one rock that uncovers a ladder, leading to the next floor of the mine, often only appearing after the player engages in combat. Depending on the player's daily in-game luck (a statistic that affects drop rates in the Mines), the ladder may be uncovered sooner or later. Comprising 120 floors split across three sections, Mines contain thirty-eight unique floor layouts with corresponding floors in each section sharing the same configuration. Through randomly generated layouts of rocks, and material themes that differ in each section, the player engages with Mines differently each on visit, despite the repetition of the basic floorplan. Unlike nature, where one environment might be ruined by human activity, a freshly replenished mine always awaits us [Fig. 12].

Beyond the player's own farm buildings, thirteen other houses are inhabited by villagers, alongside nineteen Merchant buildings, which play a part in the player's progression through the game's economy. Developing friendships and even marriages with the game's Villagers is integral to its reward system. This is facilitated by talking, completing quests, gifting and dating them according to their distinct personalities. The complex nature of the friendship mechanics is demonstrated through the vast network of gifts. Different Villagers have various reactions to these: 'love', 'like', 'are neutral towards', 'dislike' or 'hate' [Fig. 13]. Eager to advance these in-game social relations, mods such as Pathoschild's 'Lookup Anything'[11] were created to reveal this ubiquitous data about any villager, crop or animal; while kutluhan_aktar's 'Gift Preferences Bot'[12] offers a

highly novel solution to providing similar information on an external device. Whether these relationships were developed 'authentically', or advanced with the help of a mod, *Stardew Valley* stresses the importance of social interaction and community engagement to progress, relying on favours, hand-me-downs, and both structured and random encounters. This promotes a communal experience for the player rather than one of isolated escapism.

As player-created maps reveal, villagers can also work against the player by destroying items which intersect their walking routes. By overlaying this with item spawn locations on land, and fishing zones in water bodies (heat maps that indicate where different species of fish spawn) both revealed through a mod, it becomes possible to read the landscape as an interactive resource. This allows players to identify 'safe' areas in the world for crop propagation that will not be affected by any of the game's other systems, an invisible territory for productive growth [Fig. 14].

Selling over 15 million copies to date, even becoming an esport in September 2021, *Stardew Valley*'s popularity continues to expand even five years on from its initial release. To some, it may seem like a game about breaking free. But by participating in its overarching economy, this idyllic lifestyle soon develops into what feels more like a 'managerial utopia'[13]. The game mechanics operate to 'aestheticize busywork'[14] in a way that other beloved farming and life simulator games tend to do, with farms becoming densely packed with objects and crops and players sprinting down narrow pathways. Ironically, as a *PCGamesN* interview details, Ferngill Republic is also a place that actual farmers like to travel to – tending to their virtual farm on a Nintendo Switch while sat in the cabin of a self-driving tractor[15]. As we expose through this mapping, the world of Stardew Valley provides a friendly, compartmentalized environment that we can shape in our own image – square by square.

10 Alenda Y. Chang, *Playing Nature* (Minneapolis: University of Minnesota Press, 2019), 172.

11 'Lookup Anything' mod by user Pathoschild, Nexus Mods, nexusmods.com/stardewvalley/mods/541.

12 'Stardew Valley Villager Gift Preferences Bot' by user kutluhan_aktar, hackaday.io/project/182500-stardew-valley-villager-gift-preferences-bot.

13 Pan Jie, 'Why Stardew Valley Is The Perfect Game For A Recession' accessed 12/12/21, ricemedia.co/culture-life-stardew-valley-recession-game/

14 Ian Bogost, 'The Quiet Revolution of Animal Crossing' accessed 10/10/13, theatlantic.com/family/archive/2020/04/animal-crossing-isnt-escapist-its-political/610012/
National Archives, *The Homestead Act of 1862*, archives.gov/education/lessons/homestead-act

15 Rachel Watts, 'How realistic is Stardew Valley? We asked a farmer', *PCGamesN*, pcgamesn.com/stardew-valley/pc-realism

Network diagram of Villager gifting
preferences, demonstrating the
complex social relations and
friendship mechanics in the game.

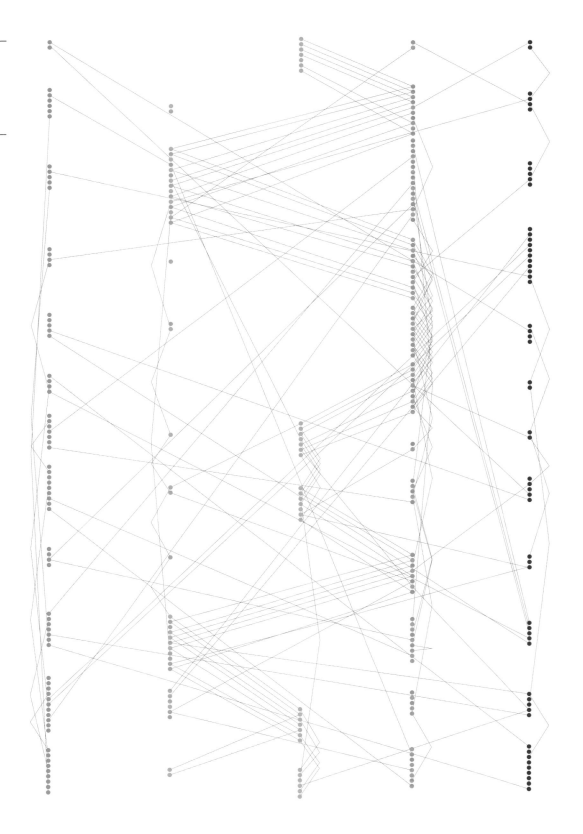

☐ Social

12 Marriage Candidates
2,500 Friendship Points
5 Universally Loved Items

14

A datascape of player-generated information on the game environment, overlaying pedestrian paths, fishing zones and spawn locations to frame the landscape as an interactive resource.

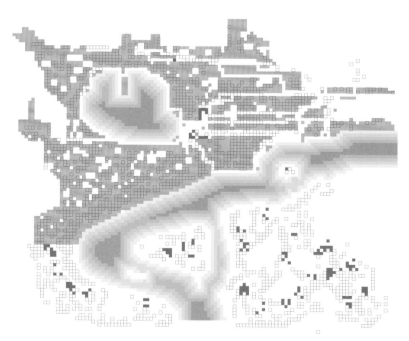

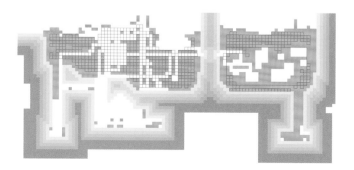

Over the course of these twelve chapters, we have seen the many ways in which game spaces can be read and interpreted, and how deeply connected the design of their worlds is to the mechanics by which we play them. This has involved trying to define the scale of worlds only experienced through fragments, keeping up with environments that are constantly being revised or trying to quantify how virtual versions of cities compare to our understanding of their real counterparts. Each of the games we have examined has provided a well of information that reflects the amount of human craft and ingenuity that underpins its design. We hope that our studies go some way to uncovering the depths in each of these environments, while also offering new ways of seeing and understanding them that neither players nor developers may have identified before.

Of course, there are many other games that have incredibly fascinating settings and architecture, which would also serve as interesting examples for analysis. We could in fact produce similar studies for any game, reading into its architectural subconscious. There will also be many yet-to-be released games that will surely demand attention through their spatial design. This might be through future books, or even by establishing new fields of research and analysis that can reflect the many complex readings these game spaces require.

As some of our game selections demonstrate, technology plays a key part in this – the types of environmental modelling, rendering and interfaces that define videogame spaces are constantly changing. In ten years' time we cannot assume that the prevailing aesthetic experience of game spaces will be the same, and maybe things will have changed by the time this book is released. While a game like *Assassin's Creed Unity* might appear strikingly like historical Paris (despite being over 7 years old), neither *Stardew Valley* nor *Dwarf Fortress* look realistic whatsoever. And if we consider the authorship of these worlds, some of these games have been made by teams comprising hundreds of people, generating billions of dollars, while others are the work of two people providing the game for free. Despite this discrepancy, all these games have compelling spatial designs and create a deep sense of community among their players.

The fact that a book like this is attempting to map architectural principles on to videogame spaces is evidence – if it were really needed any more – that games have grown far beyond a 'hobby' or even 'entertainment', and are now actively defining the way we see and conceptualize our future.

We hope that the links and ideas that have been identified through this book can strengthen the argument for looking at videogame worlds in a more visual, analytical and spatial way, using architectural methods to understand their complexities. Generating new readings of these spaces is so important because these worlds define so much of our lives today. Finnish architect Juhani Pallasmaa once said that the 'door handle is the handshake of the building', yet every time we pick up our controllers, we are greeting not only a building but a whole universe of possible new worlds.

CHAPTER 1
Assassin's Creed Unity

'A Screen Archer's Guide for Assassin's Creed Unity' by 'Tommyrro', Steam Community: steamcommunity.com/sharedfiles/filedetails/?id=1072622723

'Assassin's Creed Unity – Paris landmarks (Real Places x In game)' by Phaedrus TheExplorer: youtube.com/watch?v=9eXq7COAht4

'Assassin's Creed Unity AC: U Cinematic Tools' by Hattiwatti: github.com/Hattiwatti/CinematicTools

Fandom: assassinscreed.fandom.com

'Making Assassin's Creed Unity Part 2 – Next Generation Technology', IGN: youtube.com/watch?v=QGA0WZLp_08

'Massive Crowd on Assassin's Creed Unity: AI Recycling', GDC: youtube.com/watch?v=Rz2cNWVLncl

Reddit: reddit.com/r/assassinscreed

CHAPTER 2
Cities: Skylines

'Cities: Skylines Steam Guides': steamcommunity.com/app/255710/guides/

'Highrise Ban for Smooth Density Transitions' by u/T4rget: youtube.com/watch?v=IonUKUEhhF4

'How Cims Work in the Game': reddit.com/r/CitiesSkylines/comments/goezud/how_cims_work_in_the_game/

'How do i stop these cars appearing from nowhere' by u/robbarinn: reddit.com/r/CitiesSkylines/comments/ezdse6/how_do_i_stop_these_cars_appearing_from_nowhere/

'Vanilla Base Maps Overview': citiesskylinestips.com/all-cities-skylines-maps-part-1-vanilla/

Reddit: reddit.com/r/CitiesSkylines

Skylines Wiki: skylines.paradoxwikis.com/Cities:_Skylines_Wiki

Steam Workshop: steamcommunity.com/workshop/

CHAPTER 3
Dark Souls

'Color proportions of an image', L. Jegou: geotests.net/couleurs/frequences_en.html#

Dark Souls Walkthrough with Maps Wiki: kouryakubo.com/darksouls_en/DemonRuins.html

Dark Souls Wiki: darksouls.fandom.com/wiki/Dark_Souls_Wiki

DriftItem, Twitter: twitter.com/DriftItem

DriftItem/pawREP, GitHub: github.com/pawREP/Dark-Souls-1-P2P-Data

FRAMED. Screenshot Community: framedsc.com

Gaming, interrupted: gaminginterrupted.tumblr.com/

Illusory Wall: illusorywall.tumblr.com/

Illusory Wall, YouTube: youtube.com/channel/UCmBXkjKD8w6bbjUzNjcDtQA

Nexus Mods: nexusmods.com/darksouls

Noclip: noclip.website

Kayinworks: Dark Souls Map Explorer: kayin.moe/dark-souls-map-explorer/

Reddit: reddit.com/r/darksouls/

Souls Lore: soulslore.wikidot.com/

The brother's code, YouTube: youtube.com/c/Thebrotherscode/videos

VaatiVidya, YouTube: youtube.com/c/VaatiVidya/videos

Waypoint forums: forum.waypoint.vice.com/

CHAPTER 4
Death Stranding

'Death Stranding Maps and Locations', Game8: game8.co/games/death-stranding/archives/272288

'Death Stranding: An AI Postmortem', GDC Vault: gdcvault.com/play/1027144/AI-Summit-Death-Stranding-An

'Death Stranding', The White Pube: thewhitepube.co.uk/deathstranding

'In Death Stranding, navigating the world was harder for NPCs than players', Bryan Francis, Gamedeveloper.com: gamedeveloper.com/programming/in-i-death-stranding-i-navigating-the-world-was-harder-for-npcs-than-players

'Rapid Archaeology in Death Stranding', Archaeogaming: archaeogaming.com/2019/12/06/rapid-archaeology-in-death-stranding/

Otis_Inf: Camera Tools

Reddit: r/DeathStranding

WeMod: Game Cheat Engine

CHAPTER 5
Dwarf Fortress

'// Fall of the Succession Tower: Constructivory \\', Bay 12 Forums: bay12forums.com/smf/index.php?topic=152316.0

'40d:Design strategies', Dwarf Fortress Wiki: dwarffortresswiki.org/index.php/40d:Design_strategies

'808, Berstigil "Earthenjaws", Aluramul' by 1hNWPEyVxhCtpYSrZRca: dffd.bay12games.com/file.php?id=14886

'A return to organically designed fortresses' by u/Cutter888: reddit.com/r/dwarffortress/comments/6h7b47/a_return_to_organically_designed_fortresses/

'"Anvilrooters" (a Fortress layout)' by u/NerdyBeerCastle: reddit.com/r/dwarffortress/comments/8eo91z/anvilrooters_a_fortress_layout/

'Armok-vision' – 3D real-time visualizer for Dwarf Fortress: github.com/RosaryMala/armok-vision

'Armok Vision – 3D & First Person Dwarf Fortress' by Nookrium: youtube.com/watch?v=K7XoPbYRLqo

Arqade: gaming.stackexchange.com

Bay12 Forums: bay12forums.com

'DFMA Map Viewer' by Jacob Blomquist: blomquist.xyz/dfma/

Dwarf Fortress File Depot: dffd.bay12games.com

'Dwarf Fortress Map Archive' by John Beech: mkv25.net/dfma/

Dwarf Fortress Wiki: dwarffortresswiki.org
'For those of you who've never seen a dark fortress before' by u/Barskie: i.imgur.com/o8y3Z1J.png
'Fort Motaval "Strangelove" (Dwarf Fortress)' by Bumber64: imgur.com/gallery/xUcpJ
Human Settlements in Dwarf Fortress: imgur.com/a/lsqlK#0
'Let's Play Dwarf Fortress Extras I – Degelgongith (Isometric Tour of the Fortress via StoneSense)' by Zemalf: youtube.com/watch?v=ino-1yCouSw
PeridexisErrant's DF Starter Pack: dffd.bay12games.com/file.php?id=7622
Reddit: r/dwarffortress
'Show me your fortress designs and explain why you use them!' by u/LiddleCat: reddit.com/r/dwarffortress/comments/3aorg8/show_me_your_fortress_designs_and_explain_why_you/
UristMaps – mapping Dwarf Fortress worlds: uristmaps.org/
'Using Dwarf Fortress as a map generator' by Kyle Maxwell: technoskald.me/2014/11/15/using-dwarf-fortress-as-a-map-generator/

CHAPTER 6
Final Fantasy VII + Remake

Fandom: finalfantasy.fandom.com
'FF7 Random Battle Mechanics Guide' by XeroKynos. youtube.com/watch?v=g36-lzRCb68
Final Fantasy Forums: finalfantasyforums.net
'Final Fantasy VII Guide and Walkthrough' by Absolute Steve: gamefaqs.gamespot.com/ps/197341-final-fantasy-vii/faqs/45703
Final Fantasy Portal Site: na.finalfantasy.com/
Game8 FF7 Maps: game8.co/games/Final-Fantasy-VII-Remake/archives/278427
'"Gears": A look inside the Final Fantasy Game Engine' by Joshua Walker and the Qhimm Team"
'How Three People Crushed Final Fantasy VII In Less Than Eight Hours' by Eric Van Allen, Kotaku: kotaku.com/how-three-people-crushed-final-fantasy-vii-in-less-than-1796919938
'Makou Reactor editor' by myst6re
Playstation Blog: blog.playstation.com
'Remako Mod', CaptRobau's Place: captrobau.blogspot.com/2019/05/remako-mod-version-10-released.html
Reddit: r/FFVII & r/FFVIIRemake
Shmuplations: shmuplations.com
'The FF7 Enemy Mechanics v1.11' by Terence Fergusson: web.archive.org/web/20200208031538/gamefaqs.gamespot.com/ps/197341-final-fantasy-vii/faqs/31903
The Lifestream Forums: thelifestream.net/

CHAPTER 7
Fortnite

'All the callouts that our squad uses for Tilted Towers' by u/Lej: reddit.com/r/FortNiteBR/comments/8v106j/all_the_callouts_that_our_squad_uses_for_tilted/
'All The Ways Fortnite's Map Changed Over 10 Seasons': kotaku.com.au/2019/10/fortnite-10-seasons-all-the-way-the-map-changed/
Building Guide: gamesradar.com/uk/fortnite-building-guide/
'Fortnite Battle Royale Location Call-Outs': acornvision.blogspot.com/p/fnbr-location-specific-call-outs.html
'Fortnite Battle Royale: How To Survive The Storm': alphr.com/games/1009621/fortnite-battle-royale-the-storm-tips/
'Fortnite biome study' by u/Przard: reddit.com/r/FortNiteBR/comments/b1ydnx/so_i_decided_to_make_a_biome_map_showing_all_6/
Fortnite Milestone Guide: progameguides.com/fortnite/best-places-to-collect-wood-stone-and-metal-in-fortnite-chapter-2-season-6-fortnite-milestone-guide/
Fortnite Spawns and Map Evolution: fortnite.gg/
Fortnite Storm Guide (V8.00): rockpapershotgun.com/fortnite-storm-guide-v7-30-fortnite-storm-eye-storm-stats-storm-tips-and-tricks
Fortnite Wiki: fortnite.fandom.com/
'Know Which Storm You're In! (Fortnite Storm Size Tutorial)'u/ by Crazyguitarman: youtube.com/watch?v=Jg5JQ-7K5XY
'Revolutionizing Highground Retakes – 10 Advanced Retakes in Fortnite!' by u/KenBeans: youtube.com/watch?v=N5jz4mb9A3g&t=359s
'Understanding Zone Mechanics, Positioning and Probability' by Fortniteu/Bumpaah: youtube.com/watch?v=mECJhP1zskM
'What Type of 90's Do you Do? (Fortnite)' by u/BennyBuilds: youtube.com/watch?v=KSFslHBZ3Ok

CHAPTER 8
Katamari Damacy

1438 Objects Category Resources: speedrun.com/katamarireroll/thread/7do2m
Discord: Katamari Speedrunning
'Katamari Balls' by u/ SanekOgon: steamcommunity.com/sharedfiles/filedetails/?id=2117695640
Katamari Wiki: katamari.fandom.com/
'Make A Star 1' by u/Racing Comedian Kofize: youtube.com/watch?v=IkZAwzR1bQU&t=21s
'Make A Star 8' by u/Kuroha Zone: youtube.com/watch?v=89bPOJxTKPQ
Noclip: noclip.website/

CHAPTER 9
Minecraft

2b2t +X Nether World Border: imgur.com/a/ms7tQ3A
2b2t Maps: map.daporkchop.net/#2021_owo_isometric/0/4/5603/-5864/0
2b2t Wiki: 2b2t.miraheze.org/wiki/Front_Page
2b2t.link World Downloads
Fandom: wynncraft.fandom.com
FitMC YouTube channel, for various videos on 2b2t: youtube.com/channel/UCHZ986wm_sJT6wntdDTlIcw
'Huge Hub V3' by joker876: easyzoom.com/imageaccess/75aae8e8d21943079ff9c39d7539d1bd

Hypixel Forums: hypixel.net

'List of Grinding Spots Level 1–106' by ItzAzura: forums.wynncraft.com/threads/list-of-grinding-spots-level-1-106.255238/

'Minecraft LavaCast Tutorial: How to Cast Towers, Walls, Stairs & Pyramids With Lava & Water' by GMODISM: youtube.com/watch?v=DsACeE1BrPk

Minecraft Online: minecraftonline.com

'No Comment Explanation and Information' by nerdsinspace: github.com/nerdsinspace/nocom-explanation/blob/main/README.md

Planet Minecraft: planetminecraft.com

Reddit: r/2b2t, r/hypixel, r/Minecraft, r/WynnCraft

'The Minecraft City of the Captive Globe' by CPUser_: planetminecraft.com/project/the-minecraft-city-of-the-captive-globe/

'World Downloader Mod' by cubic72: minecraftforum.net/forums/mapping-and-modding-java-edition/minecraft-mods/1285484-world-downloader-mod

'Wynncraft 1.20 Map' by bolyai: kristofbolyai.github.io/Territory-map/

'Wynncraft Maps' by nicolashc96: blackspigot.com/downloads/wynncraft-maps.18393/

Wynndata: wynndata.tk/map

CHAPTER 10
No Man's Sky

Archaeogaming: archaeogaming.com/

Galactic Atlas: galacticatlas.nomanssky.com/

How Big is the Map?, YouTube: youtube.com/c/HowBigistheMap/videos

'NMS Save Editor', GoatFungus: github.com/goatfungus/NMSSaveEditor

No Man's Sky Coordinate Exchange: nmsce.com/nmsce.html

No Man's Sky Portals Decoder: nmsportals.github.io/

No Man's Sky Wiki: nomanssky.fandom.com/

NomNom: A No Man's Sky Multi-Tool: cengelha.github.io/NomNom/

Reddit: No Man's Sky: reddit.com/r/NoMansSkyTheGame

Reddit: No Man's Sky Coordinate Exchange: reddit.com/r/NMSCoordinateExchange/

SurvivalBob, YouTube: youtube.com/c/SurvivalBobGaming/videos

The Portal Repository: portalrepository.com/

Xaine's World: xainesworld.com/no-mans-sky-portal-glyphs-fast-travelers-graves/

CHAPTER 11
Persona 5

'"Did you want to wash some dirty items?" Found some cool Persona 5 locations in my trip through Japan last summer :)' by u/Jozu_da_meister: reddit.com/r/Persona5/comments/9spx0h/did_you_want_to_wash_some_dirty_items_found_some/

Megami Tensei Wiki: megamitensei.fandom.com/wiki/

Persona 5 – Google Maps My Maps: google.com/maps/d/viewer?mid=1zMLrFDg-yKkpgyMZ0MxY1MjokN

c&ll=35.516020157919414%2C139.8660225551753&z=11

'Persona 5 Area Maps' by up on the ladder: upontheladder.blogspot.com/2016/10/persona-5-area-maps.html

Persona 5 Locations: arcgis.com/apps/MapTour/index.html?appid=058b1fdf75df4f1fa50254d8c9264a7e

'Persona 5 metro map overlay over real-life Tokyo', Reddit u/layomayo: reddit.com/r/Persona5/comments/mjw0ft/persona_5_metro_map_overlay_over_reallife_tokyo/

'Persona 5 Pilgrimage' by ChronoCapsule: twitter.com/i/events/847148710068858881

'Persona 5 Royal – Weather Conditions Guide' by Rin Tohsaka: samurai-gamers.com/persona-5/weather-conditions-guide/

'Persona 5: Yongenjaya in Real Life', Source Gaming: sourcegaming.info/2017/04/09/persona-5-yongenjaya-in-real-life/

Persona Central: personacentral.com

Reddit: r/Persona5

The Spriters Resource: spriters-resource.com

'This vending machine and laundromat look really familiar' by u/friedstinkytofu: imgur.com/a/EHLEQrG

CHAPTER 12
Stardew Valley

Animal Crossing: New Horizons – Official Companion Guide (Future Press, 2020)

'AUTOMATE – A Stardew Valley mod guide with real playthrough examples' by BiiPolar Potato: youtube.com/watch?v=ytX6DKYlge0&t=287s

Discord: Stardew Valley

Mods: Automate, CBJ Cheats Menu, Lookup Anything: nexusmods.com/stardewvalley

'Optimal Bee House Layouts': hypercarry.com/games/stardew-valley/guides/optimal-bee-house-layouts/

Stardew Planner: stardew.info/

'Stardew Valley Best sprinkler/scarecrow layout for maximum crop harvest': reddit.com/r/StardewValley/comments/48u7s9/stardew_valley_best_sprinklerscarecrow_layout_for/

'Stardew Valley Everything Junimo Huts' by ezlilyy: youtube.com/watch?v=1plYNCEOKBc&t=34s

'Stardew Valley Hi-Res Full World Map' by u/Wolfittish: reddit.com/r/StardewValley/comments/c2op6w/hires_full_world_map/

'Stardew Valley Speedrun | Mines% Level 120 in 1:10:54' by TheHaboo: youtube.com/watch?v=9bDexv1ySR8

Stardew Valley Wiki: stardewvalleywiki.com/Stardew_Valley_Wiki

'ULTIMATE Bee House Guide & Best Layout for Honey in Stardew Valley' by CapoTho: youtube.com/watch?v=qVZfl45H6L0

Luke Caspar Pearson is an Associate Professor at the Bartlett School of Architecture, UCL. Luke has written widely on the relationship between architecture and games for publications such as *FRAME, eflux Architecture* and *Disegno*. Luke's previous books are *Architectural Design: Re-Imagining the Avant-Garde* (Wiley, 2019) and *Drawing Futures* (UCL Press, 2016).

Sandra Youkhana is a Lecturer at the Bartlett School of Architecture, UCL and a registered Architect. Sandra has consulted for game developers, technology companies, and city planners and is currently undertaking a funded PhD at UCL. Her research investigates how the real world is extracted, altered and applied to the design of virtual environments.

Luke and Sandra are co-founders of You+Pea, a design research studio working between architecture and videogames. They co-lead the Videogame Urbanism studio at UCL, examining how games can help shape the future of urban design.

Marie Foulston is a leading curator and creative director specializing in play and digital culture. Previously she was curator of videogames at the V&A and is a co-founder of the UK's alternative videogame collective the Wild Rumpus. In her practice she has developed headline exhibitions, immersive installations, virtual displays in the metaverse, playful festivals and DIY arcade club nights, all alongside a host of international organisations including the Smithsonian, the Design Museum, the British Council, Netflix, MoPOP, ACMI and Somerset House.

On the cover: Videogame Atlas Vignettes: Illustrating a journey through 12 unique videogame worlds

First published in the United Kingdom in 2022 by Thames & Hudson Ltd, 181A High Holborn, London WC1V 7QX

First published in the United States of America in 2022 by Thames & Hudson Inc., 500 Fifth Avenue, New York, New York 10110

Videogame Atlas: Mapping Interactive Worlds © 2022 Thames & Hudson Ltd, London

Foreword © 2022 Marie Foulston

Text © 2022 Sandra Youkhana and Luke Caspar Pearson
Illustrations © 2022 Sandra Youkhana and Luke Caspar Pearson

Design by Julia in collaboration with Darren Wall

Research Assistant: Ness Lafoy (funded by the Bartlett School of Architecture, UCL: Architecture Research Fund)

British Library Cataloguing-in-Publication Data
A catalogue record for this book is available from the British Library

Library of Congress Control Number 2022931874

ISBN 978-0-500-02423-2

Printed and bound in China by C&C Offset Printing Co. Ltd.

Be the first to know about our new releases, exclusive content and author events by visiting
thamesandhudson.com
thamesandhudsonusa.com
thamesandhudson.com.au